VALUES AND TEACHING:

Working with Values in the Classroom

MERRILL'S

INTERNATIONAL EDUCATION SERIES

Under the Editorship of

Kimball Wiles

*Dean of the College of Education
University of Florida*

VALUES AND TEACHING:

Working with Values in the Classroom

Louis E. Raths
State University College at Fredonia

Merrill Harmin
Southern Illinois University

Sidney B. Simon
University of Massachusetts

Charles E. Merrill Publishing Co.
Columbus, Ohio
A Bell and Howell Company

Library of Congress Catalog Card Number: 66-13815

PRINTED IN THE UNITED STATES OF AMERICA

18 19 - 77 76 75 74

With grateful acknowledgment for the support, devotion and concern shown by our wives:

Mildred D. Raths, Tamaji Harmin and Marianne P. Simon

Foreword

Years ago when I was in graduate school Louis Raths intrigued me with his reactions to my comments. As far as I could detect he never really approved any statement I made. He would ask a question, make a noncommittal observation, test my assertion by supplying additional data, ask if I had considered a different alternative.

The experience was disconcerting to me. My previous educational experience had led me to expect to use the teacher as a means of determining the correctness of my answers. He was the person who knew and his role was to keep me informed of my progress in the search for truth. He was to provide reinforcement. And this teacher did not! I expected positive affirmation and support. And I received more questions and the expectation that I would continue to probe.

Years later, when we were colleagues at New York University, I saw Louis Raths playing the same role in faculty meetings and in informal discussions with fellow faculty members. By this time I had come to understand teaching as assistance in the search and support as concern for the students' continuing growth.

The process of valuing and helping others to value has been a way of life for Louis Raths for the thirty years I have known him.

In this book Raths, Harmin, and Simon have stated a value theory that can guide a teacher and

have described a process and specific instructional strategies which
implement the theory. The illustrations are concrete examples of
how a teacher may cultivate pupil skill in the process of valuing.
However, the assumption is clear throughout the book, that the
process is a creative one in which each teacher formulates the actions that he deems appropriate at each moment.

This description of a theory and practices of one instructional
role will be helpful and provocative to any teacher who conceives
his function to be assisting students to develop skill in valuing and
questing.

Kimball Wiles

May, 1965

Table of Contents

Part One   **Introduction**   **1**

    Chapter 1   *Overview of the Book*   3

Part Two   **A Theory of Values**   **13**

    Chapter 2   *The Difficulty of Developing Values* . .   15

    Chapter 3   *Values and Valuing*   27

    Chapter 4   *Teaching for Value Clarity*   38

Part Three   **The Value Clarifying Method**   **49**

    Chapter 5   *The Clarifying Response*   51

    Chapter 6   *The Value Sheet*   83

    Chapter 7   *Other Classroom Methods* 112

Part Four   **Using the Value Theory**   **163**

    Chapter 8   *Getting Started: Guidelines and Problems* . 165

    Chapter 9   *Emotional Needs, Thinking, and Valuing* . 197

    Chapter 10   *Research Completed and Needed* . . . 205

Appendixes   **231**

Notes   **259**

Bibliography   **263**

Index   **269**

Part One

Introduction

Chapter 1

Overview of the Book

A major theme of this century has been child study, and a major outcome of this study has been awareness of the role that emotions play in the life of a growing child. In fact, as the emotional aspects of childhood began to gain prominence, a trend developed which implied that almost all problems of children arose from emotional disturbances. This is understandable; emotions explain so much that it is easy to assume they explain everything. The work of Freud, the development of psychoanalysis and psychiatry, and the mental-health movement contributed to this preoccupation with the role of emotions, but one other major theme of this century, the measurement of intelligence, had a similar kind of influence. The result has been that all too often a behavior problem of a child, and especially a school problem, is attributed to either an emotional disturbance or something called a low I.Q.

There is a parallel here with work that was done in medicine in the last century and the early years of this century. When it was discovered that some illnesses were "caused" by germs, and when further inquiry showed that a number of illnesses were associated with penetration by germs, it became a common practice to assume that practically all manifestations of bad health were caused by germs. It was very difficult, for example, to convince certain segments of the medical profession that pellagra had its origin in dietary deficiency. The idea of germs was so strongly entrenched that it was very difficult for some to accept any alternative explanation.

With children it was never quite as simple as that. Emotions and I.Q. were, and are, often prime suspects to explain behavior problems, but there have been some understandings as well of the way physical conditions influence behavior and, especially in recent years, the influence of group pressures and group climates.

However, there has been little more than vague understanding of the influence that values might be having on behavior. Many of us have spoken of values as if they were important, perhaps crucial. Could it be that a number of children's problems currently attributed to emotions, for example, are more usefully seen as resulting from value disturbances? The study and research upon which this book is based answer that question affirmatively. We have found that several kinds of problems children often exhibit in school and at home are profitably seen as being caused by values, or, more precisely, by a *lack* of values. To put this another way, we have found that when children with certain behavior problems are given value experiences of a particular kind, those problems often ease in intensity and/or frequency. In short, there is strong support for the notion that values must be added to the possible explanations of children's behavior problems.

To get at a central idea of this book, let us make use of an image. Imagine a giant continuum with persons standing at various points along it, some in clusters, some alone, some in motion, and some quite immobile. And imagine a sign above the people's heads that says, CLARITY OF RELATIONSHIP TO SOCIETY. At one end of the continuum, we see a smaller sign that says, simply, CLEAR, while the other end is similarly labeled UNCLEAR. We move forward to examine this puzzling sight.

We find a large cluster of persons at the CLEAR end of the continuum and, as we look closely, each person at this end does seem to be clear about what the relationship is between himself and the society that he is in. Each seems to be dealing with life in a consistent and purposeful way. We talk to a few and each appears to know what he wants in life and how to work for it. Although in somewhat different styles, each person in this cluster seems to relate to the forces and events and persons around him with considerable verve, purpose, and pride. It's not at all as if these persons have "adjusted" to their environments in any passive sense. In fact, many of them have important misgivings about large parts of their surroundings, but there is a strong interest in dealing with those displeasing elements constructively, usually by seeking ways to improve things. If we seek words to describe the persons who live their lives at this extreme point on the relationship-to-society continuum, we think of *positive, purposeful, enthusiastic, proud.*

All is not so rosy at the other end of the line. The persons there decidedly do not seem to be clear about how to relate to the things and people around them. There is much personal confusion, and we are quick to observe that these persons seem much less secure than do those at the other end.

As we become familiar with persons in this group, it is interesting to note how their common confusion about how to relate their lives to their surroundings has led to quite different patterns of behavior:

1. Some are *apathetic.* They are listless and uninterested, willing to let the spinning world carry them along whichever way it will.

2. Others are *flighty,* interested in many things but only for fleeting moments. They often are involved in something with high spirit; but with equal spirit and in short order, they abandon it for another favorite.

3. Some are *very uncertain,* seemingly unable to make up their minds about the many choices with which the world continues to face them.

4. Then there are *very inconsistent* ones, persons involved in many things that are mutually inconsistent if not mutually destructive. Unlike their flighty compatriots, they may have patterns in their lives but, if so, the patterns tend to be incompatible. One thinks of the student who is alternately generous and selfish, or who is hard working this week and totally without energy the next week.

5. Others at this end of the continuum might aptly be called *drifters.* For these persons there is a pattern of behavior characterized by planless and unenthusiastic drift from this to that, like humans without power or rudder in the sea of life.

6. A large number are *overconformers.* Not having a clear idea of what they want to do with their lives, many take the road of conformity, accommodating themselves the best they can to what they perceive to be the dominant viewpoint of the mo-

ment. Other-directed with a passion, are those in this subgroup.

7. Some are *overdissenters*, not occasional and reasoned dissenters, but chronic, nagging, and irrational dissenters. It's as if some confused persons try to obtain an identity by opposing the prevailing winds. This behavior pattern is, of course, no more independent of others than is that of the overconformer.

8. Finally, we note a group of *poseurs* or *role players*, persons who cover their lack of clarity about what life is for by posturing in some role or other that is no more real for them than a made-up cardboard image. One thinks of the class clown or the bully on the block as often being of this type. Each poseur adopts a counterfeit existence to conceal his lack of a real one.

A strange group at this unclear end of the relationship-to-society continuum,[1] most of them fall into some eight subclusters, none of which has behavior patterns like their counterparts at the "clear" end of the scale. The persons in that first group seemed to be positive, purposeful, enthusiastic, and proud. The persons in the second group seem apathetic, confused, or irrational; in different ways, each seems to have learned a pattern of behavior that compensates for his not knowing how to deal with the dynamics of the surrounding world.

If we define the term "values" as those elements that show how a person has decided to use his life, it would be as if the first group's members knew what they valued and the members of the second group had very unclear values. The second group's members could be viewed as having failed a critical test, for, to use the words of Hunt and Metcalf* (1955, p. 52): "The critical test of a person's insights is whether they provide him with a set of beliefs about himself in relation to his social and physical environment which are extensive in scope, dependable in action, and compatible with one another." The differences between the lives of persons who pass and fail this test are dramatic and, we think, important.

This is important, not in any abstract way, but in the way it illuminates what may be a central problem for our times. Many social

---

[1] The continuum suggested by this image is similar to those presented by others. See, for example, Krathwohl, Bloom, and Masia (1964), and, for a more psychologically-oriented continuum, Peck and Havighurst (1960).

* Complete information for this and all other references is found in the Bibliography beginning on p. 263.

observers (see, for example, Lerner, 1957; Whyte, 1956; Fromm, 1955; and Reisman, 1950), have noted that large numbers of persons in this country seem to fall into the lower half of that relationship-to-society scale, toward the pole of apathy, confusion, and irrationality. In fact, it is sometimes said that the proportion of our population at that pole is increasing. Be that as it may, few would deny that there are far too many children in the schools today who do not seem to learn as well as they might because they simply are not clear about what their lives are for, what is worth working for. We put into this category those children whom teachers recognize as being very *apathetic, flighty, uncertain,* or *inconsistent,* or who are *drifters, overconformers, overdissenters,* or *role players.* Many underachievers, those whose problems are not physical or emotional in origin, also are in this group. One thing which unites them all is that they have not yet found a meaningful role for their lives and are therefore unable or unwilling to marshal up their full intellectual resources for use in the crucial game of living.

Could it be, we wonder, that the pace and complexity of modern life has so exacerbated the problem of deciding what is good and what is right and what is worthy and what is desirable that large numbers of children are finding it increasingly bewildering, even overwhelming, to decide what is worth valuing, what is worth one's time and energy? Life is certainly less neat and simple than it was even a few generations ago. "A perfection of means and a confusion of goals" is the way Einstein characterized this age. Could this be a cause for much of the apathy, confusion, and irrational behavior that seems to make concentration on school work so difficult for some students?

It is against this backdrop of issues and problems that the value theory of this book developed. The senior author considered for some time what might be the implications of value development for teaching and, based on some of the work of Dewey (see, especially, Dewey, 1939), built a theory of values that seems to offer concrete and effective aid to teachers. For years, we gave special treatment to those students who suffered from physical disabilities. Later, we learned many approaches to those children whose problems indicated an emotional disturbance.[2] Now we believe similar under-

---

[2] See Raths and Burrell (1962).

standings and practices can be directed to children who have value-related disturbances. These children are often identifiable by idiosyncratic behavior patterns—apathy, flightiness, extreme uncertainty, and inconsistency; drift, overconformity, overdissension, and chronic posing; and, frequently, underachievement. The common malady of these children seems to be *confusion in values*.

Value theory and the teaching strategies associated with it are presented in this book. Although preliminary research shows it to be especially potent for those children who suffer from value confusion, it is doubtlessly appropriate for all children living in today's complex world.

This theory is particularly noteworthy in the sense that it is a *teaching* theory and, as such, is easily tested. No teacher need accept the approach that grows from this value theory on the basis of distant research or persuasive argument, although both are available. The theory can be tested by any teacher in any classroom. Indeed, we strongly recommend that the reader who finds the theory at all worthy at first reading go so far as to give it a try in his classroom. Procedures for doing this and for evaluating the outcome are outlined elsewhere in this volume.

It may be reassuring or disappointing, depending on how one looks at it, to know that this value theory is not a panacea for all that ails children and education. It provides unique and powerful tools for some problems of many children, but it does not pretend to help solve behavior difficulties whose causes lie outside of value issues.

In this modest mood, it is worth noting that the approaches of this book will not be radically new for all teachers. Many sensitive teachers have been working along these lines, even if they have been calling it something else, for many years. This book may only help them organize and conceptualize those practices, perhaps permitting them to use them more systematically and pointedly. It is likely that new teaching ideas will be suggested to even the most experienced and sensitive teacher, however. Our experience in presenting this theory to hundreds of teachers, and the ideas in this book include ones they have found most useful, is that it helps the larger number of them to multiply their effectiveness in important ways. It is enough of a goal to justify a book for teachers.

Many readers will note the similarity between the value theory and certain approaches to critical thinking.[3] In general, we might say that we apply critical thinking techniques to matters that are largely in the affective domain.[4] It is also reasonable to say that the value theory provides that amalgam of subject matter, personal concerns, and attitude development that has been such an elusive educational problem for so many years. In this regard, subject-matter specialists, such as most college and secondary-school teachers, may be especially interested in Chapter 9, "Subject Matter and Values."

There is much similarity between the basic orientation of this value theory and the work of a number of authors. The reader who desires to see some writings in a related view or to examine different implications of this general approach might consider Dewey, and especially his 1939 essay *Theory of Valuation,* and his *Moral Principles in Education;* Gordon Allport, *Becoming: Basic Considerations for a Psychology of Personality;* Gardner Murphy, *Human Potentialities;* Asch, *Social Psychology;* the 1962 yearbook of the Association of Supervision and Curriculum Development, *Perceiving, Behaving, Becoming;* Edgar Friedenberg, *The Vanishing Adolescent;* and Carl Rogers, *On Becoming a Person.*

Also of special interest are Peck and Havighurst, *The Psychology of Character Development;* Hunt and Metcalf, *Teaching High School Social Studies;* Brinton, *A History of Western Morals;* Fromm, *Man for Himself* and *The Sane Society;* Havighurst, *Human Development and Education;* Reisman, *Lonely Crowd;* Krathwohl, Bloom, and Masia, *Taxonomy of Educational Objectives: Handbook II: Affective Domain;* Soderquist, *The Person and Education;* Smith, *Value Convictions and Higher Education;* Wheelis, *The Quest for Identity;* Whyte, *The Organization Man;* Lynd, *Knowledge for What?;* and Witkin, *Psychological Differentiation.*

The meaning of the term "value" is by no means clear in the social sciences or in philosophy (Macmillan and Kneller, 1964). One can find consensus for no definition. About the only agreement that emerges is that a value represents something important in human existence. Perhaps because it is such a pivotal term, each school of thought

---

[3] For example, Hunt and Metcalf (1955) discuss an approach that overlaps some of the approaches of this value theory.

[4] See Krathwohl, Bloom, and Masia (1964) for a definition and discussion of the affective domain.

invests it with its own definition. For the same reason, a particular definition is not often acceptable elsewhere. The definition of this book, developed more fully in Chapter 3, is closest to ones used by those who talk of the *process* of valuing, rather than of a value in any identifiable institutional sense. We believe that it is more useful to consider the posture of a person facing his world, how he uses his muscle and spirit to relate to his surroundings, than to consider what he might find valuable at any one time or in any one particular circumstance or in a series of similar times or circumstances, for that matter. "How did he get his ideas?" is a more fundamental question for us than "What did he get?"

We believe that each person has to wrest his own values from the available array. As is elaborated later, values that actually penetrate living in intelligent and consistent ways are not likely to come any other way. Thus it is the process of making such decisions that concerns us. "Instead of giving young people the impression that their task is to stand a dreary watch over the ancient values," says John Gardner (1964), "we should be telling them the grim but bracing truth that it is their task to recreate those values continuously in their own time." Giving students a process of valuing is giving them something that should serve them well and long.

Our emphasis on *valuing* rather than on *values* is not universally shared. In the recent work of Krathwohl *et al.* (1964), the emphasis is on values as entities, and most of the research dealing with values has tried to measure what values people have and not the processes they used to get them (J. Raths, 1964). For us, the concern would be less whether or not so-and-so says he values thrift than it would be where did so-and-so get his ideas of thrift; for example, did they come unthinkingly from his father, is he thrifty only because thrifty persons surround him, did he come to it freely and thoughtfully, or what? We would, of course, also be interested in knowing if our mythical Mr. So-and-so is, in fact, thrifty, a dimension of values that has all but been ignored in the research on values to date, and for good reason: actual behavior is virtually impossible to measure for large numbers of individuals.

There is an assumption in the value theory and the teaching strategies that grow from it that humans *can* arrive at values by an intelligent process of choosing, prizing, and behaving. At least we assume that humans can arrive at *something* via that process and, with some support in the literature, we prefer to call that something "values." That assumption (which may seem essentially semantic) need not unduly bother the practical-minded classroom teacher, however, for operationally the assumption is transformed into a hypothesis of a different order: If children are helped to use the valuing process of this book, we assert that they will behave in ways that are less apathetic, confused, and irrational and in ways that are more positive, purposeful, and enthusiastic. And that hypothesis is readily testable by anyone wishing to do so.

SUMMARY

As our society enters the stage in which persons' physical needs are increasingly easily satisfied by an increasingly productive and efficient economy, other problems come into focus. One of these, already evident to many in the Western world, deals with the question of what to do with the extra time and energy left over after work is done. The problems older and younger people in our society have in confronting this question can be seen most dramatically. How pitiful is the older person left with time and energy but nothing to do with them. In a similar situation are those young people, perhaps the majority of them, for whom schoolwork and family life are not adequately fulfilling. And, is the situation different for the increasing numbers of housewives who kill time by running in circles? Devoting one's life to picking up the children after Cub Scouts only to deliver them to dancing class does not seem very satisfying to many. And what about the working man who finds his increasing leisure as much a burden as a blessing?

The problem is simply stated: What is to be done with one's life and force? Once a question mainly for philosophers, in these times of increasing complexity and change and abundance, it is a question that challenges almost all of us, although often we move through our lives unaware of it. This is its terrible power: it is a question that cripples us as long as it remains unanswered. A growing tragedy is that it is not usually even asked. Witness the teenager who does little other than escape to temporary, sometimes desperate, excitements. Witness the job-hopper who seems unable to find any work satisfying. Witness the student who daydreams, unmoved by the combined exhortation of teachers and parents and with an occa-

sional threat from the principal thrown in. Witness, too, the successful adult who achieves what he was supposed to achieve only to
wonder what it was all for: "If this is success, why did I want it?"
We would say that these people, and they are legion in our increasingly affluent society, may well suffer from unclear sets of
values. Such persons seem not to have clear purposes, to know what
they are for and against, to know where they are going and why.
Persons with unclear values lack direction for their lives, lack criteria for choosing what to do with their time, their energy, their very
being. It seems unlikely that animals other than humans can have
values. It is one of our most precious potential gifts. Yet it seems
increasingly apparent that all too few humans do, indeed, have clear
values.

That is why we have written this book. It outlines a theory of
values and a methodology for the clarification of values. It shows
how to work with others so as to help them clarify their own values.
It should be useful to persons of all ages and walks of life, but is
directed most specifically to those who work professionally with
children, such as teachers. It is an eminently practical book in that
it shows how the theory of values operates and how procedures
grow from the theory. Furthermore, the theory is set up in such a
way that the reader can give it a test of his own.

This can be, we feel, a very important book. The evidence already
in shows that the reported procedures have helped many students
change patterns of behavior that were characterized by apathy, drift,
conformity, and underachievement. In different words, many students have been helped to become more purposeful, more enthusiastic, more positive, and more aware of what is worth striving for.
This, of course, is the kind of behavior teachers and parents have
wanted to promote for some time but, until recently, clear procedures based on adequate theory have not been available. It is hoped
that the theory and the procedures discussed in this volume will help
with this important, and gratifying, task.

Part Two

A Theory of Values

Chapter 2

The Difficulty of Developing Values

Modern life in the United States is rich with choices and opportunities, but it is also very, very confusing for a child to comprehend. Although few of us would willingly return to the simple and more austere life of earlier days, we must recognize the penalty we pay for the complexities of the present. One of those penalties deals with values. It is certainly much more difficult today than it was at the turn of the century for a child to develop clear values.

Look at the family, for example. Many persons believe that values develop in and around the family. But the changes in the family from more stable days are dramatic if not frightening. According to recent figures, one out of every three mothers is working. It is estimated that in one out of every five families the mother is not home when children return from school.

Recent estimates suggest that one out of every five families represents a broken home. In this context the word *broken* means that one of the parents is dead, the parents are divorced or separated, or one of them is institutionalized. As in the case with working mothers, the result is a decrease in the amount of contact which a child might have with either parent.

The character of the father's job and its relation to family life has changed considerably. It is almost universally true today that the children really do not know very much about what the father does to earn a living. They do not see him at his work and they are not informed enough about it to enter into meaningful discussions about the nature of his career, its problems, and its successes. In other words, a major part of the father's life is almost beyond the possibilities of communication with his children.

It is said that one out of every five American families moves every year. Think of what this means for the stability of the life of children. Friendship patterns are often destroyed. There are new children and new teachers to meet. There is the requirement of becoming oriented to new communities, new neighbors, new congregations, and perhaps to new and different patterns of living. This very high geographical mobility is something quite unique in our history. Even so, it is becoming an expected part of family life; and today it can be said that parents are not very much upset when it becomes necessary or desirable to take the children and move to a new community.

There is some little truth in the saying that the family has become a refuge from the world. Father, mother, and children go there to hide from the pressures of life outside. Very often fathers commute several hours daily. They leave the house too early in the morning to have intelligent conversations with children. They come home late at night, tired out, not only from their work, but from the travel. They would like the home to be quiet. They wish that the children would be still. Before long it is time for the children to go to bed, and another opportunity is lost for discussing the meanings of the day's activities, whatever they may have been.

In recent years tremendously potent new means of communication have been introduced into standard family life rituals. In the early days of the century the telephone was brought into more and more families. Then, in the second decade, radio came into being; almost immediately children began to listen; those in charge of programming began to develop programs which they thought would be interesting to children. (Not much attention was paid to the question: What programs would be *good* for children?) Just previous to the advent of radio, the motion picture began to have a great impact upon life in the United States. And then, after World War II, television arrived and with great rapidity captured vast adult and child audiences.

If values represent a way of life, if values give direction to life, if values are those things which make a difference in living, one might expect that, in our concern for developing values among children, there might be a focus upon one or two ways of life which might give stability to the child. Yet the rapid incursion of these new media of communication meant the presentation to the child of many, many *different* ways of life. The output was vast on radio, in the movies, and on the television screen. He saw numerous things and heard many views, which in the ordinary run of life would never have been presented to him as a part of family living. Inanity, crime, violence were hour-by-hour occurrences. Acts that can truly be called depraved were committed by people who were seemingly well-educated, while people watched, listened, and took it in. Surely children must have imbibed some ideas from all of this.

There is another possible inference: being exposed to so many different alternatives, perhaps the child was left with *no* ideas, but instead absorbed just the confusion. It is possible that the biggest contribution these media made was to baffle the child's nascent understanding of what is right and what is wrong, what is true and what is false, what is good and what is bad, what is just and what is unjust, what is beautiful and what is ugly.

Radio, movies, and TV were not the only forces at work. In the same period of time, new and cheaper ways of distributing printed materials were discovered. The comics came into being, and there were publishers who saw great riches in the children's market. "Comic" books became another purveyor of crime stories, horror stories, and all sorts of strange ways of life. They found a market, for children bought these books, and bought them in large quantity.

At about the same time, the family newspapers changed greatly. More crime stories, more sex stories, more corruption were reported; more suggestive pictures were printed; and our children read them along with the comics.

We are not suggesting here that the alternatives which life offers should be blacked out. Nor are we suggesting that the children cannot learn something from all of this exposure. We are suggesting, however, that by themselves children cannot profit greatly from exposure to this myriad of choices. If the family as a *unit* had been exposed to all these choices, if the family as a *unit* could discuss the reasonableness or unreasonableness of what had been presented, every child might have learned something of the meaning of these new ways of living. But, as has been suggested, with the mother working, with more homes broken, with the father away all day, there was even less family sharing. The consequence, we submit, has been a growing confusion in the life of children as to what is good and what is bad, what is right and what is wrong, and what is just and what is unjust.

In addition to all of these other technological innovations, one must not lose sight of the impact of the automobile. At the beginning of the century it was probably quite unusual for a family or children to have traveled very much. In general, the family stayed home except for short excursions on trolley cars, if it were lucky enough to live near one, or on trains. With the advent of the automobile, it became the usual custom to travel quite a bit. The family car moved from luxury to necessity; and under these circumstances, one met new people more often. One was in more frequent contact with customs of another town or another region. One saw other children doing things which perhaps were unthought of in one's own community.

Out of this welter of traveling and communication, there came not only confusion and uncertainty but also the idea that perhaps anything was all right, nothing really mattered, that while many people were different, there was nothing particularly significant in the differences. One way of life was as good as another. Nobody really was an example of what was the right way to be.

Another factor operated in the life of children which may or may not be significant for our discussion of values. At the turn of the century the teacher in her local classroom was almost always a local girl. She knew the ways of the community, and she most often knew each child's family. There was a local standard of life, and she was familiar with it. The policemen were often known personally. The storekeepers were often known by name, and the man who ran the store knew a child's parents and they knew him. As a child lived in such a world, he was aware that he was noticed. His behavior was personal in the sense that he was a member of a family and this family was known by the teacher, by the minister, priest, or rabbi, by the storekeeper, by the neighbors. All of this acted as a kind of brake on innovations in behavior. The child was more likely to absorb the mores of the community. There was a kind of common understanding of what behavior was good and what was bad, of which attitudes and aspirations were appropriate and which were inappropriate. In other words, it was easier for a child at that time to come to understand what society expected of him now and would expect of him later as an adult.

It is commonplace to point out that in the early years of this century the church also seemed to have a much greater influence on the growing child than it does today. Father and mother, grandfather and grandmother had an attitude toward the church and its teachings which was forcefully conveyed to the children of the family. As the family changed, and as new influences came into the family, the impact of the church began to wane. The way of life represented by a long religious tradition began to be neglected. It would be too much to say that the church was opposed. It wasn't opposition that began to appear. It was, first of all, a weaning or separation. With all this moving around, with so many new stimuli coming into the family, there was a gradual but continuing separation of family life from frequent church and Sunday school participation. This meant a decrease in the quantity and quality of contact with religious traditions and their emphasis upon values. This should not be underestimated as a factor in today's world of confusion and apathy. As this separation from frequent contact with the church continued, clergymen were seen more frequently as people who merely officiated at baptisms, deaths, weddings, and the rites associated with the idea of confirmation.

World events also had an incalculable effect upon family life. In the first forty years of this century, there were two terrible world wars; and in the past twenty years, the newspapers have shouted almost continual news of cold wars and hot wars. Under these circumstances it must be very difficult for children to believe in nonviolence and in peace as a reality. Atomic bombs have been developed by educated men and have been used on human populations. Even now they are held as a threat to slaughter millions of people.

During these same years, there have been disastrous famines at a time when, in other places, large amounts of excess food overflowed storage bins. In the last world war, millions of human beings were exterminated by a country which had been regarded as one of the most civilized and educated in the world. Children are now being told that the Communists are "ahead" in education—whatever that means—and are also told that these educated Communists want to capture the world, to crush liberty everywhere, and to make human beings the slaves of the party or the state. Under these circumstances, isn't it natural for children to come to believe that education has very little to do with what is good and what is bad, what is right and what is wrong, what is just and what is unjust?

Out of this uncertainty and confusion, it has come to pass that our schools can hardly stand for a single set of values. For example, there was a time when the schools celebrated the Christian holidays, Christmas and Easter. Groups other than Christian called this practice into question and suggested that the school should not represent one religion any more than another, and it wasn't long before the celebration of Christmas was very different from what it had been. The schools used to put an emphasis upon a daily prayer, but the rulings of the Supreme Court of the land have decided that a common prayer may not be demanded of all children in the schools. As it is with religious matters, so it is with other matters of deep concern. If someone was for something, someone else was against it; and to avoid controversy, schools began to stand for nothing.

Teachers turned toward "teaching the facts." If controversy was to be troublesome, one should stay away from it. Administrators tended to prefer teachers who did not raise issues. In communities of strangers living together, people who did not know one another well, people with many different backgrounds, it became easier to have schools which themselves represented an absence of consensus. Moral, ethical, aesthetic values were quietly abandoned as integral parts of the curriculum. Thus the gap widened between what we *said* the schools were to foster and what was actually taught. Children saw this gap between reality and something perhaps more promising. They saw many other gaps, too. A child who asks his parents to buy a gadget advertised on television and who quotes its supposed good qualities is very often told that you cannot believe what the television says. When he repeats to his mother what the clerk in the store has said about a product, his mother lets him know that you cannot believe what clerks say. As he attempts to accept some of the things that appear in newspapers and magazines, he is again told to be suspicious. What can one believe? Is it true that most people in the adult world regularly lie, and, in general, lie for money? Why isn't something done about this?

The child sees pretty much the same thing when it comes to most serious matters. He is surrounded by repetitive statements pledging a dedication to peace, and all around him are signs of war. He is told that we must be militarily strong; might is at least as important as right. In school and out of school, our country is held up to him as a model of equal rights before the law. He also receives reports over and over again that Negroes in our culture do not receive equal rights. But he is so accustomed to duplicity that he very often does not wonder how this can be so.

In school and out, he is told that to co-operate is not only excellent but is practically a necessity in our world. At the same time, he is told that everybody should look out for himself, that if you don't look out for yourself nobody else will. You are to get yours and everyone else is to get his. He is told that women are the equal of men, and as he grows up he sees that in many situations they are not. In school he learns a romanticized version of the vigilantes in California history. He comes to believe that they were fine people. And at the same time he is supposed to pledge loyalty to a society that is ruled by law. He learns about some of the great patriots who initiated our revolution, people who stood up and spoke their minds; and while he is learning these things, people close to him advise him to be careful of what he says, not get into any trouble, go along with the authorities, and make the best of whatever the situation is.

He learns a lot of verbalisms about religion; and as he grows up, he also learns that one should not let religion interfere with making money. He is told again and again that education is a fine thing and that it helps to enrich life; but he is apt to learn that it is the certificate, the diploma, or the degree which is really significant. It is not education itself which is so important, but the accepted symbols of education that open up the door to success. While he is told that knowledge is power and that skill is to be respected, he is also told that it is not what you know but who you know that really counts.

Many more of these kinds of conflicts could be added but enough have been listed to suggest that the child's world is indeed a confused one. It must not be easy to grow in a society characterized by these conflicts.

Does this suggest that human beings are more inconsistent now than ever before in the history of mankind? Probably not. What it does suggest is that with the development of all these new means of mass communication, with the increased travel, with the increased moving around of people, *more children are exposed to more of these inconsistencies. This means that it is probably increasingly difficult for the growing child to develop clear values of his own.* There is so much confusion surrounding him and so little attention paid to the child's dilemma, so few persons with the time and patience to listen to him and to help him untangle some of the confusion, that he simply remains without sufficient clarity of beliefs or purpose.

One way of summing up what has been said is to indicate that the child of today confronts many more choices than the child of yesterday. He has so many more alternatives. In one sense, this makes him less provincial and more sophisticated. In another sense, the complex array of choices makes the act of choosing more difficult. How can one size up all of the available alternatives? How can one examine the grounds on which each rests, and how can one anticipate the consequences toward which each one points? In short, how does one know what to believe? The job seems so staggering that one is tempted to throw up his hands at the outset.

Just take this matter of choosing: think of the alternatives which confront the child in the world of products. There are all these different automobiles with their presumed uniqueness. Think of the toothpastes, the soaps, the toys, and the clothes which are offered. How do you choose? Is it true that one thing is as good as another and that discrimination is fairly useless? Is it not possible that in situations like this a kind of apathy about choice develops, and one begins to think that almost nothing makes a difference?

On the international scene, TV, radio, newspapers, and magazines bring to children news of violence and conflicts and disaster from all over the world. It assails the eyes and ears of our children; and in some vague, unknown way, the idea is communicated that we should all be concerned about these happenings. Concerned in what way? Will someone help us to relate these particular happenings to some general notions of value, of what is good and just?

There is yet another factor. It is widely proclaimed that there has been a significant shift in social class relationships, that many people have emerged from the working class and are now to be regarded as middle class. In a sense this means that the kind of work the parents are doing has changed. Probably the parents have joined the march to the suburbs. It almost certainly means that the parents have become more dedicated to schooling and education for their children. It is apt to mean, too, that parents are beginning a longer range type of planning, that they are not consuming their total earnings week by week or month by month. There may well be some plan for the future of the children, perhaps college. More money is spent on insurance. The house, even with its mortgage, is seen as an asset which will increase in value with the years. In other words, children are growing up in families where there is an emphasis upon security, and there is a minimizing of the value of taking risks. Parallel to the literature of daring and adventure, running beside a national emphasis on exploration of space and trips to the moon, there is a family atmosphere of "Don't stick out your neck," "Don't take a chance," "Play it safe."

The new social class alignments also tend to raise some new kind of insecurity on the part of parents. Parents are not yet accustomed to the new roles they have chosen to play. In these new suburbs they do not know their neighbors very well, and they do not know the standards which their neighbors have or do not have. In this absence of knowing there is a tendency to withdraw; and as the months go by, very little knowledge about each other's ways of living is exchanged. If a child comes home from high school and wants to stay up for the late news and argues that other children in his class do so, his parents are quite apt to accede reluctantly to his request, and they do this without knowing in fact whether such a practice is common in other homes. If this kind of situation is repeated often enough, it may be one of the bases for saying the children now have too much to say about their own conduct. As a matter of fact, they probably say so much because no one else is in a position to say very much at all. It suggests a weakening of the authority of parents with no substitute authority to fill the vacuum beyond the temporal standards of the boys and girls themselves.

These standards do not always work. We do know that there is much more delinquent behavior *reported* now than fifty years ago. We hear of many more cases of children using various kinds of narcotics. We know that there are large numbers of babies born out of wedlock, and we know that there are tens of thousands of abortions each year. We know that rates of criminality have increased. We have reports that ever so many children have ulcers, and we know that the rate of suicide amongst children is growing. Increasingly we are recognizing that there are many children who are in need of psychological assistance of a very specialized kind.

We know, too, that along with the growing emphasis upon commodities as symbols of status, there has been great unemployment, that the number of the *very poor* has changed hardly at all in the past sixty years, and that those who are poor today tend to be even poorer in relation to the other social classes. In many classrooms poverty is a very great problem. Interestingly, while this condition persists, the very children who are poor hear about national and local efforts to help the poor in Africa and in Asia and in Central America. Many of them must wonder deeply why the poor here at home are not receiving the attention which they deserve. How does one know what is right under these circumstances? Is poverty the problem, really, or is it an image of the United States which is to be created in the eyes of a world split between communism and noncommunism? What will these young people in our schools come to believe about our attitudes toward poverty, toward segregation, toward civil rights, toward law, toward freedom and liberty?

Although many more things might be suggested which make it difficult for a child to develop values, only one more will be added to the list: the standardized role which seems to be played by most adults when they are in the presence of children. Somehow or another the idea is held by adults that their chief function—in relationship to children—is to *tell* them things: to tell them what to do, when to do it, where to do it, how to do it, how often to do it, and when to stop doing it. If the child resists, he is apt to be characterized as disobedient, impertinent, unstable, or rebellious. In other words, typically, the adult only *adds* to the array of directives already urged upon the child by TV, radio, movies, newspapers, magazines, textbooks, teachers, other children, etc. The real problem is that almost no one sees the necessity for helping a child to make some order out of the confusion which has been created inside his head. Almost no one sees the necessity for questioning a child, to help him sort out and examine all those confusing ideas.

In one sense, the adult is led to believe that children are not people. Children are to follow the proposals of adults. They are to follow the aspirations which adults have for them. Children are to have the same feelings as adults, *without,* by the way, having had the same experiences as those adults. Children should have the "right" attitudes, and the "right" attitudes are those which correspond to those held by the adults who have control over them at the moment. Notwithstanding the tremendous amount of new knowledge which has accumulated in recent decades, and assuming that beliefs are related to knowledge, there is nevertheless a tendency on the part of grownups to assume that adult beliefs should persevere unmodified, that children should have the beliefs of their elders.

And when, as is frequently the case, children do not have the same beliefs as adults say they should have, grownups become frustrated and sometimes angry. They begin again to tell the child what he is to believe. They push more ideas into his confused mind. They pressure him, bribe him, sometimes frighten him. This manipulation only further confuses many children. One person will tell the child one thing. His father insists something different. The child's friends are certain of something else. Successful people all around demonstrate yet other notions. What is one to believe? How is one to know? Who is to help the child unravel this bewildering array of ideas? Would it help for a teacher to sit the child down and add another lecture or reasoned argument to the turmoil? How *is* the child to know what to believe?

This distressing and not totally unfamiliar survey of what problems and dilemmas confront a young person growing up in this culture need not go on any longer. We do not wish to return to a simpler and less rich life, but we do wish to develop methods for helping children deal with the complexities of modern living. The important thing is that we agree that it is indeed a confusing and complex world into which we welcome our youth. We must now ask, how does all of this affect the behavior of children? In what ways does it show up in how they think, how they react, how they plan, and how they dream? Just what does it mean for teachers?

For a long time now teachers have been able to identify children who do not hear very well or who do not see very well. We have finely developed tests to reveal those students who are not reading up to grade level and whose mathematical skills will most likely require special tutoring. Now, are there signs to indicate a child who has had serious trouble in coping with the development of values? It is one of the principal contentions of this book that there are such signs.

We believe that we have the means for identifying many of the children who are having difficulty in forming values and, having identified them, we have found that teachers can do a great deal about the problem. It need not plague the child throughout his life. On many occasions we are going to need help from the family, from other teachers, and perhaps from a counselor, but—as is outlined below—the main burden in this confused and confusing world can be borne by the classroom teachers of America.

Chapter 3

Values and Valuing

Persons have experiences; they grow and learn. Out of experiences may come certain general guides to behavior. These guides tend to give direction to life and may be called values. Our values show what we tend to do with our limited time and energy.

Since we see values as growing from a person's experiences, we would expect that different experiences would give rise to different values and that any one person's values would be modified as his experiences accumulate and change. A person in the Antarctic would not be expected to have the same values as a person in Chicago. And a person who has an important change in patterns of experience might be expected to modify his values. Values may not be static if one's relationships to his world are not static. As guides to behavior, values evolve and mature as experiences evolve and mature.

Moreover, because values are a part of living, they operate in very complex circumstances and usually involve more than simple extremes of right and wrong, good or bad, true or false. The conditions under which behavior is guided, in which values work, typically involve conflicting demands, a weighing and a balancing, and finally an action that reflects a multitude of forces. Thus values seldom function in a pure and abstract form. Complicated judgments are involved and what is really valued is reflected in the outcome of life as it is finally lived.

We therefore see values as constantly being related to the experiences that shape them and test them. They are not, for any one person, so much hard and fast verities as they are the results of hammering out a style of life in a certain set of surroundings. After a sufficient amount of hammering, certain patterns of evaluating and behaving tend to develop. Certain things are treated as right, or desirable, or worthy. These tend to become our values.

In this book we shall be less concerned with the particular value outcomes of any one person's experiences than we will with the process that he uses to obtain his values. Because life is different through time and space, we cannot be certain what experiences any one person will have. We therefore cannot be certain what values, what style of life, would be most suitable for any person. We do, however, have some ideas about what processes might be most effective for obtaining values. These ideas grow from the assumption that whatever values one obtains should work as effectively as possible to relate one to his world in a satisfying and intelligent way.

From this assumption comes what we call the *process of valuing*. A look at this process may make clear how we define a value. Unless something satisfies *all* seven of the criteria noted below, we do not call it a value. In other words, for a value to result, all of the following seven requirements must apply. Collectively, they describe the process of valuing.

Process of valuing:

1. *Choosing freely.* If something is in fact to guide one's life whether or not authority is watching, it must be a result of free choice. If there is coercion, the result is not likely to stay with one for long, especially when out of the range of the source of that coercion. Values must be freely selected if they are to be really valued by the individual.

2. *Choosing from among alternatives.* This definition of values is concerned with things that are chosen by the individual and, obviously, there can be no choice if there are no alternatives from which to choose. It makes no sense, for example, to say that one values eating. One really has no choice in the matter. What one may value is certain types of food or certain forms of eating, but not eating itself. We must all obtain nourishment to exist; there is no room for decision. Only when a choice is possible, when there is more than one alternative from which to choose, do we say a value can result.

3. *Choosing after thoughtful consideration of the consequences*

of each alternative. Impulsive or thoughtless choices do not lead to values as we define them. For something intelligently and meaningfully to guide one's life, it must emerge from a weighing and an understanding. Only when the consequences of each of the alternatives are clearly understood can one make intelligent choices. There is an important cognitive factor here. A value can emerge only with thoughtful consideration of the range of the alternatives and consequences in a choice.

4. *Prizing and cherishing*. When we value something, it has a positive tone. We prize it, cherish it, esteem it, respect it, hold it dear. We are happy with our values. A choice, even when we have made it freely and thoughtfully, may be a choice we are not happy to make. We may choose to fight in a war, but be sorry circumstances make that choice reasonable. In our definition, values flow from choices that we are glad to make. We prize and cherish the guides to life that we call values.

5. *Affirming*. When we have chosen something freely, after consideration of the alternatives, and when we are proud of our choice, glad to be associated with it, we are likely to affirm that choice when asked about it. We are willing to publicly affirm our values. We may even be willing to champion them. If we are ashamed of a choice, if we would not make our position known when appropriately asked, we would not be dealing with values but something else.

6. *Acting upon choices*. Where we have a value, it shows up in aspects of our living. We may do some reading about things we value. We are likely to form friendships or to be in organizations in ways that nourish our values. We may spend money on a choice we value. We budget time or energy for our values. In short, for a value to be present, life itself must be affected. Nothing can be a value that does not, in fact, give direction to actual living. The person who talks about something but never does anything about it is dealing with something other than a value.

7. *Repeating*. Where something reaches the stage of a value, it is very likely to reappear on a number of occasions in the life of the person who holds it. It shows up in several different situations, at several different times. We would not think of something that appeared once in a life and never again as a value. Values tend to have a persistency, tend to make a pattern in a life.

To review this definition, we see values as based on three processes: choosing, prizing, and acting.

CHOOSING: (1) freely
             (2) from alternatives
             (3) after thoughtful consideration of the consequences of each alternative

PRIZING: (4) cherishing, being happy with the choice
             (5) willing to affirm the choice publicly

ACTING: (6) doing something with the choice
             (7) repeatedly, in some pattern of life

Those processes collectively define valuing. Results of the valuing process are called values.

The reader might pause for a moment and apply the seven criteria for a value to one of his hobbies, be it sewing, skiing or hi-fi. Is it prized, freely and thoughtfully chosen from alternatives, acted upon, repeated, and publicly known? If so, one might say that you *value* that hobby.

VALUE INDICATORS

Obviously not everything is a value, nor need it be. We also have purposes, aspirations, beliefs, and many other things that may not meet all seven of those criteria. However values often do grow from our purposes, aspirations, beliefs, and so on. Let us briefly discuss some things that could indicate the presence of a value but that are different from values. We call these expressions which approach values, but which do not meet all of the criteria, *value indicators*.

1. *Goals or purposes*. To have purposes gives direction to life. If the purpose is important to us, we cherish it and we organize our life in ways by which we can achieve the purpose. This doesn't mean that every stated purpose is a value. Instead, we should think of a stated purpose as a potential value or a value indicator. If, in our presence, a child should state a purpose, it is, until we inquire further, merely a stated purpose—and we have an opportunity to pursue with him whether or not he prizes it, has freely chosen it,

has wanted it for some time, and is willing to do what is necessary to achieve it. Some stated purposes are dropped when these processes are applied. The child finds out that what he said is not what he really wants. He might have had what amounts to a passing interest in the idea, but even brief examination often results in depreciation of the stated purpose. Thus a purpose *may* be a value, but, on the other hand, it may not be.

2. *Aspirations*. We sometimes indicate a purpose that is remote in terms of accomplishment. It is not something that we wish or expect to accomplish today or tomorrow, or within a week or sometimes even a month. The statement of such an aspiration frequently points to the possibility of something that is valued. We shall not know if it is truly a value until we have asked questions which relate to the seven criteria which have been mentioned. When the responses are consistent with those criteria, we can say that we have touched a value.

3. *Attitudes*. Sometimes we give indications that we may have values by expressing attitudes. We say that we are *for* something or *against* something. It is not always a sound practice to infer that such a statement represents a value. Is it really cherished? Has some consideration been given to alternatives? Does it come up again and again? Is it related to the life activities of the person who expresses it? Unless these criteria are met, it may be just so many words. That is, it may just be an attitude and not a value.

4. *Interests*. Very often you hear people say that they are interested in something. Care should be taken, however, in concluding that this means that a value is present. Very often when we say we are interested, we mean little more than that we would like to talk about it or to listen to someone talk about it, or that we might like to read a little more in that area. It isn't a combination of the criteria which have been proposed. It may be a bit more than a passing fancy, but very frequently it does not work out to be a value.

5. *Feelings*. Our personalities are also expressed through our feelings and through statements about how we feel. Our feelings are sometimes hurt. Sometimes we feel outraged. On other occasions we are glad, sad, depressed, excited; and we experience dozens of other feelings. We cannot always say that a value is present. In terms of a definition of a value, our feelings may be responses which are dissipated by very brief reflection. We should have to ask a number

of questions in order to find out if the feeling reflects an underlying value.

6. *Beliefs and convictions*. When we hear someone state what he believes, it is all too easy to accept the statement as a value. A man may believe that there should be discrimination with respect to race, but he may be ashamed of that belief. He may not prize holding it. Moreover, upon examination, he may have doubts about the truth or goodness of his belief. It is the examined belief, the cherished belief, the freely chosen belief, and the belief that pervades life that rises to the stature of a value. The verbal statement provides a pointer, but it is only through careful examination that we get to know whether it represents a value.

7. *Activities*. We sometimes say about a figure in public life, "That's what he says, but what does he do?" We seem to be saying that not until a person does something do we have some idea of what he values. With values, as with other things, actions speak louder than words. Of course, it isn't true that every thing we do represents our values. For example, we are pretty sure that going to church does not necessarily mean a commitment to religion. One may go to church for many reasons. One may go often and regularly to bridge parties, all the while wishing that he didn't have to go. One may do a certain kind of work every day without having chosen that work or prizing it very much. In other words, just by observing what people do, we are unable to determine if values are present. We have to know if the individual prizes what he is doing, if he has chosen to do what he is doing, and if it constitutes a pattern in his life, etc. All by themselves, activities do not tell us enough, but they may indicate a value.

8. *Worries, problems, obstacles*. We hear individuals talk about worries that they have, or problems that they have, and we sometimes infer from the context that we know the values that are involved. Here again we may be giving undue importance to verbal statements. If we were to ask questions bearing upon the seven criteria which have been proposed, we might find out that nothing of great importance is involved; that the statement represented "a conversation piece." Many of us talk a good deal, and we may mention problems or worries only as ways of entering into a conversation. Examining the worry or the problem may reveal that something *is* deeply prized, that a belief *is* being blocked, that one's life *is* being

disturbed, and under these circumstances we can be more confident with the judgment that a value is involved.

We have explained something about eight categories of behavior which have a significant relationship to valuing. There is no implication that other categories of behavior may not be just as important. However, these eight categories—goals and purposes, aspirations, feelings, interests, beliefs and convictions, attitudes, activities, and worries—are often revealed in the classroom. We believe it is important that opportunities for revealing these become a vital part of teaching, for the next step—as will be discussed in later chapters—is for the teacher to help those children who choose to do so to raise these value "indicators" to the level of values, that is, to the level on which all seven of the valuing processes operate.

We now want to turn our attention to one of the value processes that seems to have particular importance in our work with children growing up in this confused and complex world, the process of choosing.

THE CRUCIAL CRITERION OF CHOICE

Because we see choosing as crucial to the process of valuing, it may be useful at this point to expand on the conditions that must exist if a choice is really to be made.

The idea of choosing suggests the notion of alternatives. One chooses something from a group of things. If there is only one possibility, we cannot make a choice and, according to our definition, we cannot have a value in that area. Yet so often we eliminate all but one alternative or we restrict alternatives available to children. For example, we say to a child that he must either sit silently in his chair or stay after school. Or we ask, "Wouldn't you like to learn your multiplication table, John?" If we restrict alternatives, so that the child's preferred choice is not among them, we cannot say that his choice represents a value. It is common practice to give children either-or choices, both of which may be undesirable from his standpoint, then wonder why he does not value his own behavior.

Unless we open up decisions, and include alternatives that a child might really prefer, we may only give the illusion of choice, at least in terms of this value theory. Values must grow from thoughtful, prized choices made from sufficient alternatives.

When we take the lead in presenting alternatives to children, we should also take some care in seeing to it that *the alternatives have meaning* for them. A student may be familiar with only one of the possible choices and may not be aware of what the others involve. We can discover this by asking questions; and if he doesn't know what other choices could mean, we can help him to understand them better. It is useless, therefore, to ask a young child to make choices from among alternatives he doesn't understand, and it is inaccurate to *think* a choice has been made when, for example, a child selects democracy over autocracy without much understanding of either.

We should also help children to see the probable *consequences of a choice* and find out if they are willing to accept the consequences which may follow. Where a child has put himself on record as willing to take the consequences, the situation has been clarified, and his choice has some meaning. Without such an understanding of and acceptance of the consequences, we can hardly call the choice meaningful.

Also there is the idea that the child needs to be really *free to choose.* If for many reasons we don't want him to choose a particular alternative, like setting fire to the house, we should let him know that this is not within the realm of choice. We should not try to fool him into thinking that he is a free agent and then disappoint him when we refuse to honor his choice. We should be clear and forceful when we deny choices. Otherwise we subvert the faith of the child in the very process of deciding and choosing. But when we are concerned with values, we must be willing to give the child his freedom to choose. In short, we are saying that a coerced choice is no choice at all. It is not likely that values will evolve from a choice imbued with threat or bribery, for example. A condition of choosing that the value theory suggests is freedom to choose. One important implication for teachers is the diminution of the punishment and reward systems so widely used in schools. Choices cannot be considered sufficiently free if each one is to be weighed, approved or disapproved, or graded by someone in charge.

Does this mean that the whole world should be open for choice and that we should respect a child's choice no matter what it is?

Most teachers, in the light of policies suggested by a school board or school administrators, make quite clear to students that there are areas where choice is not possible. One of these relates to life itself. We do not allow children to engage in activities which might result in serious danger. This is almost always directly stated and carried out without exception. We say to children that in matters like this they cannot choose, that their behavior is restricted; and the reason we give is that the consequences of an unwise choice are not tolerable or that the alternatives can probably not be well enough understood to make a choice meaningful.

Many of us are also against vulgarity in many forms. Profane language, obscene behavior, filth, and dirtiness are matters on which many of us take a stand. We may indicate to children that they may not engage in things of this kind; that the policies for which we stand do not allow such things to go on; that deviations from our standards bother us too much to be tolerated. When an individual reveals this kind of behavior, we may directly intervene and, perhaps privately, talk with the student. Thus may some teachers want to restrict choices in areas that are important to adults.

In almost every culture and in many communities there are areas which are sometimes called "hot" or "very delicate." In some communities it may be matters pertaining to religious issues; in some other communities it may be matters relating to political issues; sex is frequently such an issue. Where these so-called hot issues are matters of civil rights, rights which belong to all individuals, teachers may wish to challenge restrictions or taboos. It is good policy, however, to do this on a professional level, working among colleagues first, and not to take up things with children in a public way which may be against public policy. It is usually wiser to make attempts to clarify public policy and to modify it before involving the children in affairs that might be extremely embarrassing and extremely provoking. Whether children should be encouraged to reflect and choose in a controversial area is not the point. They *must* reflect and choose if values are to emerge. The question is one of what teachers might do first in communities which frown upon opening certain issues.

In summary, we are saying that if children—or adults, for that matter—are to develop values, they must develop them out of personal choices. We are also saying that these choices, if they are possibly to lead to values, must involve alternatives which (1) include ones that are prized by the chooser; (2) have meaning to the chooser, as when the consequences of each are clearly understood; and (3) are freely available for selection.

THE PERSONAL NATURE OF VALUES

The point has been made that our values tend to be a product of our experiences. They are not just a matter of true or false. One can not go to an encyclopedia or to a textbook for values. The definition that has been given makes this clear. One has to prize for himself, choose for himself, integrate choices into the pattern of his own life. Information as such doesn't convey this quality of values. Values come out of the flux of life itself.

This means that we are dealing with an area that isn't a matter of proof or consensus. It is a matter of experience. So, if a child says that he likes something, it does not seem appropriate for an older person to say, "You shouldn't like that." Or, if a child should say, "I am interested in that," it does not seem quite right for an older person to say to him, "You shouldn't be interested in things like that." If these things have grown out of a child's experience, they are consistent with his life. When we ask him to deny his own life, we are in effect asking him to be a hypocrite. We seem to be saying in an indirect way, "Yes, this is what your life has taught you, but you shouldn't say so. You should pretend that you had a different life." What are we doing to children when we put them into positions like this? Are we helping them to develop values or are we in effect saying that life is a fraud and that one should learn to live like a fraud very early in life.

We have an alternative approach to values, and this will be presented in the following chapters. For now, it is important to note that our definition of values and valuing leads to a conception of these words that is highly personal. It follows that if we are to respect a person's life, we must respect his experience and his right to help in examining it for values.

As a matter of fact, in a society like ours, governed by our Constitution, teachers might well see themselves as obliged to support the idea that every individual is entitled to the views that he has and to the values that he holds, especially where these have been examined and affirmed. Is this not the cornerstone of what we mean by a free society? As teachers, then, we need to be clear that we cannot dictate to children what their values should be since we cannot also dictate what their environments should be and what experiences they will have. We may be authoritative in those areas that deal with truth and falsity. In areas involving aspirations, purposes, attitudes, interests, beliefs, etc., we may raise questions, but we cannot "lay down the law" about what a child's values should be. By definition and by social right, then, values are personal things.

As a matter of cold fact, in the great majority of instances, we really don't know what values an individual child has. We are apt to make inferences which go beyond the available data and to attribute values to children which they do not hold. We probably will be better off if we assume in almost every case that we really don't know. If we are interested in knowing, we might well initiate a process of investigation and inquiry, and more attention will be given to this notion later.

One last point needs to be made before we go on. Some people, when they travel, seem to be much more interested in the motels or hotels at which they stop than in the experiences which they have along the way. Some other people are much more interested in the road than the inn. In what has been said thus far, the reader may see that we associate ourselves with the latter group. We are interested in the processes that are going on. We are not much interested in identifying the values which children hold. We are much more interested in the process because we believe that in a world that is changing as rapidly as ours, each child must develop habits of examining his purposes, aspirations, attitudes, feelings, etc., if he is to find the most intelligent relationship between his life and the surrounding world, and if he is to make a contribution to the creation of a better world.

The development of values is a personal and life-long process. It is not something that is completed by early adulthood. As the world changes, as we change, and as we strive to change the world again, we have many decisions to make and we should be learning how to make these decisions. We should be learning how to value. It is this process that we believe needs to be carried on in the classrooms, and it is at least partly through this process that we think children will learn about themselves and about how to make some sense out of the buzzing confusion of the society around them.

Chapter 4

Teaching for Value Clarity

Earlier we noted some of the uncertain and confusing aspects of society and speculated upon the difficulties children have in making sense of it all. We also said that we use the term "value" to denote those beliefs, purposes, attitudes, and so on that are chosen freely and thoughtfully, prized, and acted upon. We suggested, further, that since the development of society and the people in it is best seen as dynamic, it is perhaps wiser to focus upon the process of *valuing* than upon any particular values themselves.

Now let us be a bit more explicit about that process. What, according to the theory that we propose, does one *do* if one wants to take on the problem of helping children develop values? Briefly, one assists children in using the process of valuing. The process flows naturally from the definition of values presented earlier. That is, an adult who would help children develop values would be advised to:

1. Encourage children to make choices, and to make them freely.
2. Help them discover and examine available alternatives when faced with choices.
3. Help children weigh alternatives thoughtfully, reflecting on the consequences of each.

38

4. Encourage children to consider what it is that they prize and cherish.
5. Give them opportunities to make public affirmations of their choices.
6. Encourage them to act, behave, live in accordance with their choices.
7. Help them to examine repeated behaviors or patterns in their life.

In this way, the adult encourages the process of valuing. The intent of this process is to help children (although it is equally applicable to adults) clarify for themselves what they value. This is very different from trying to persuade children to accept some predetermined set of values. It is based on a conception of democracy that says persons can learn to make their own decisions. It is also based on a conception of humanity that says human beings hold the possibility of being thoughtful and wise and that the most appropriate values will come when persons use their intelligence freely and reflectively to define their relationships with each other and with an ever-changing world. Furthermore, it is based on the idea that values are personal things if they exist at all, that they cannot be personal until they are freely accepted, and that they cannot be of much significance if they do not penetrate the living of the person who holds them.

The next section of this book describes the value clarifying process in much more detail and gives many examples of how it might be used by teachers at many grade levels and in many subject areas. At this point it might be useful to contrast the value clarifying approach with more traditional approaches to values.

TRADITIONAL APPROACHES TO VALUES

Here are some ways that have often been advocated for helping children develop values.

1. *Setting an example* either directly, by the way adults behave, or indirectly, by pointing to good models in the past or present, such as Washington's honesty or the patience of Ulysses' wife.

2. *Persuading and convincing* by presenting arguments and rea-

sons for this or that set of values and by pointing to the fallacies and pitfalls of other sets of values.

3. *Limiting choices* by giving children choices only among values "we" accept, such as asking children to choose between helping wash the dishes or helping clean the floor, or by giving children choices between a value we accept and one no one is likely to accept, such as asking children to choose between telling the truth and never speaking to anyone again.

4. *Inspiring* by dramatic or emotional pleas for certain values, often accompanied by models of behavior associated with the value.

5. *Rules and regulations* intended to contain and mold behavior until it is unthinkingly accepted as "right," as through the use of rewards and punishments to reinforce certain behavior.

6. *Cultural or religious dogma* presented as unquestioned wisdom or principle, such as saying that something should be believed because "our people have always done it this way."

7. *Appeals to conscience*, appeals to the still, small voice that we assume is within the heart of everyone, with the arousing of feelings of guilt if one's conscience doesn't suggest the "right" way, such as telling a child that he should know better or that he shamed his parents.

We have no doubt that such methods as those listed, and there are others that could be listed, have in the past controlled behavior and even formed beliefs and attitudes, but we assert that they have not *and cannot* lead to values in the sense that we are concerned with them—values that represent the free and thoughtful choice of intelligent humans interacting with complex and changing environments.

In fact, those methods do not seem to have resulted in deep commitments of any sort. The values that are supposedly being promoted by those methods in our society—honor, courage, devotion, self-control, craftsmanship, thrift, love, etc.—seem less than ever to be the values that guide the behavior of citizens. On the pragmatic test of effectiveness alone, the approaches listed above must receive a low grade. They just do not seem to work very well. This alone would suggest that we try a new approach.

We emphasize that these methods are not without some useful effect. It is certainly useful, for example, for adults to set examples for the kinds of behaviors that they say they support. Also, most of us have had our lives stirred and enriched by inspiring words and deeds. And many have found that religion is able to nourish virtue and hope, even in an otherwise desperate and dark life. Our main point, then, is not that the above approaches to values have been without use, but that they have not worked as well as we might have hoped and that we now have some understanding of why this might have been.

The reader will note that with each of the above approaches there is the idea of persuasion. The "right" values are predetermined and it is one method or another of selling, pushing, urging those values upon others. All the methods have the air of indoctrination, with some merely more subtle than others. The idea of free inquiry, thoughtfulness, reason seems to be lost. The approach seems not to be how to help the child develop a valuing process but, rather, how to persuade the child to adopt the "right" values.

When we ask persons why such persuasive approaches are employed, why there is little effort to have the child think through issues and freely choose what *he* prizes, we tend to receive certain answers.

1. "Children are not old enough or experienced enough or wise enough to choose values for themselves. We are responsible for starting them off on the right track. We have to drill values into children now; later they will learn to value for themselves."

The assumption here is that one does not have to practice valuing for oneself at an early age and that after twenty years or so of indoctrination one can readily break the habit of conforming to the values of others.

2. "It takes too much time to help children figure out their own values. It's faster and simpler to merely show them the best way."

There are probably assumptions here about what is most important for a limited amount of time and energy, with an implication that something other than values is most important. Also implied is the assumption that everyone can get values from being shown "the best way," even as we note that a child is exposed to many varied models of what are touted as "best ways." Note also the implication that the best ways are already defined in such a form as to be generally applicable.

3. "You can't really trust children to choose the values that would serve them best. Both their inexperience and some tendency to obstinacy may lead them to poor choices. We may have disastrous results, and most certainly we will have many regrettable results."

This view assumes that one would have children choose in all areas, whether they understood the alternatives or not and whether the choice could lead to disaster or not. It also reflects some limited faith in the intelligence and good will of children.

4. "Think of the problems that will develop from wrong choices! Time wasted, unnecessary hurt and pain, and perhaps even irreparable human damage. Besides, how can adults contain themselves when they see children going astray? What, after all, are adults for if they do not point the way to wisdom and righteousness?"

There are two separate sets of assumptions here. One set has to do with the problem of "poor" choices, which assumes that children cannot learn from such choices, that the consequences of such choices are not educational, and, in fact, that children can learn about values *without* making some poor choices. There is the idea that one is helping if he prevents a child from making a mistake.

The second set of assumptions, more by implication, seems to say that adults will feel some loss of function, perhaps of power, if they do not intervene in the decisions of children. One almost imagines an adult looking back at a long childhood of being manipulated at the whimsy of the surrounding adults and hoping that his turn to assert himself will not be denied.

5. "Look, what can I do? Everyone else tries to give values to children. My children will think I'm crazy if I do otherwise, and certainly other adults will look at me and wonder at my laxness."

This says quite plainly that many adults feel pressure from others to conform in some way. It would be unwise to underestimate the strength behind that pressure, but it tends to assume that adults under pressure have not the wherewithal to assert whatever values they hold. For some, this may be true. But it may be a result of an adult's own lack of values. One might assume that if a person didn't have a clear set of values in a certain area, he would be likely to look around and see what others are doing. Thus, some conformity is not the result of a desire to conform, but represents a desire to do what is best in circumstances which are unclear. Perhaps, then, clarity here as elsewhere is what is needed.

6. "I really do not want to get too deeply into examinations of values. It is too confusing and I do not understand it well enough myself. Maybe professionals can do it, but it is much easier to let things be and direct my attention to other things."

The assumption that is clearest here is that an adult should not work with children in areas in which he is not expert, that it would be too threatening to do so. There may also be an implication that some adults do not want to recognize how ineffective their own valuing process has been.

7. "It is a matter of will power. If one wants to do something, all he needs is the will to do it."

This assumes, of course, that one does want to do something, that purposes are clear, that something is blocking the achievement of personal goals. It does not seem to take in the possibility that purposes are not clear and that ambivalence is in control.

8. "Frankly, children are more difficult to handle if they are deciding too many things for themselves. If children expect to learn what they should believe and value from us, it is easier all around. There will be fewer discipline problems."

The assumption here is that children who are tractable are more valuable than children who have values. There is the additional assumption that the indoctrination of values does lead to more obedient children and fewer behavior problems.

9. "Children appreciate being told what to do and what to believe. It gives them security. Freedom is frightening to many of them."

The assumption here would seem to deal with the cause of insecurity that arises when duties cease to direct children. Are children insecure only because they now would have free time and free choice, or are they insecure because they have had no help in acquiring real values to direct their use of that freedom? Is the answer to keep children under pressure, keep them busy, keep them under control? Or is the answer to help them to develop values so that they can be responsibly self-directing in an ever-changing world?

Now these reasons for wanting to persuade children to take on certain values seems to us to be based on questionable assumptions, although some of the assumptions seem more temptingly tenable than others and some are probably reasonable for some situations and not for others. There is at least one additional reason for adults trying to impose their values on children, and it is perhaps the overriding reason: *no other alternative that is clear and testable has been provided.* Not being aware of another choice, who can blame adults for doing what they think best? The observation that many children and adults do not, in fact, seem to have many clear values may have raised questions about the efficiency of trying to sell adult beliefs to children, but what alternative choice is there? This book, of course, hopes to offer one.

WHY A NEW APPROACH?

There is widespread concern that youth, and adults in some cases, do not seem to live by any consistent set of values. They act impetuously, erratically, and sometimes with malice. Many children find nothing enjoyable to do with their free time. Even in school many seem purposeless and listless, motivated only—but not always consistently—by outside pressures. Our population is becoming other-directed, it is asserted; we guide our lives not by what we believe is right and proper, but by what others do or say. Does this not suggest that many persons have unclear values?

We note the wide discrepancy between what people do and what they say. Many political leaders, business executives, military leaders, workers of all sorts, and even professional people are known to *do* things that are inconsistent with what they *say* are their values. Corruption is not an unusual occurrence. So many people can be "bought." Does this not suggest that the approaches to values that have been so widely used in the past have been less than effective?

Adults have been trying to set examples for years. They have tried often with ingenious manipulation to persuade children to accept certain values. They have carefully limited choices given to children. They have attempted to inspire identification with particular values. They have made rules and insisted on certain patterns of behavior. They have relied upon religion and cultural truisms. They have appealed to the consciences of young people. But even a casual look at the results of these approaches is discouraging. They just do not seem to have worked.

In the past we have told children, children who have been exposed to so many different and confusing stimuli, that they should believe in one thing or another. We have said this in many ways: by our example, our rules, our arguments, and so on. But as we spoke, they were surrounded by other examples and arguments which stood for different values; and when a child indicated by a lack of purpose or a disregard of purpose that he was confused by all this, we insisted, punished, pleaded, and otherwise campaigned even harder for one of the many values that we were convinced he must adopt. More than likely this only further confused many children and made them less able to decide in what to believe. Consequently, many children pretend to believe. Or if they do believe, they try not to do it very keenly. Or they deal with the dilemma by taking whatever belief is popular and convenient at the moment, switching frequently.

Why must teachers see their role only as putting things into the mind of the child? Why can't a role be defined that would help a child take all the confusion that already exists in his mind, remove it, look at it, examine it, turn it around, and make some order out of it? Why can't teachers learn to spend some of their time helping children understand what the bewildering array of beliefs and attitudes that saturate our modern life are all about and which suits him best? Is this not the road to values, to *clear* and *personal* values?

We believe it is. We believe that as children are helped to use what we call the valuing process, they will move toward value clarity in a more sensible and dramatic way than ever before. Peck and Havighurst (1960, p. 191) put it succinctly:

It is temptingly easy and insidiously gratifying to "mold" children, or to "whip them into line" by exercising one's superior status and authority as an adult. It is often personally inconvenient to allow children time to debate alternatives, and it may be personally frustrating if their choice contradicts one's own preferences. If there is any selfish, sensitive "pride" at stake, it is very hard for most adults to refrain from controlling children in an autocratic manner. Then, too, like any dictatorship, it looks "more efficient"—to the dictator, at least. However, the effect on character is to arrest the development of rational judgment and to create such resentments as prevent the growth of genuine altruistic impulses. For thousands of years, the long-term effects have been ignored and sacrificed to short-term adult advantages, most of the time. Probably it is no accident that there are relatively few people who are, or ever will become, psychologically and ethically mature.

SUMMARY OF PART TWO

So far we have presented a view of the concept of value that is based on a particular notion of human potential, one which emphasizes man's capacity for intelligent, self-directed behavior. We have said that it would be well to reserve the term "value" for those individual beliefs, attitudes, activities, or feelings that satisfy the criteria of (1) having been freely chosen, (2) having been chosen from among alternatives, (3) having been chosen after due reflection, (4) having been prized and cherished, (5) having been publicly affirmed, (6) having been incorporated into actual behavior, and (7) having been repeated in one's life. In different words, we might say that something will not qualify as a value if *any* of the following conditions apply.

1. It has not been *freely* chosen (no room in this theory for values that are imposed upon one by outside pressures).

2. It is without one or more available alternatives (a real choice must exist, not a spurious choice).

3. It has been chosen without thoughtful consideration (this excludes impulse or highly emotional choices from the category of values).

4. It is not prized or cherished (we exclude from the level of values those things which we have or do of which we are not proud and would rather not have or do—as when one chooses the least objectionable of several undesirable alternatives).

5. It is denied upon public confrontation (to be ashamed or unduly fearful of something is to indicate that one does not value it highly).

6. It is not in some way reflected in one's actual behavior (one who chooses democracy and never does anything to put that choice into practice may be said to have an attitude or belief about democracy but not a value).

7. It is a passing fancy and lacks any persistence over time (a one-shot effort at pottery-making, for example, would not qualify as a value).

The meaning here for schools and, more particularly, the busy classroom teacher is implicit in the definition. If one wishes to help children develop clearer values, one must help children use the process of valuing. That is, one must help children: (1) make free choices whenever possible, (2) search for alternatives in choice-making situations, (3) weigh the consequences of each available alternative, (4) consider what they prize and cherish, (5) affirm the things they value, (6) do something about their choices, and (7) consider and strengthen patterns in their lives. It is as simple, and complex, as that. As the teacher helps students use these processes, he helps them find values.

It should be increasingly clear that the adult does not force his own pet values upon children. What he does is create conditions that aid children in finding values *if* they choose to do so. When operating with this value theory, it is entirely possible that children will choose not to develop values. It is the teacher's responsibility to support this choice also, while at the same time realizing that value development is likely to be one of the goals of the school and, if so, it should be encouraged by providing regular experiences that will help raise to the value level the beliefs, feelings, interests, and activities children bring with them.

The next section of the book details procedures that teachers can use to do this. Procedures are presented that teachers can use without taking time away from on-going programs or activities. Also outlined are techniques for relating value lessons to the familiar subject matter.

The teacher who activates the value theory in some of the ways suggested in those chapters can expect that children will have more values, be more aware of the values that they have, have values that are more consistent with one another, and, especially, be ready to use the valuing process as they continue to grow and learn.

But there are also purposes that are more concrete, more relevant to the typical school task, and more readily measurable that seem to be promoted by the valuing process. For example, research (discussed more fully in Chapter 11) shows that when the valuing process was promoted with children who were very apathetic, over-conforming, flighty, and likely to act in a variety of poses or "phony" roles, this type of behavior became noticeably less acute and less frequent. There is also evidence that these techniques help children who are very indecisive, who are very inconsistent, or who are chronic dissenters. Other research showed the valuing process to help underachievers improve in the following:

Attitudes toward learning
Raising of questions and alternatives
Initiation and self-direction of classroom activity
Perseverance
Active participation

In general, the research shows that students become more vital and purposeful when given opportunities to clarify their values. How, specifically, this may be done is the subject of the chapters which follow.

Part Three

The Value Clarifying Method

Chapter 5

The Clarifying
Response

The basic strategy of this approach to value clarifying rests on a specific method of responding to things a student says or does. This basic responding technique is discussed in this chapter.

Fundamentally, the responding strategy is a way of responding to a student that results in his considering what he has chosen, what he prizes, and/or what he is doing. It stimulates him to clarify his thinking and behavior and thus to clarify his values; it encourages him to think about them.

Imagine a student on the way out of class who says, "Miss Jones, I'm going to Washington, D.C., this weekend with my family." How might a teacher respond? Perhaps, "That's nice," or "Have a good time!"

Neither of those responses is likely to stimulate clarifying thought on the part of the student. Consider a teacher responding in a different way, for example: "Going to Washington, are you? Are you glad you're going?" To sense the clarifying power in that response, imagine the student saying, "No, come to think of it, I'm not glad I'm going. I'd rather play in the Little League game." If the teacher were to say nothing else at this point other than perhaps "Well,

51

we'll see you Monday," or some noncommittal equivalent, one might say that the student would be a little more aware of his life; in this case, his doing things that he is not happy about doing. This is not a very big step, and it might be no step at all, but it might contribute to his considering a bit more seriously how much of his life he should involve in things that he does not prize or cherish. We say it is a step toward value clarity.

Or note this example. A student says that he is planning to go to college after high school. A teacher who replies, "Good for you," or "Which college?", or "Well, I hope you make it," is probably going to serve purposes other than value clarity. But were the teacher to respond, "Have you considered any alternatives?", the goal of value clarity may well be advanced. The "alternatives" response is likely to stimulate thinking about the issue and, if he decides to go to college, that decision is likely to be closer to a value than it was before. It may contribute a little toward moving a college student from the position of going because "it's the thing to do" to going because he wants to get something out of it.

Here are two other samples of exchanges using clarifying responses.

STUDENT: I believe that all men are created equal.

TEACHER: What do you mean by that?

STUDENT: I guess I mean that all people are equally good and none should have advantages over others.

TEACHER: Does this idea suggest that some changes need to be made in our world, even in this school and this town?

STUDENT: Oh, lots of them. Want me to name some?

TEACHER: No, we have to get back to our spelling lesson, but I was just wondering if you were working on any of those changes, actually trying to bring them about.

STUDENT: Not yet, but I may soon.

TEACHER: I see. Now, back to the spelling list. . . .

TEACHER: Bruce, don't you want to go outside and play on the playground?

STUDENT: I dono. I suppose so.

TEACHER: Is there something that you would rather do?

STUDENT: I dono. Nothing much.

TEACHER: You don't seem much to care, Bruce. Is that right?

STUDENT: I suppose so.

TEACHER: And mostly anything we do will be all right with you?

STUDENT: I suppose so. Well, not anything, I guess.

TEACHER: Well, Bruce, we had better go out to the playground now with the others. You let me know sometime if you think of something you would like to do.

The reader may already sense some criteria of an effective clarifying response, that is, a response that encourages someone to look at his life and his ideas and to think about them. These are among the essential elements.

1. The clarifying response avoids moralizing, criticizing, giving values, or evaluating. The adult excludes all hints of "good" or "right" or "acceptable," or their opposites, in such responses.

2. It puts the responsibility on the student to look at his behavior or his ideas and to think and decide for himself what it is *he* wants.

3. A clarifying response also entertains the possibility that the student will *not* look or decide or think. It is permissive and stimulating, but not insistent.

4. It does not try to do big things with its small comments. It works more at stimulating thought relative to what a person does or says. It aims at setting a mood. Each clarifying response is only one of many; the effect is cumulative.

5. Clarifying responses are not used for interview purposes. The goal is not to obtain data, but for the student to clarify his ideas and life if he wants to do so.

6. It is usually not an extended discussion. The idea is for the student to think, and he usually does that best alone, without the temptation to justify his thoughts to an adult. Therefore a teacher will be advised to carry on only two or three rounds of dialogue and then offer to break off the conversation with some noncommittal but honest phrase, such as "Nice talking to you," or "I see what you mean better now," or "Got to get to my next class," or "Let's talk about this another time, shall we?", or "Very interesting. Thanks." (Of course, there is no reason why a student who desires to talk more should be turned aside, the teacher's time permitting.)

7. Clarifying responses are often for individuals. A topic in which John might need clarification may be of no immediate interest to Mary. An issue that is of general concern, of course, may warrant a

general clarifying response, say to the whole class, but even here the *individual* must ultimately do the reflecting for himself. Values are personal things. The teacher often responds to one individual, although others may be listening.

8. The teacher doesn't respond to everything everyone says or does in a classroom. There are other responsibilities he has. (In Chapter 8, we discuss how clarifying responses can be used with those students who need them most.)

9. Clarifying responses operate in situations in which there are no "right" answers, such as in situations involving feelings, attitudes, beliefs, or purposes. They are *not* appropriate for drawing a student toward a predetermined answer. They are *not* questions to which the teacher has an answer already in mind.

10. Clarifying responses are not mechanical things that carefully follow a formula. They must be used creatively and with insight, but with their purpose in mind: when a response helps a student to clarify his thinking or behavior, it is considered effective.

The ten conditions listed above are very difficult to fulfil for the teacher who has not practiced them. The tendency to use responses to students for the purpose of molding students' thinking is very well established in most of our minds. The idea that a function of a teacher is to help the child clarify some of the confusion and ambiguity already in his head is an unfamiliar one for many of us. After all, most of us became teachers because we wanted to *teach* somebody something. Most of us are all too ready to sell our intellectual wares. The clarifying strategy requires a different orientation; not that of adding to the child's ideas but rather one of stimulating him to clarify the ideas he already has.

Here is another classroom incident illustrating a teacher using clarifying responses, in this case to help a student see that free, thoughtful choices can be made. The situation is a classroom discussion in which a boy has just made it clear that he is a liberal in his political viewpoints.

TEACHER: You say, Glenn, that you are a liberal in political matters?

GLENN: Yes, I am.

TEACHER: Where did your ideas come from?

GLENN: Well, my parents I guess, mostly.

TEACHER: Are you familiar with other positions?

GLENN: Well, sort of.

TEACHER: I see, Glenn. Now, class, getting back to the homework for today . . . (returning to the general lesson).

Here is another actual situation. In this incident the clarifying response prods the student to clarify his thinking and to examine his behavior to see if it is consistent with his ideas. It is between lessons and a student has just told a teacher that science is his favorite subject.

TEACHER: What exactly do you like about science?

STUDENT: Specifically? Let me see. Gosh, I'm not sure. I guess I just like it in general.

TEACHER: Do you do anything outside of school to have fun with science?

STUDENT: No, not really.

TEACHER: Thank you, Jim. I must get back to work now.

Notice the brevity of the exchanges. Sometimes we call these exchanges "one-legged conferences" because they often take place while a teacher is on one leg, pausing briefly on his way elsewhere. An extended series of probes might give the student the feeling that he was being cross-examined and might make him defensive. Besides it would give him too much to think about. The idea is, without moralizing, to raise a few questions, leave them hanging in the air, and then move on. The student to whom the questions are addressed, and other students who might overhear, may well ponder the questions later, in a lull in the day or in the quiet moments before falling asleep. Gentle prods, but the effect is to stimulate a student who is ready for it to choose, prize, and act in ways outlined by the value theory. And, as the research reported in Chapter 11 demonstrates, these one-legged conferences add up to make large differences in some students' lives.

THIRTY CLARIFYING RESPONSES

There are several responses that teachers who have worked with the clarifying approach have found very useful. A list of some of these is presented below. As the reader goes through the list, he might make note of some he would like to try; that is, make his own list. There are too many noted here to keep in mind at one time. It is probably best then, to gather a dozen or so together, ones which sound as if they could be used comfortably, and try them out, perhaps expanding or revising the list as experience dictates.

Be reminded, however, that the responses listed here are recommended as useful clarifying responses only when they are used in accordance with the ten conditions listed earlier. The acid test for any response is whether or not it results in a person reflecting on what he has said or done, clarifying, getting to know himself better, examining his choices, considering what he prizes, looking at patterns in his life, and so on. If the response makes the student defensive, or gets him to say what the adult wants him to say, or gives him the feeling that the adult is nagging at him, it is being used improperly or with poor timing. An accepting, noncommittal attitude on the part of the person making responses is crucial.

The reader might note that some of the responses listed below are geared directly to one or another of the seven valuing components: prizing, searching for alternatives, thinking critically, choosing freely, incorporating choices into behavior, examining patterns of living, and affirming choices. Some other responses stimulate reflection in a more general sense. But, in _all_ cases, responses are open-ended— they lead the student to no specific value. No one must deliver a "right" answer to a clarifying response. Each student must be permitted to react in his own personal and individual way.

1. Is this something that you prize?

To respond in a way that gets the student to consider whether he prizes or cherishes something he has said or done helps him to clarify his values. The response could, of course, be in a different form and have the same intent, e.g., "Are you proud of that?", "Is that something that is very important to you?", "Is that idea very dear to you; do you really cherish it?" The particular situation in which the response is being made, as well as the age of the child to whom it is directed, will help determine the precise wording.

2. Are you glad about that?

This encourages the student to see whether things he feels, says, or does are things that he is happy about and make him feel good. One could also ask if the student is unhappy about something. Such questions stimulate a child to evaluate his life and to consider changing it if *he* finds it does not bring him satisfactions. Note how different the effect of this response is from the scolding "Aren't you ashamed of that?" Clarifying responses are accepting and illuminating, not rejecting and moralizing.

3. How did you feel when that happened?

It advances clarification for a person to understand that his feelings are part of his understandings and awareness and that they have to be considered in decision-making. He needs to know that feelings are important, that we respect his right to have his own feelings, and that feelings do not have to be suppressed.

4. Did you consider any alternatives?

Note how this tends to widen, to open up the thinking of children (and adults). With this response, as with *all* the others in this list, teachers will need to accept whatever the student replies without judgment. After he answers the question, leave him with an honest "Oh. Now I see," or "I understand," or "You stated your views clearly," or "I appreciate hearing what you say," or some non-judgmental phrase or gesture.

5. Have you felt this way for a long time?

Questions that get at the same thing are, "When did you first begin to believe in that idea?" and "How have your ideas or understandings changed since the time you first considered this notion?" Here the person is pushed to examine the history of his beliefs or attitudes, to look at their origins, and to see if they are really his or if they have been absorbed unthinkingly. Note how the next response might follow after a student replies to this one.

6. Was that something that you yourself selected or chose?

This reminds persons that they *can* make their own choices, if they want to do so. An affirmative reply to this response might well be followed by response Number 7.

7. Did you have to choose that; was it a free choice?

Here, no matter what the student says, it is probably wise to say no more but to discontinue the conversation with some non-judgmental closing.

8. Do you do anything about that idea?

This response helps persons see the responsibility for incorporating choices into actual living. A verbalization that is not lived has little import and is certainly not a value. Another way of saying the same thing: "How does that idea affect your daily life?", or "In what ways do you act upon it?"

9. Can you give me some examples of that idea?

This helps push generalizations and vague statements of belief toward clarity. Note also the relevance of the next response.

10. What do you mean by————: can you define that word?

This also pushes understanding to clarity and helps prevent the mouthing of words students cannot really mean because they do not really understand them.

11. Where would that idea lead; what would be its consequences?

This encourages the student to study carefully the consequences of ideas. No meaningful choice can be made unless the consequences of alternatives are understood. Therefore, it is often very useful to help children examine the consequences of each available alternative. Accordingly, one could also ask, "What would be the results of each of the alternatives?", or "How would those ideas work out in practice?"

12. Would you really do that or are you just talking?

Again the encouragement to see the importance of living in accordance with one's choice.

13. Are you saying that . . . [repeat]?

It is sometimes useful merely to repeat what the student has just said. This has the effect of reflecting his ideas and prompting him to ask himself if he really meant that. It is surprising how many persons seldom hear what they say. Sometimes the phrase "Did I hear you correctly?" can be used for this purpose.

14. Did you say that . . . [repeat in some distorted way]?

Sometimes a teacher does well to purposely twist what a student has said. Will the student attempt to correct the distortion? After trying it, one senses that the effect is much the same as response Number 13.

15. Have you thought much about that idea (or behavior)?

Of course one accepts whatever reply a student makes to this. It is destructive to the valuing process to attack a negative answer to this question with something like, "Well, in the future it would be wise to think before you speak (or act)." An accepting and non-judgmental mood is vital for the valuing process.

16. What are some good things about that notion?

A simple request for justification of expressed ideas in some such non-judgmental words often brings dramatic re-evaluation of thinking on the part of students. Many persons rarely realize that there could or should be good, desirable, worthwhile aspects of ideas they hold. The ideas are just there, unexamined and unevaluated.

17. What do we have to assume for things to work out that way?

Many persons have neglected to examine the assumptions upon which rest their ideas, aspirations, and activities. This probing helps persons understand better, make choices more wisely, and make valuing more possible. It is sometimes useful, in this context, to suggest an assumption that the student seems to be making and ask him if he has considered it, e.g., "Are you assuming that there was *nothing* good about the depression?"

18. Is what you express consistent with . . . [note something else the person said or did that may point to an inconsistency]?

To present such a disconcerting challenge, to note an exception, to relate things with other things, can produce real clarification_ *if* it is not done with an "I think I have trapped you in an error" tone of voice. The idea is not to slap students down, but to open things up for them so that they can think with new insight, if they want to do so. (Happily, teachers trying this approach seem to find that most students do want to do so.)

19. What other possibilities are there?

This raises alternatives to students and thus it aids them in valuing. Sometimes this question is posed to a group and all alternatives are listed on the board, without judgment again. Of course, other students and the teacher, too, can say which alternative *they* prefer, but there is no judging a child because he chooses a different alternative. No teasing or otherwise deriding others' choices is tolerated or else there is no free choice.

20. Is that a personal preference or do you think most people should believe that?

To inquire whether a statement is intended as a personal preference or whether it is something that should be generally endorsed is one way of helping to distinguish an attitude or prejudice from a social principle. "Is this idea so good that everyone should go along with it?" is another way to get at this.

21. How can I help you do something about your idea? What seems to be the difficulty?

This question reminds the student that *action* is a component of life and intentions are incomplete until acted upon. Sometimes such questions uncover suppressed feelings or misunderstandings. Obviously, they locate real or imagined obstacles, too. Also try: "Where are you stuck?", or "What is holding you up?" (But be prepared to offer help if it's asked for.)

22. Is there a purpose back of this activity?

Asking students what, if anything, they are trying to accomplish, where they are headed with ideas or activities, sometimes brings the realization to students—and for the first time—that they might really have purposes and goals and that they might relate their ongoing activities to those purposes and goals.

23. Is that very important to you?

This gets students to consider more seriously what is and what is not important to them. It is also often useful to ask students to put several things in order of rank. Assigning priorities is a variation, and a useful one.

24. Do you do this often?

"Is there any pattern to your life that incorporates this idea or activity?", one might inquire. The idea here is to help students see what is repeated in their lives and what is not and to leave them with the decision of whether or not to build a pattern.

25. Would you like to tell others about your idea?

Inviting a student to explain his ideas to the class or others provides two challenges. It tests to see whether he is committed to his beliefs strongly enough to affirm them in public. It also puts him in the position of thinking through his ideas well enough to explain them, and perhaps justify them, to others.

26. Do you have any reasons for (saying or doing) that?

This tests whether or not a choice has been made and to what extent that choice was based on understanding. DANGER: Avoid using that question to pull up short on a student who is obviously not thinking. If you want to tell a student that you believe that he is not thinking, tell him so. But use the above question when you really want to have a student consider his beliefs or actions.

Incidentally, when a student does (or says) something and the teacher inquires, "Sonny, why did you do that?", the student often hears, "Sonny, now why in the world did you ever do something as foolish as that?" "Why" questions are usually to be avoided when attempting to help students clarify their values. "Why" questions tend to make a student defensive, tend to prod him into making up reasons or excuses when he really has none in mind. Besides, the question "Why did you do that?" carries with it the assumption that the student *knows* why, and that is perhaps the reason he tends to concoct a reason when he has none. It is much more effective, for value clarifying purposes, to ask "Do you *have* a reason?" and then sometimes follow up an affirmative reply with, "Would you mind telling me?"

27. Would you do the same thing over again?

This helps a student to evaluate things that he has done, to consider why he has done them, and perhaps to affirm the wisdom of doing it in the future. Do not use this question everytime someone does something that *you* do not like. That would be an example of not-so-subtle moralizing. Use the question when you want to stimulate thinking, and strive to keep it non-judgmental.

28. How do you know it's right?

When a child makes a moral or ethical judgment about something by saying that a thing is right or lovely or good, it is useful to ask how he knows that that judgment is correct. Sometimes we ask how he was able to decide. Note this dialogue.

> TEACHER: "I see you're hard at work on that project, Jimmy."
> STUDENT: "It's not good to be lazy, you know."
> TEACHER: "How do you know it's not good?"
> STUDENT: "Everybody knows that. My parents always say it."
> TEACHER: (Walking away) "I see."

Thus may a teacher subtly and persistently suggest that one might think about such matters as rightness, or beauty, or goodness if one wants to do so.

29. Do you value that?

Merely picking out something a student has said or done and asking "Is that something that you value?" helps to stimulate clarifying thinking. Perhaps such a question could have been added by Jimmy's teacher in the above dialogue, e.g.,

> TEACHER: "I see. Is working something that you value then, Jimmy?"
> STUDENT: "Huh? I suppose so."
> TEACHER: "O.K., Jimmy. Thank you."

30. Do you think people will always believe that? Or, "Would Chinese peasants and African hunters also believe that?" Or, "Did people long ago believe that?"

Such questions are useful to suggest to a student that his beliefs may be unknowingly influenced by his surroundings, by his social milieu. It helps him gauge the extent to which he may be conforming. See also response Number 5.

Note Chart 1 for examples of how some of the above clarifying responses, and others, are related to the seven components of the valuing process. Those seven criteria are helpful for thinking of other useful clarifying responses and for keeping in mind the ones above. All clarifying responses in one way or another encourage the student to choose, prize, or act in terms outlined by the value theory.

CHART 1

Clarifying Responses Suggested
by the Seven Valuing Processes

1. Choosing freely
   a. Where do you suppose you first got that idea?
   b. How long have you felt that way?
   c. What would people say if you weren't to do what you say you must do?
   d. Are you getting help from anyone? Do you need more help? Can I help?
   e. Are you the only one in your crowd who feels this way?
   f. What do your parents want you to be?
   g. Is there any rebellion in your choice?
   h. How many years will you give to it? What will you do if you're not good enough?
   i. Do you think the idea of having thousands of people cheering when you come out on the field has anything to do with your choice?

2. Choosing from alternatives
   a. What else did you consider before you picked this?
   b. How long did you look around before you decided?
   c. Was it a hard decision? What went into the final decision? Who helped? Do you need any further help?
   d. Did you consider another possible alternative?
   e. Are there some reasons behind your choice?
   f. What choices did you reject before you settled on your present idea or action?
   g. What's really good about this choice which makes it stand out from the other possibilities?

3. Choosing thoughtfully and reflectively
   a. What would be the consequences of each alternative available?
   b. Have you thought about this very much? How did your thinking go?
   c. Is this what I understand you to say . . . [interpret his statement]?
   d. Are you implying that . . . [distort his statement to see if he is clear enough to correct the distortion]?
   e. What assumptions are involved in your choice. Let's examine them.
   f. Define the terms you use. Give me an example of the kind of job you can get without a high-school diploma.

    g. Now if you do this, what will happen to that . . . ?
    h. Is what you say consistent with what you said earlier?
    i. Just what is good about this choice?
    j. Where will it lead?
    k. For whom are you doing this?
    l. With these other choices, rank them in order of significance.
    m. What will you have to do? What are your first steps? Second
       steps?
    n. Whom else did you talk to?
    o. Have you really weighed it fully?

4. Prizing and cherishing
    a. Are you glad you feel that way?
    b. How long have you wanted it?
    c. What good is it? What purpose does it serve? Why is it impor-
       tant to you?
    d. Should everyone do it your way?
    e. Is it something you really prize?
    f. In what way would life be different without it?

5. Affirming
    a. Would you tell the class the way you feel some time?
    b. Would you be willing to sign a petition supporting that idea?
    c. Are you saying that you believe . . . [repeat the idea]?
    d. You don't mean to say that you believe . . . [repeat the
       idea]?
    e. Should a person who believes the way you do speak out?
    f. Do people know that you believe that way or that you do that
       thing?
    g. Are you willing to stand up and be counted for that?

6. Acting upon choices
    a. I hear what you are for; now, is there anything you can do
       about it? Can I help?
    b. What are your first steps, second steps, etc.?
    c. Are you willing to put some of your money behind this idea?
    d. Have you examined the consequences of your act?
    e. Are there any organizations set up for the same purposes? Will
       you join?
    f. Have you done much reading on the topic? Who has influ-
       enced you?
    g. Have you made any plans to do more than you already have
       done?

    h. Would you want other people to know you feel this way? What if they disagree with you?

    i. Where will this lead you? How far are you willing to go?

    j. How has it already affected your life? How will it affect it in the future?

7. Repeating
   a. Have you felt this way for some time?
   b. Have you done anything already? Do you do this often?
   c. What are your plans for doing more of it?
   d. Should you get other people interested and involved?
   e. Has it been worth the time and money?
   f. Are there some other things you can do which are like it?
   g. How long do you think you will continue?
   h. What did you *not* do when you went to do that? Was that o.k.?
   i. How did you decide which had priority?
   j. Did you run into any difficulty?
   k. Will you do it again?

TOPICS RIPE FOR CLARIFYING RESPONSES

Let us now consider what kinds of student expressions might fruitfully be followed by clarifying responses. One does not follow all student statements and behaviors with clarifying responses. They are not for teaching subject matter, for example. They are for promoting student thought of a particular kind, the kind we call valuing. But when does one use clarifying responses?

We have arrived at five important categories having a relationship to values: *attitudes, aspirations, purposes, interests,* and *activities.* We call these "value-indicators"; and they are just that, they point out that the expression (a statement or an action) indicates something about values. Of course, we save the precious word "value" itself only for those expressions which meet all seven of the valuing criteria outlined in previous chapters. Value indicators are expressions which are *headed* toward values, but they have not yet "arrived." They are, however, ideal matter for value clarifying responses.

The teacher who would help students must learn to listen for the specific comments students make which are in the realm of value indicators. With just a little practice, most teachers can hear these indicators. After a while, they come at a teacher with red flags flying. Below are some charts showing several value indicators and some examples of the kinds of things students are apt to say which tell a teacher that things are ripe for a clarifying response.

No value indicator operates alone, but suffice it to say that a teacher who listens for those comments from his students that fall in the several categories and who then responds within the framework of the valuing methodology should do much to advance the clarification of values and, in turn, should witness significant behavioral changes. Students who had been listless and apathetic should become more purposeful and self-directed. Students who had been over-conforming should more often stand on their own two feet and come closer to discovering their own identity. So it will be with other students with value-related behavior problems. This is part of the reward for the teacher who begins to work in the area of value clarification.

On Attitudes

As seen in Chart 2 people express an ATTITUDE when they reveal what they are *for* and what they are *against*. Beliefs, opinions, and convictions are often similarly used. In number 1 on Chart 2, it is clear that the student is against letting in too many immigrants. In number 2 the student is for the "buyer beware" principle. (We might say that he is against revealing every flaw. Most of the things we are against can be expressed as something we are for and *vice versa*.) In number 3 the student is for giving Negroes more than just equal opportunities. In number 4 we have someone against doll playing, at least for him; and in number 5, an impatience with a particular law. Such statements are ripe for a clarifying response.

CHART 2

Value Indicators: Attitudes

Statements students have made:

1. "If you let in too many immigrants, I believe it just makes it tough for everyone else."

2. "When I sold him my bike, I didn't feel I had to tell him *every-thing* that was wrong with it."
3. "I think we just have to overcompensate Negroes at this time, because they're so far behind."
4. "You wouldn't catch me playing with dolls."
5. "I don't see why we have to wait until we're eighteen to drive."

Typical keywords that signal the statement of attitudes:

I'm for . . . .
I'm against . . . .
I feel that . . . .
I think if . . . .
The way I see it . . . .
If you ask me . . . .
In my opinion . . . .
My choice is . . . .
My way of doing it is . . . .
I'm convinced that . . . .
I believe . . . .

One useful tool for teachers to work with in the area of attitudes is to listen carefully to what students say and then to mentally "plus" and "minus" their statements. We plus what they are for and minus what they say they are against. This is particularly easy to do in students' written work, but more on that later. We have found that students are not always aware when they have revealed that they are for and against something. They are, of course, quite surprised to see their inconsistencies. We must be careful to avoid making our students feel they will lose face as these things are exposed, however. It is important, terribly important, to maintain that accepting atmosphere and to say over and over again, and mean it, "All of us are inconsistent from time to time, and all of us tend to be confused about certain things that we are for and against. One of the things we hope to learn is how to think about our attitudes and clarify them."

It may be helpful for the reader to try to match up the expression of an attitude, such as those in Chart 2, with a reasonable clarifying response, such as from the list of thirty. (Responses 10, 11, and 12, among others, are often suited to expressions of attitudes.) One need not commit this to memory; after trial-and-error practice, a sense of it is likely to emerge, permitting one to improvise freely.

On Aspirations

As seen in Chart 3, students express ASPIRATION when they reveal some long-range plan or goal. Sadly, without help from sensitive teachers, so many plans never can come to fruition; and when a series of one's hopes goes down the drain, it becomes difficult to continue to aspire. Such is the soil in which grow listlessness, indifference, and apathy. One of the most important things we can do when we deal with aspirations is to bring some of the dreamers face to face with the necessary steps between the first dream and the final achievement, and to do this without throwing cold water on what may be a reality greater than we are able to recognize. It reminds us again that there are no right answers in clarifying. It demands in the clarifier a quiet humility. Nevertheless, one can see how statements of aspirations invite a value clarifying response.

CHART 3

Value Indicator: Aspirations

Statements students have made:

1. "Someday I'd like to join the Peace Corps."
2. "If only I were better in math, I'd try for engineering."
3. "My hope is to someday buy a summer home on a lake and to have my own boat."
4. "My dream is to someday run a little nursery school of my own."
5. "We want to have six kids, three boys and three girls, eighteen months apart."

Typical keywords that signal the statement of aspirations:

In the future . . . .
When I grow up . . . .
Someday, I'm going to . . . .
My long-range plan is . . . .
In about ten years I'm . . . .
If all goes well . . . .
One of these days . . . .

On Purposes

As seen in Chart 4, students express PURPOSE when they reveal some short-range goal or hope. They require planning, sometimes writing letters or making phone calls, getting commitments from others occasionally, and almost always some money (working for it, saving it, borrowing it). When a student has a plan, his excitement often spills out. Plans and goals give a much needed lift to life, and people with many plans (if they don't get frenetic) tend to be zestful and purposeful. The teacher can help students test the consequences of some coming adventure, can pose alternatives for what else might use this energy, time, and money, and can help the student see what else could grow from the coming event. These are legitimate clarifying efforts. Moralizing, preaching, and generating guilt are not.

CHART 4

Value Indicator: Purposes

Statements students have made:

1. "This weekend we're going to play."
2. "At the end of the month three of us fellows are going skiing."
3. "If I can find the right rear end from an old car, I'm going to make a trailer."
4. "I called my buddy and he's going to write for the appointment to see this man about the summer job."
5. "When I save up the twenty dollars, I'm going to buy that guitar."

Typical keywords that signal the statement of purposes:

We're thinking about doing . . . .
On the fifteenth, I'm going . . . .
On the way downtown we're . . . .
I wrote for the plans . . . .
When I get this . . . . I'm going to do that . . . .
We're waiting to hear from him . . . .
Boy! Will Saturday ever come?
I'd like to . . . .

On Interests

As seen in Chart 5, students express INTEREST when they reveal some of the things they like to do in their spare time. Included are those things which excite us, which occupy our minds and hands, and which cause us to spend time, money, and energy on them. Hobbies are the most obvious expressions of interests, but so, too, are our reading and what we go out of our way to see or experience, such as sporting or theatrical events.

One of the interesting side effects for a teacher when he begins to listen and really show an interest in something a student is excited about is that the teacher's own life can take on some added flavor, for students have many delightful and really creative pastimes. Not all of them are values, however, and this is one of the ways we can help students, by getting them to clarify which are those that are merely passing whims or thoughtless behaviors and which are headed well along the road to becoming values.

CHART 5

Value Indicator: Interest

Statements students have made:

1. "I read everything I can lay my hands on about nursing."
2. "I'd rather listen to Bach than almost anyone else."
3. "I'm saving up to subscribe to this photography magazine."
4. "I'm going to enter this glider into the contest."
5. "No, I won't be home Saturday. I'm going to the town drag strip."

Typical keywords that signal a statement about activities:

I love making [or doing] . . . .
My hobby is . . . .
Yes, I subscribe to . . . .
I really enjoy reading about . . . .
If I had my choice I'd take the ticket to . . . .
Most weekends I'm over at the . . . .
Every night after school I . . . .
Boy, nothing makes me feel better than . . . .
I got this catalogue on . . . .

On Activities

As seen in Chart 6, students express ACTIVITY when they reveal how they use time. Actually, the activity category is a part of each of the other value indicators, and that is why we list it last. When one has attitudes, often activities will follow, and so it is with aspirations, purposes, and interests. In short, what we *do* with our waking hours hints at what values we may have. As an ideal, we might strive to value everything we do and to do only what we value.

To merely *kill* time might be a value for some people, but for most of us the measurement of how we survive the onslaught of time tells much about the values we hold.

It is so prevalent nowadays to mouth the right words but to do very little about them. We must come, more of us, to do more about what we value. A list of our activities tells us more about what we prize and cherish than does an eloquent statement of beliefs. As teachers we do well to hold up a mirror to our students, to help them reflect on what they do with each day's 86,400 seconds, and to help them clarify the issue of the use of time and energy.

To summarize a bit, a teacher learns to spot value indicators and to follow them up, at least part of the time, with clarifying responses, sometimes in brief one-legged conferences, sometimes in written comments in the margins of student papers, and in other ways to be discussed. Expressions, verbal or behavioral, that are value indicators include attitudes, aspirations, purposes, interests, and activities. This list could be expanded to include opinions, convictions, beliefs, feelings, appreciations, and worries. The general intent is clear: Find value indicators, expressions that may not yet meet all seven criteria, and help students use the valuing process to see if they are at the value level or can be raised to the value level.

CHART 6

Value Indicator: Activities

Statements students have made:

1. "I took my dog for a long walk."
2. "I worked five hours Saturday waxing the car."
3. "Friday night we watched the late show and then the late-late show."
4. "These two fellows and I made a hut."
5. "I lay down to take a nap, but just slept right through the night."

Typical keywords that signal a statement about activities:

After school, I usually . . . .
Last weekend, we . . . .
On my day off, I went . . . .

One of the best things we did Halloween . . . .
. . . . All yesterday afternoon
We just like to play . . . .

SOME EXAMPLES

It might be well now to give some additional examples which show how the clarification process operates. Several cautions might be reiterated first, however. For one thing, there is no set formula for clarifying. It is very personal and individualized, both in the ways clarifiers proceed and in the range of problems that come up for clarification. There is a danger in seeing a clarifying incident in print. It is not to be taken as the only way it could have been done. There are easily a dozen variations on this theme, and all could readily be said to advance clarification.

Another danger occurs to us. Seeing the dialogue in print sometimes makes it seem bland or even silly. We ask you to accept the idea that these conversations are held, on the contrary, with dead earnestness. The person being "clarified" usually senses the power of this methodology and generally does not fritter away an opportunity to get clear on something related to his values. In other words, the dialogues do not print as movingly as they sound. Finally, we might remind the reader that the examples we cite do not stand alone. Clarifying is not a one-shot business. Each incident may stand by itself, but the sensitive teacher is constantly looking for other incidents and, especially if a teacher uses some of the techniques noted in the following chapters, there will be more incidents than can ever be used.

Let us look at this dialogue,

TEACHER: You were late again today. Do you like coming to school late?

STUDENT: Well, no.

TEACHER: How long have you been coming to school late?

STUDENT: Quite a while. I guess most of the time since I've been coming to school.

TEACHER: How do you feel about being tardy?

STUDENT: Well, I feel funny about it sometimes.

TEACHER: What do you mean by "funny?"

STUDENT: Well, that I'm different from other kids. I feel embarrassed.

TEACHER: As I get it, you feel uncomfortable about being late.
STUDENT: That's right.
TEACHER: What can I do to help you get here on time?
STUDENT: Well, my mother usually calls me in the morning—but sometimes she oversleeps.
TEACHER: Do you have an alarm clock?
STUDENT: No.
TEACHER: Could you get one? I could help you get one if that is what you think you need.
STUDENT: It would be kind of fun. I'll try to get one.

Later in the semester, this student's mother said: "What have you and my son been talking about? He is getting to school on time and he hustles around to get ready. When I asked him what had been happening he said, "Oh, my teacher and I have been talking.""[1]

Here is dialogue which grew out of a classroom discussion in a high-school social studies class.

JOHN: If you let in too many immigrants it just makes it tough for everyone else.
TEACHER: Tough in what way, John?

Here great courage was needed on the part of the teacher not to leap in with the usual chestnuts about "Was not your grandfather once an immigrant?" or "Don't you know that this country was founded by immigrants, that George Washington was an immigrant, etc., etc.?" The sum effect of that kind of question would have been to make John wish he hadn't brought up the topic. This is a most important point; every effort must be made to cull out of our questions those which moralize, get preachy, or back a student into the wall so that what appears to be a question is in reality a statement. Too often a question is asked in a way that tells us that only one right answer is acceptable, i.e. "Don't you think . . . ?", or "Wouldn't you agree . . . ?", "Is it not true that our ancestors were all immigrants?" Instead, this teacher has asked a real clarifying question, "Tough in what way?" It is a clarifying question for several reasons:

1. It keeps open the invitation to dialogue.

---

[1] James Raths, "Clarifying Children's Values," *National Elementary Principal*, November, 1962, pp. 37-38.

2. It talks to the real concern, which is probably more closely related to some problem about money than it is to immigration.
3. It works at making things clearer.

Back to our dialogue.

JOHN: Well, they work so much cheaper that a decent American can't get a job.
TEACHER: Can you give me an example of that happening, John?
JOHN: Well, I went to this supermarket which had an advertisement, but this kid with an accent got there first.
TEACHER: And he was willing to work cheaper?
JOHN: Well, I don't know that for sure.

Again, the teacher resists the temptation to make John feel like a naughty boy, for he knows that would not advance clarification. Instead he offers a clarifying question.

TEACHER: What did you feel when you found out that you didn't get the job?
JOHN: Boy I was mad.
TEACHER: Would you have been mad say if Pete over there had gotten the job?
JOHN: I guess I would have been just mad at anybody, because I really need that job.
TEACHER: Have you tried any of the other markets? Maybe we could make a list of them together and you could check them out one at a time.

Teacher makes a mental note: Why does John want that job after school? Is he going to buy a car? Does he have one already and must work for it? Big dance coming up? Saving for college? Perhaps explore these in some future clarifying contacts, for money, what we spend it on and what we don't spend it on, is one important bellweather of values.

What about the prejudicial statement about immigrants which John made and which started off this dialogue? Can a teacher, in good conscience, ignore such poor critical thinking? One answer is that a frontal attack is not always the most effective. The teacher in this dialogue worked under the assumption that the statement about immigrants, although obviously not entirely innocent, was triggered more by John's frustration over not getting the job he needed. At another time, in another context, the teacher may well pursue the prejudice expressed.

Here is another example, this time based on an expression of an aspiration.

CLARA: Some day I'd like to join the Peace Corps.
TEACHER: What are some good things about that, Clara?
CLARA: Oh, the chance to be of service excites me and going to faraway places does too.
TEACHER: Of those two, which would you put in first place?
CLARA: I guess the faraway places part.
TEACHER: Are you glad that that one is first?
CLARA: No, I guess people would respect me more if the service part was first.

Now, the teacher has some interesting alternatives at this point. Which of the following should he pursue?

1. The area of how important it is for Clara to feel respected.
2. The area of what services she has performed and might perform right now.
3. The area of what other possibilities does she have for getting to faraway places?
4. The teacher also has the possibility of not going forward at all and saying, "Well, it's been interesting talking with you Clara, but I must get back to my papers. Perhaps we can talk about it another time."

In the transcript of the incident above, the teacher did just that. When questioned, the teacher said that he felt that Clara had been a bit embarrassed when she realized what she had been doing and was anxious to terminate the conversation herself. The teacher's sensitivity must always be alert.

Other directions this discussion could have taken might have been equally as productive. The reader might want to look back at the list of clarifying responses and think about which of those might have reasonably followed Clara's opening statement.

A teacher may wonder when these conversations take place and where they are held. One obvious place is after school or between lessons. Other conversations occur in the morning before school, or in line in the cafeteria, or before class starts, or when you see students downtown. Often they grow right out of the subject matter during class, as did the incident about immigration mentioned above.

More such dialogues would occur, we feel, if teachers cared more about them and went out of their way to hold them. Students seem to welcome them. Certain teachers have already established such rapport with students that they can talk often and easily with them. We advocate that such talks more often focus upon values via the clarification process. For example, a young teacher was walking down the hall and overheard this snatch of conversation.

JERRY: When I save up the twenty dollars, I'm going to buy that guitar.

The teacher heard the expressed purpose, turned and said that he overheard the comment.

TEACHER: Can you play a guitar, Jerry?
JERRY: A little, but I'm going to really learn when I get my own.
TEACHER: Is playing the guitar important to you, Jerry?
JERRY: Yes, very.
TEACHER: What are the possibilities for making the twenty dollars?
JERRY: Not too good right now, I'm afraid.
TEACHER: Any chance of cutting down on what you now spend and saving it?
JERRY: You mean giving up smoking?
TEACHER: That's one alternative.
JOE: (Jerry's friend): Or staying out of the bowling alley for three weeks.
TEACHER: Well, good luck to you, Jerry. See you later.

The school day is really full of opportunities for these "one-legged conferences," for they are not interviews and not therapy. (We do _not_ recommend the clarifying technique for the solution of emotional problems.) The clarification methodology is concerned only with values and as such it seems to be a process well within the boundaries of the work of teachers.

Sometimes a student will view a clarifying response to something he has said or done as an intrusion.

TEACHER: I see, Vic, that you are still hard at work on that map. Is that something that you are very happy to do?
VICTOR: (No clear response. Appears to want to avoid a conversation. Continues to work at map.)
TEACHER: Just thought I'd ask. See you later, Vic.

This example shows what often happens with clarifying: sometimes some children just do not seem to want to respond and the teacher, ever respectful and permissive about the clarifying process, attempts to let the student off the hook without any embarrassment or pressure. A clarifying teacher encourages the valuing process but does not insist upon it. In fact, the teacher smiles to himself whenever the student shows that he knows he is respected enough to be able to say to a teacher, "I'd rather not talk about it." The wise teacher walks off with something like a "Well, bring it up again someday if you would like," knowing that at least the child has passed the point of total acquiescence.

Two final comments. Although when we deal with values, we emphasize the need for a non-judgmental approach, for acceptance, for the student to arrive at his *own* ideas on the basis of his *own* critical thinking and evaluation, we do not mean to suggest that the teacher must remain neutral. The teacher may take a clear position about a value-related issue—but the student must be encouraged to take his own position and to use his knowledge of the teacher's position only as interesting information, perhaps worth considering when he makes up his own mind. If, however, a teacher senses that students are not yet accustomed to critical thinking and taking independent positions, he might well conceal his beliefs and attitudes until they are weaned from this intellectual and moral dependence upon authority. Note this conversation:

> TEACHER: June, it seems to me that you very seldom talk in class discussions. Does it seem that way to you? (In this case, the teacher was picking up on something that a student did, or failed to do, and working at clarifying it.)
>
> JUNE: Yeah. I suppose so.
>
> TEACHER: Is that a pattern in your behavior? I mean are you pretty quiet in other groups and outside of school?
>
> JUNE: Well, maybe. Yes, usually.
>
> TEACHER: It seems to me that it would be more fun participating and getting your ideas into the group, but there is nothing wrong with not participating if you want to, either. Have you thought about this?
>
> JUNE: Well, no, not much I guess.
>
> TEACHER: Well, I won't interrupt your studying any longer, June. You can get back to your work.

In this exchange, the teacher clearly stated his position—it seemed to him that a lack of participation was not good—but also left open the possibility that others could disagree. The teacher did not leave the student, hopefully, with the feeling that there was a "right" way to behave, but rather left the student with a bit of food for thought. One can almost hear June meditating after this incident: "Now, I usually am quiet aren't I? I wonder why. Should I push myself to talk up and participate? Would Mr. Nelson want me to? I guess he doesn't really care. But what do *I* want?"

Again, if this teacher did not have an open and accepting atmosphere and if the students were not accustomed to hearing the teacher's opinions and knowing that those opinions were only some of many possible ones, it might have been better for the teacher to omit the statement of his position in the above exchange. The conversation could have been exactly the same, except that the sentence preceding "Have you thought about this?" would be omitted.

It seems to us desirable that a teacher's ideas, feelings, and opinions are made known to students. This demonstrates to students that one can talk openly about such things. And this provides alternatives for students to consider when making up their own minds. But if the teacher cannot do this without fear that students will copy those ideas, feelings, or opinions routinely and meekly, they might better be concealed—or even disguised—until the students learn to use the valuing process for themselves.

And lastly, an important word about getting started with this use of clarifying responses. (A more detailed discussion of how one might put the value approach of this book to a test, how to get started, and upon whom to focus this approach is contained in Chapter 8.)

Students are accustomed to having teachers ask questions. The standard recitation lesson is basically a question and answer process. In value-related areas, many teachers also use questions to guide student behavior and thinking, e.g.,

Johnny, didn't I tell you to be quiet?
Don't you think it would be a good idea to wash your hands before lunch?
Why do you tease the girls? When are you going to stop? Do I have to punish you again?
Don't you think it would be good for you to get higher grades?

You know that the way you're going you'll never get into college, don't you?

However, these questions have very little to do with the clarifying approach we are discussing. A clarifying response respects the right of the individual student to make decisions; the above questions are really not questions at all but statements of the teacher's decisions, and one can sense that they are not likely to trigger a clarification process.

Because of this, because many students expect that when a teacher asks them a question it is really a concealed directive, it is wise to begin to use clarifying questions at times when the student knows that you are *not* trying to disapprove of what he is saying or doing. Do not begin the use of clarifying responses by saying "Have you thought of any alternatives to what you are doing?" after a student hits another student—such a question will most likely be interpreted as a rebuke. Rather, when you first try the process, use such a response after a student has *helped* another student, or worked hard to pass a test, or volunteered to do extra work, or done something else he knows that you are not likely to disapprove of. After students become familiar with the use of clarifying responses, you can, of course, use them with little fear that students will view them as disguised criticisms.

The point here, then, is that a teacher would be wise to begin using clarifying responses only in situations that will prevent students from equating those responses with criticism or rebuke. The simplest way to do this is to use clarifying responses, in the beginning, in situations of which you either approve or have no preferences.

Incidentally, after students become familiar with the clarifying responses, they will begin to use them on one another and on other friends, and that is a delightful development. Somehow, persons like to have genuine clarifying responses directed to them. It doesn't threaten, and they know it helps clarify ideas and feelings.

SUMMARY

Basic to the use of the approach to values of this book is the clarifying response. The clarifying response is usually aimed at one student at a time, often in brief, informal conversations held in class, in hallways, on the playground, or any place else where the teacher comes in contact with a student who does or says something to trigger such a response.

Especially ripe for clarifying responses are such things as expressions of student attitudes, aspirations, purposes, interests, and activities. These sometimes indicate a value or a potential value and thus we refer to them as value indicators. Also in this category are expressions of student feelings, beliefs, convictions, worries, and opinions. A teacher who is sensitive to these expressions finds many occasions for useful clarifying responses.

The purpose of the clarifying response is to raise questions in the mind of the student, to prod him gently to examine his life, his actions, and his ideas, with the expectation that some will want to use this prodding as an opportunity to clarify their understandings, purposes, feelings, aspirations, attitudes, beliefs, and so on.

Undergoing this, some students may find the thoughtful consistency between words and deeds that characterizes values. But not everything need be a value. Beliefs, problems, attitudes, and all the rest are part of life too, although in most of our lives they might be even clearer and more consistent one to the other.

It may be useful to list some things that a clarifying response is *not*.

1. Clarifying is not therapy.

2. Clarifying is not used on students with serious emotional problems.

3. Clarifying is not a single one-shot effort, but depends on a program consistently applied over a period of time.

4. Clarifying avoids moralizing, preaching, indoctrinating, inculcating, or dogmatizing.

5. Clarifying is not an interview, nor is it done in a formal manner.

6. Clarifying is not meant to replace the teacher's other educational functions.

If clarifying is none of the above, what is it? It is an honest attempt to help a student look at his life and to encourage him to think about it, and to think about it in an atmosphere in which positive acceptance exists. No eyebrows are raised. When a student reveals something before the whole class, he must be protected from snickers from other class members. An environment where searching is highly regarded is essential.

We emphasize that students will probably not enter the perplexing process of clarifying values for themselves if they perceive that the teacher does not respect them. If trust is not communicated— and the senses of students for such matters can be mystifyingly keen —the student may well play the game, pretending to clarify and think and choose and prize, while being as unaffected as by a tiresome morality lecture. This is a difficult and important point, for it is not easy to be certain that one is communicating trust, whether or not one believes he is doing so. (A moot point is whether some persons can communicate a trust that they, in fact, do not have.) One must be chary about concluding that a teacher who says the right words is getting the results desired. There is a spirit, a mood, required that we cannot satisfactorily describe or measure except to say that it seems related to a basic and honest respect for students. It may be fair to say that a teacher who does not communicate this quality will probably obtain only partial results.

For many teachers a mild revolution in their classroom methodology will be demanded if they are to do very much with the clarification of values. For one thing, they will have to do much less talking and listen that much more, and they will have to ask different kinds of questions from the ones they have asked in past years. Teachers usually favor questions that have answers that can be scaled from "right" to "wrong." No such scoring can be applied to answers to clarifying questions.

The rewards for giving up the old patterns may not come right away, but there is mounting evidence that teachers who act "responsively" begin to have small miracles happening in their classrooms. They often see attendance go up, grades rise, and interest and excitement in learning crackle. They witness students who had been classified as apathetic, listless, and indifferent begin to change. In the words of one teacher, "students get their heads off their elbows and use those elbows to wave hands in the air."

In brief, one might see the clarifying response as fitting into the value clarifying method in the following framework:

1. First, look and listen for value indicators, statements or actions which suggest that there could be a value issue involved.

It is usually wise to pay special attention to students who seem to have particularly unclear values. Note especially children who seem to be very apathetic, or indecisive, or who seem to be very flighty, or who drift from here to there without much reason. Note, also, children who overconform, or who are very inconsistent, or who play-act much of the time.

2. Secondly, keep in mind the goal: children who have clear, personal values. The goal, therefore, requires opportunities for children to use the processes of (a) choosing freely, (b) choosing from alternatives, (c) choosing thoughtfully, (d) prizing and cherishing, (e) affirming, (f) acting upon choices, and (g) examining patterns of living. One does this with the expectation that the results of these processes are better understandings of what one stands for and believes in and more intelligent living.

3. Thirdly, one responds to a value indicator with a clarifying question or comment. This response is designed to help the student use one or more of the seven valuing processes listed above. For example, if you guess that a child doesn't give much consideration to what is important to *him*, you might try a clarifying response that gets at prizing and cherishing. Or the form of the value indicator may suggest the form of the clarifying response. For example, a thoughtless choice suggests responses that get at choosing, and a fine-sounding verbalization suggests responses that get at incorporating choices into behavior.

The rest of the chapters in Part Three provide additional techniques that teachers can use to get students involved in value-related discussions, thinking, and activities. Each of these, of course, provides threads for a teacher to use in helping children clarify values.

Chapter 6

The Value Sheet

The technique for the clarifying response presented in the last chapter is used to help one student think more clearly and independently about something he has said or done. Other students may well overhear the exchange and profit indirectly—as they learn to use the valuing process themselves and as they hear talk about an issue that may also be relevant to their lives—but the clarifying response is essentially an individually focused strategy. The strategy of this chapter, the value sheet, is focused on the group.

There are many things in our complex world that are worth getting clearer about,[1] and the value sheet offers a strategy for bringing some of these to the attention of students in a non-threatening and stimulating way. This is consistent with the value theory because each student is faced with the issue and its alternatives; and each one is encouraged to make an intelligent choice freely and thoughtfully and to act in ways consistent with that choice.

A value sheet in its simplest form consists of a provocative statement and a series of questions duplicated on a sheet of paper and

---

[1] The question of finding topics for the valuing process is further discussed in Chapter 8, "Getting Started: Guidelines and Problems."

distributed to class members. The purpose of the provocative statement is to raise an issue that the teacher thinks may have value implication for students. And the purpose of the questions is to carry each student through the value clarifying process with that issue. Since valuing is an individual matter, each student completes the value sheet by himself, preferably by writing answers on a separate sheet of paper. Later, that writing may be shared with other students or the teacher and/or used as a basis for large or small group discussions. Value sheets can also be used as programmed instructional material. But perhaps some examples will help make this clearer.

Value Sheet 1

The Meditation Room at the U.N.

DIRECTIONS: Please answer as many of the questions below as you wish, but answer them thoughtfully and honestly. I will collect the papers at the end of the study period and return them to you with occasional comments later in the week. This is an optional assignment, and has no effect on grades, of course.

There is a chapel or meditation room at the U.N. General Assembly building in New York that has had all symbols of particular religions removed. There is nothing there but some rows of chairs, a potted plant, and a shaft of light. Marya Mannes writes of this room:

"It seemed to me standing there that this nothingness was so oppressive and disturbing that it became a sort of madness, and the room a sort of padded cell. It seemed to me that the core of our greatest contemporary trouble lay here, that all this whiteness and shapelessness and weakness was the leukemia of non-commitment, sapping our strength. We had found, finally, that only nothing could please all, and we were trying to make the greatest of all generalities out of that most singular truth, the spirit of man. The terrifying thing about this room was that it made no statement whatever. In its capacity and constriction, it could not even act as a reflector of thought."

1. Write your reaction to this quotation in just a few words.
2. Does it produce a strong emotion in you? What emotion does it produce?

3. Do you think Miss Mannes's quotation is "anti-religious"? If not, why? If yes, in which ways?

4. In your mind, does Miss Mannes, in the quotation above, exaggerate the danger which she sees? Explain.

5. Can you list some more examples in our society which tend to support Miss Mannes's point?

6. Can you list any which tend to refute her point of view?

7. If this quotation suggests a problem which worries you, are there some things you might personally do about it? Within yourself? With some close friends? With the larger society?

8. Is there any wisdom from the past which you can cite to ease Miss Mannes's concern? Is there any wisdom from the past which might alarm her even more?

9. What do you get aroused about? Are you doing anything about it?

The second value sheet has directions that indicate that it is to be completed in a study period. This is only one of several ways it could be used, of course. Value sheets are suitable for home work assignments and for individual class work, for example. The important consideration in the use of value sheets is that each student has an opportunity to grapple with the questions *before* getting involved in any discussion that might tempt him to avoid thinking for himself and listen passively to others. Once each student has done some independent judging and thinking, a discussion is often useful. In any case, the directions given for the value sheets in this chapter are merely meant to be suggestive. Value sheets are used differently by different teachers.

This second example is a controversial one. It confronts the student with something that can be highly charged. Perhaps because of this, many students have found this sheet provides a rich educational experience.

It would be useful for the reader to count the number of times the questions on this sheet use the words "you" or "your." "You" questions are the hallmark of an effective value sheet.

There was an effort in the sheet, as in all value lessons, to allow for the fullest range of opinions, to avoid loading the dice in favor of any one point of view. There is no position taken by the teacher, although we hope each teacher does indeed know where he stands on this issue. When a teacher is seriously concerned with the clarification of values, he does not moralize, preach, indoctrinate, or inculcate. He must rely upon the informed and considered thought of students, while feeling free, of course, to confront students with alternatives not yet recognized and consequences not yet considered.

Question 7 on Value Sheet 12 deserves particular attention. In many sheets, we strive to move students toward the recognition that there is a large gap between most of our words and our deeds. If values are to be part of who we are, then we must constantly strive to close that gap. We need to do what we value. We need to value what we do.

Question 8 recognizes the subject matter responsibilities each of us as teachers have, and question 9 simply and directly asks, "What do *you* get aroused about?" It is frightening to realize how few things most of us do indeed care deeply about. We believe students need to examine such a position, and the next sheet illustrates that point further.

Value Sheet 2

Illegal Behavior

DIRECTIONS: Write out answers to the questions below. Later, you will have a chance to discuss your answers with a small group of students. You need not reveal your answers to anyone if you choose not to do so.

New Rochelle, N. Y., Oct. 27*—When the red light turns to green and reads "Thank you" at any one of the automatic toll booths of the New England Thruway here, it does not always mean what it says. At least not if the motorist has short-changed the machine or dropped lead washers or foreign coins into it.

The state police reported today after a two-week campaign against toll cheaters that they had arrested 151 persons. They have been fined in City Court from $25 each for first offenders to $250 for multiple offenders.

Lieut. Thomas F. Darby reported that the offenders included a clergyman, a doctor, a dentist, an atomic scientist, lawyers and quite a number of engineers, advertising men and salesmen.

What the offenders did not know, the lieutenant said, was that new toll-booth glass with one-way vision prevented them from seeing watchful troopers inside.

Neither did they know, the lieutenant continued, that the license plate of each offender was recorded, along with the objects he dropped into the machine.

° Date line "New Rochelle," *The New York Times,* October 28, 1961. © 1961 by The New York Times Company. Reprinted by permission.

1. Under what circumstances would *you* try to pass a toll machine without properly paying the fee? Check the most applicable reply below.

___Only if I was certain that I would not be caught.

___If I felt I had a good chance of not getting caught.

___Never, under any circumstances.

___Only if I needed the money desperately, like for family food supplies.

___(Write any other choice that better suits you:)

2. Among the 151 persons arrested, there was only one clergyman, doctor, dentist, and atomic scientist. On the other hand, there were several lawyers, engineers, advertising men, and salesmen. Do you think this means that persons in the first group of occupations are more honest than those in the second group? Discuss.

3. Do you think that this behavior is serious? Do you think these persons are likely to be dishonest in other ways that would be more serious? Discuss.

4. Return to Question 1 and put an X by the reply that you would make to this: Under what circumstances would you keep a dime that was returned in error in a phone booth?

5. How do you account for any differences in your answers to Questions 1 and 4, if any?

6. Are you clear about how you feel about illegal behavior? Discuss.

Value Sheet 2, appropriate for young and old students, shows how a little news item can be tied into a general theme, in this case illegal behavior. Note how the sequence of questions leads the student into the theme, gently but interestingly.

Question 1 gets the student to take a position, often a useful clarifying tactic. Question 2 calls for a bit of critical thinking and takes the heat off the student for a moment. Question 3 is similarly impersonal and calls for thinking about some of the consequences and correlates of slug passing. Questions 4 and 5 bring the issue back home, often dramatically, and point up possible inconsistencies in a person's stance. Noting inconsistencies is another important clarifying tactic and is especially useful before posing the jackpot question, number 6.

This sheet has directions that lead from individual thinking to small group deliberations, but other directions could be used, of course.

Value Sheet 3

Leisure

INSTRUCTIONS: Please respond in writing to the questions below and turn your work in on Monday. I will pick a few of the responses to read to the class, anonymously, and we may have time for an open discussion of a few of the questions after our other lessons.

The cartoonist, Osborn, has said:

"If we are to have any Leisure—we must set limits to our efforts and to do this requires some truly adult decisions and no fudging or blurring of the outlines!

"How much *lawn* are we going to *mow?* If we choose too little, we have lots of Leisure, but a vapid face. If we choose too much we become tired, irritable, dislocated, insensate."*

---

* From R. Osborn, *On Leisure* (New York: The Ridge Press, Inc., 1956), p. 58.

1. Just what is Osborn saying? What is this "lawn" he mows?

2. Can you expand on your own observations of "vapid faces"? What are some of the things people with vapid faces *do?*

3. What does Osborn say to *you,* personally.

4. Are you in basic agreement with him? In what ways would you change what he says so that it more nearly describes what *you* actually believe (or value) in this area?

5. Well, what do you actually DO about changing the way you operate in the realm of this problem? How do you begin? What do you do first? Second? Third? When do you start? What are some things you can do over the next three months? Six months? Next year? Today?

6. What about your own lawn? Do you seem to be mowing too little? How do you measure if you're mowing too much? In what ways can you cut down? In what ways can you mow more? How do you decide? (Please tell us later if you make any changes in your life on the basis of this sheet.)

The sources for value sheets are varied and, in a sense, endless. Teachers who use them tend to read with a scissors in hand. Value Sheet 3 came from a cartoon book which was distributed to doctors by one of the large pharmaceutical firms. However, it discusses a problem of concern to people other than members of the medical profession. The important point here is that each teacher will discover for himself just which sources of ideas are most effective for him and the particular children he teaches.

Ideas that lend themselves nicely to value sheets are those that touch directly or indirectly the lives of the students. Some topics touch the students mainly in their current stage of growth, such as bicycle safety and cheating on tests, and these are *less* significant than topics that will face students throughout their lives, such as carefulness in general, honor in general, etc.

Value Sheet 3 deals with the question of the worthy use of leisure time and, as such, is a question which persists throughout life. It also nicely reflects our activities and thus gets at a useful value indicator.

SUBJECT MATTER AND VALUE SHEETS

It may be apparent by now that there is a viable connection between value sheets and the standard subject matter of the schools. Of course we believe that there is good reason for having "pure" value lessons, that is, lessons that stand all by themselves. We know that boys and girls need to have time and help to think through certain issues of life, and that they enjoy and seem to profit from such thought. Consequently, we believe a teacher would be wise to use value sheets just for the sake of value clarity. But we have also found that they provide an exciting and provocative *introduction and motivation* for typical subject-matter lessons.

Look at the sheet on the Meditation Room at the U.N. That could lead to units, in the social studies, on the great religions of the world, or on prejudice, or on the history of religious tolerance, or on the United Nations, etc. In mathematics, the teacher might use such a value sheet to lead, via the arcs and lines found in the classic church designs, to a unit on geometry. The alert English teacher could tie such a sheet to units on symbolism, religious poems, modern fiction, journalistic objectivity, etc. Other teachers might well find other ways to use that sheet to carry student enthusiasm to a subject-matter unit.

The following possibilities occur to us:

Social studies. Exploration. Westward expansion. Invention and discovery. Immigration. Geography. National Banking system. Big business and big government. Public utilities, etc.

Mathematics. Division. Graphs. Percentage. Extrapolation. Analysis of data. Large numbers. Place value of numbers, etc.

Science. Space. Astronomy. Disease. Nature of research. Newton's Laws. Nutrition. Etc.

Reading and English. Add new words to vocabulary lists and spelling lists. Find grammar errors or examples of certain usage forms. Use to motivate stories dealing with travel, money, exploration, science fiction, etc. Require that written responses to questions use topical sentences, gerunds, the semicolon, colorful verbs, etc. Have the passage read for speed and then for detail. Etc.

Foreign Language. Translate the opening passage into the foreign language. Translate the questions into the foreign language. Respond to the questions both in English and in the foreign language. Have the students respond in English, but have the value sheet written in whole or in part in the foreign language. Etc.

As a value sheet can lead into a subject-matter unit, so can it *culminate* such a unit. A number of teachers have given out value sheets as the last assignment in each unit, to help students go beyond the information to the values concerned. The examples above generally suit that approach.

Finally, value sheets can be *incorporated* into the middle of subject-matter lessons. They can be used merely as interesting interludes in the unit. Or they can be an integral part of the subject matter itself.

For example, an arithmetic unit on weights and measures used a value sheet on deceptive packaging. In this case the teacher did not begin his sheet with some dramatic opening, but himself wrote a few sentences saying that such practices do exist and then asked questions that got at the students' thinking about such packaging (and deceptions in their own lives) and had students calculate weights and sizes from sample boxes and cans seeking examples of packaging that might be termed deceptive.

A social-studies teacher made up her own value sheet during a unit that, in part, dealt with the Chinese Exclusion Acts. The teacher wrote out a few questions that stimulated students' thinking about exclusion, for the nation and for themselves, then went on with the history lesson.

For reading, English, literature, and foreign language teachers, the value sheet is a natural teaching device. For reading, there are few things more stimulating for reluctant readers than value sheets. Slow readers strive with new interest when so confronted. For English, value sheets provide a neat and exciting way toward vocabulary and grammar illustrations and practice. For foreign language classes, we believe that the motivation and learning in a language is increased immeasurably when what is read in the foreign language is, in whole or in part, a value sheet, and/or what writing practice there is comes in response to value questions.

Literature and reading lessons are bursting with value possibilities. Note the following example.

Note how Value Sheet 4 presents literature and then connects it to the lives of the children. Perhaps this is the richest use of literature to help the reader better understand himself and his relationships to his world. Since value sheets have this as their purpose, they are well suited for use with reading and literature lessons.

Value Sheet 4

Worksheet:
*"Silas Marner" by George Eliot**

INSTRUCTIONS: Read chapters V through VIII for Monday, March 2.
Write out answers to the following questions, ready to be turned in and/or discussed in class.

Chapter V
1. What is the focus of the narrative in this novel?

Chapter VI
1. What is the function of this chapter? How is it different from other chapters?

---

* From Joyce Cox, Connetquot High School, Long Island, N. Y.

2. Briefly characterize the major people you meet at the Rainbow.

3. Do you know any people who are similar to those at the Rainbow? Discuss briefly.

4. Consider the topics of conversation at the Rainbow. Do those topics persist to this day with the people you know? How much of your discussions involve those topics?

5. How would you define gossip? Why do you think we gossip?

6. How much time do you spend in gossip in an average week?

7. What are some alternative ways of spending this time?

8. Compare the consequences of time spent in gossip to the consequences of time spent at the alternative you listed and make some judgment as to which consequences you would want for yourself.

Chapter VII

1. What reasons can you think of for the people being glad that the "reality of ghosts remained still an open question"?

2. Any implications in question 1 for your thinking and your life?

3. Some people say that Macey and the farrier do not remain true to their character in questioning Silas on page 652. Discuss this assertion.

Chapter VIII

1. Consider Godfrey's statement about Dunstan, "He'll never be hurt—he's made to hurt others." Do you know of a person who could never be hurt? Is it possible to be that way, do you think?

2. Do people ever consciously hurt you? Can you explain this?

3. Do people ever unconsciously hurt you? Can you explain this?

4. Can you think of something you can do to help persons understand what they are doing when they are hurting you and how they might cease this kind of behavior?

5. Will you do it? (Please let us know if and when you do such a thing and how it works out. Write me a brief note.)

Often when a class is all reading the same story book or textbook, there is no need to write out an opening passage. One merely makes reference to it at the top of the sheet and then lists the questions, as in Value Sheet 4 which deals with the classic *Silas Marner*.

Note how "subject-matter" questions and "value" questions are interspersed. We believe that teachers have both responsibilities, and each type of learning reinforces the other. Children cannot develop clear and workable values without some understanding of the alternatives and the consequences of each alternative; this understanding is the responsibility of the teacher to help provide. But children can make little real use of understandings until they are turned into personal meaning for actual living, and that is the role of the valuing process, which teachers also must nourish. Both are indispensable for an educated man.

The reader may infer that we do not believe that the learning of understandings has to precede the valuing process. We see clearly that they usually *both* proceed best when they proceed apace. Valuing is superficial without understanding. Understanding is superficial without valuing. Neither can wait until the other is accomplished. Thus we reject the position that says that children should learn their subject matter first and do their valuing later. Because knowledge not turned into values has a short half-life in memory and can be almost as easily used destructively as constructively (witness the informed Germans of the Second World War and the educated social irresponsibility reflected in our own newspapers today), we recommend that teachers consider moving valuing right along as a part—a vital and exciting part—of the learning process. Besides, unless children learn to use the valuing process when they are growing up, there is danger that they will have a much more difficult time finding their way to the process, and thus to clear, independent thinking about moral issues, when they are older.

Value Sheet 5

Civil Liberties

Below are several paragraphs relating to one issue. Select the paragraph that comes closest to your own position and change the wording in it until it represents your thinking as exactly as possible. Or you may write a new position if none of the ones listed is close to the one you prefer. The idea is to get a statement about which you can say, "This is where I now stand."

A useful way to decide between alternatives is to identify the *consequences* of each of the positions and then to decide which set of consequences it is that you prefer to come about. You may, of course, use other sources of information before committing yourself to a position.

1. Freedom is basic to the existence of a democratic society. This does not mean license to do as one sees fit. Within the limitation of not interfering with someone else's freedom, it is desirable for the individual to pursue his own self-interest.

2. In our society, everyone has freedom. One may do, think, and say that which he believes. We draw the line at a point, however. In the best interests of our society, we cannot permit anyone to hold doctrines or to preach anything that might undermine our society as it stands now. Erroneous beliefs, therefore, cannot be treated with the same tolerance as the normal and accepted doctrines, since their sole purpose is to destroy the very foundation of our society. Any dangerous opinions and beliefs must, therefore, be curbed.

3. Many persons think of freedom as the right of suffrage, but this is only an illusion that one is free. He who thinks that his power of freedom comes from his vote has only to compare the power he has with that of the international financier, or a big businessman; voting provides freedom only in a flimsy parliamentarian sense. It is an illusion in which man is like the trained dog who thinks he learned the tricks by himself.

4. The only true freedom that can ever exist comes about when we allow so-called truth and error to clash in the open market place of ideas. We cannot suppress any heresies nor can we censor thoughts, ideas, or practices; *nothing* is heretical. We must promote and encourage differences of opinion, and we must discourage uniformity of thinking. It is only this way that we can prevent a tyranny of the mind and body from ever imposing itself.

5. True freedom is non-existent. Man acts out a plan that is set for him before he is five years old. His emotions reflect the society into which he is born. All his actions also reflect that society and are determined by it. Even his conception of freedom is one which has been drummed into him by the particular society. Convinced that he is free, it never occurs to him to question the fact that even in the ability to leave society, he is a slave to its laws.

This is the last value sheet upon which we will make specific comments, and it is a valuable one. It represents a neat and effective value sheet form.

The directions for this kind of value sheet can remain unchanged no matter what the topic. Students are asked to examine a number of alternative positions on a given issue, in this case "civil rights," and each is asked to frame his own position. No questions are needed when using this format. The challenge to examine alternatives and choose a position is built into the directions.

These value sheets are easy to construct. Choose any issue that penetrates the lives of persons in our society. Examples are:

1. Selfishness vs. altruism
2. Sloppiness vs. neatness
3. Individual initiatives vs. governmental controls
4. The role of advertising
5. Independence vs. dependence
6. Sexual promiscuity vs. abstinence
7. Acting on emotions vs. acting on intellect
8. Capitalism vs. socialism
9. Democracy, autocracy, and anarchy
10. Wealth vs. pleasant life
11. Tardiness vs. promptness

Write out a few paragraphs identifying possible positions on an issue. Ask each student to study the alternatives (and other available data) and to write out his own position. Finally, collect the papers and/or discuss the issue. The teacher can make good use of the students' positions when revising the sheet to add to his original list of alternatives. It is, of course, important that all conceivable and identifiable alternatives—not just the "acceptable" ones—be brought to the attention of the student if he is to make a choice that can lead to a value.

Value Sheet 6

Friendship

1. What does friendship mean to you?
2. If you have friends, did you choose them or did they get to be your friends by accident?
3. In what ways do *you* show friendship?
4. How important do you think it is to develop and maintain friendships?
5. If you plan to make any changes in your ways, please say what changes you will make. If you do not intend to make any changes in your ways, write "No changes."

Value Sheet 7

Minding Your Own Business vs. Helping Those in Need

I. Some persons say that men are basically selfish, that one must watch out for himself, that it's best to serve your own purposes, avoid hurting others, and "Mind Your Own Business."

II. Other persons say that men must stick together and help one another, or they will fall separately, that no man is an island, that each man's fate is intertwined with other men's fates, and one should "Help Those in Need."

1. What label might be appropriate for each of those positions?

2. Is this a case of "either-or," *either* you support one position *or* the other? Are there other positions that one could take concerning this issue? If possible, identify some other positions.

3. Professor Laurence Hopp of Rutgers University suggests that persons who have experienced social injustice, who have experienced feelings of being unfairly treated, are likely to take the second position. Would you agree? Have you any evidence for your ideas about this?

4. It has also been suggested that those who have experienced success, who have power and privilege, would likely take the first position, regardless of whether or not they have earlier experienced social injustice. Would you agree? Have you any evidence for your ideas about this?

5. What other explanations might account for persons preferring one position over the other? List them and discuss each briefly.

6. Read each of the eight situations below and try to identify *what you would do* in each case. Although not all the information is provided for any of the situations, make the best estimate you can of *what you would do if you were faced with such a situation in the future*. Try to be as realistic as possible in your choice of actions. When you are finished, try to summarize *your* position regarding the issues: Minding Your Own Business *vs.* Helping Those in Need.

Situation A

You are walking down a busy shopping street in the middle of the afternoon. You hear screams across the street and see a man choking a woman in a doorway. Several persons on both sides of the street notice, but nobody moves as the woman continues to scream and as the man tries to drag her indoors by the throat.

Situation B

You are in a group of persons with whom you would like to be friends. Two members of the group begin to tease a nearby girl who has a very strange face. Others in the group join in, although a few are silent.

Situation C

The young married couple that lives next to you has a little boy.

three years old. During a friendly visit with them, you observe that they are energetically teaching that boy to hate a minority group.

Situation D

An unpleasant-looking man approaches you on a corner and asks you for a dime for a cup of coffee.

Situation E

Someone asks your advice on a tax law that must be voted on in the forthcoming election. The proposed law would not change the total amount of money collected, but it would increase taxes for those in the middle and upper income brackets and decrease taxes for those in the lower income brackets.

Situation F

You hear that the Indians on the reservation in the next state are suffering from severe poverty and that nobody is doing much about it.

Situation G

You read that Negroes in some areas of the South continue to suffer discrimination and that they are sometimes beaten or even murdered and that the white persons in those areas are angry with those trying to interfere with the way things are.

Situation H

You are asked to make a judgment about U.S. foreign policy. The leaders of country XYZ are about to be thrown out by the citizens there because they are not doing the kind of job that the majority of the citizens desire. Those leaders appeal to the U.S. for armed support, to keep the citizens from removing them. The U.S. government is concerned because the current leaders vigorously support the U.S.A. in international disputes while the new leaders that would probably emerge in that country are not expected to support the U.S.A. in international matters and would probably request the removal of a large American air base on their territory.

Value Sheet 8

On Thomas Jefferson

"His duplicity sinks deeper and deeper into my mind. His hatred of Hamilton was unbounded; of John Marshall, most intense; of my father, tempered with compunctious visitings, always controlled by his ambition ° ° ° he died insolvent, and on the very day of his death received eleomosynary donations from the charity of some of those whom he had most deeply injured."°

° Joseph Berger, "Diary of John Quincy Adams," *The Times Magazine,* March 13, 1960. © 1960 by The New York Times Company. Reprinted by permission.

1. In what ways does this picture of Jefferson differ from the one you have been taught?

2. How do you explain the difference?

3. What *is* the truth and how do you know it?

4. Is it possible for one to go through life without making enemies? Explain.

5. How much of your life should you live so you don't make anyone criticize you? Is criticism good? Is it bad? Explain?

6. Take some well-known person living in our world today. Write three different paragraphs expressing three different points of view about this person, and base each paragraph on facts.

7. How can we judge people? It has been said that the purpose of education is to know a good man when you see one. How has your education helped you in this?

Value Sheet 9

On Civil Liberties

The National Defense Education Act of 1958 stipulated that a student wanting a federal loan for education purposes had to sign an affidavit stating that he "does not believe in, and is not a member of and does not support any organization that believes in or teaches, the overthrow of the United States Government by force or violence or by any illegal or unconstitutional methods."

1. What do you think of such a requirement? (Check one)

_____Seems reasonable. I would not mind signing such an affidavit.

_____Seems unreasonable, but not seriously so. Not worth making a fuss over.

_____Seems unreasonable, and seriously so. I would not accept money under such conditions and believe the law should be changed.

_____(Any other position; write it out here:)

2. Some persons did think such a "loyalty oath" serious and refused to accept money on that basis. In fact, some thirty-two of the

nation's leading colleges and universities had officially notified the Office of Education that they had withdrawn from or declined to participate in the program specifically because of that requirement. Another sixty-three institutions participated, but under protest.

Why do you think some schools protested that oath?

3. The provision was repealed by Congress in the 1962 session. President Kennedy said when he signed the repeal that the oath was "offensive" to college students.

Under what conditions do you think the government should change laws when the people object?

4. Discuss your feelings about this matter further. Perhaps you will want to discuss the general relationship between citizens and government, or what you would have done in the specific situation described above, or what you will do in the future under such circumstances.

Value Sheet 10

Courage*

"Courage is generosity of the highest order, for the brave are prodigal of the most precious things."—C. C. Colton.

"True courage is to do without witness everything that one is capable of doing before all the world."—La Rochefoucauld.

"Courage is like love: it must have hope to nourish it."—Napoleon Bonaparte.

"Courage leads starward, fear toward death."—Seneca.

"Brave men are brave from the first."—Corneille.

"The courage of the tiger is one, and the horse another."—Ralph Waldo Emerson.

"Ultimate bravery is courage of the mind."—H. G. Wells.

"Grace under pressure."—Ernest Hemingway.†

† Peggy Streit, editor, *The Times Magazine*, November 24, 1963. © 1963 by The New York Times Company. Reprinted by permission.

1. What does the word "courage" mean to you?
2. Do you think courage manifests itself? How?

* By Sima Schuman

3. Do you think everyone possesses courage? How? If not, why?
4. Are you proud of your level of courage? Discuss.

Value Sheet 11

Home of the Brave?

I used to be an idealist. When there was a picket line, I would
picket. When there was a sitdown, I would sit. When there was a
demonstration, I would demonstrate. I sat for two days in front of
a store that wouldn't hire "minority type" people—I felt that they
should have a fair chance in the land of opportunity, that all men
are created equal. They told me to go to Russia. I was born in
Brooklyn!

Then there was the time I marched around the U.N. and handed
out leaflets saying that we shouldn't use bombs to kill each other,
and that man should study war no more. They called me an atheist!

Once I was arrested for going into a school with a sign saying
that all children are entitled to an equal opportunity to education,
like the Supreme Court says the Constitution means. They called me
a Communist!

Soon I got tired of being called all these names, so I gave up. I
don't care if half of them starve. I don't care if tl ey don't all get
educated. I don't care if they kill each other with bombs. I don't
care if their babies die from radiation. Now I'm a good American.*

---

* Gary Ackerman, Castle, Oct. 8, 1963.

To think on and to write on:

1. What is this writer for and what is he against?
2. Have you had any experiences like his?
3. Who are some people who should be concerned about the
problems he mentions?
4. Are there any things which *you* are working to change, to set
right, to improve? Discuss briefly.

Value Sheet 12

On Mexico

"After the taking of Mexico, Cortez divided the land among the
conquerors and on the ruins of the Aztec City he began to build
the Spanish city of Mexico, proclaiming its future greatness. He
organized a city corporation, established markets, repaired the aqua-
duct of Chapultepeo, which had been cut during the siege, laid

down moral laws, thus beginning the government of the colony whose wealth he protected by wise measure. . . .

"Then Pizzaro showed his admirable gifts as organizer and colonizer; he divided the land into districts, he organized the administration of justice and the working of the mines . . . and in short time, thanks to his energy and will, the church, town hall, palaces, and houses formed a beautiful city (Lima) which grew and prospered."*

---

* From Bleye Pedro de Aquado, *Compiedo de Historia de Espana* (1933), II, 115, 123-24, as quoted in A. C. Walworth, Jr., *School Histories at War* (Cambridge, Mass.: Harvard University Press, 1938).

"Pizzaro, in imitation of Cortez, laid hands on the Inca Atahualpa, and held him as security for the good behavior of his people.

"In return for his freedom the Inca promised to fill a large room with objects of gold to a depth of nine feet. Almost immediately porters began to come in bearing golden vases, goblets, and jars; miniature gold birds and beasts, golden leaves, flowers, beads, and roots. Melted down, this mass yielded 1,326,539 pesos de oro, the equivalent of $15,500,000 in American money. Having secured this treasure, the Spaniards treacherously led their prisoner out to the plaza of Caxamarca and strangled him with a bowstring."†

---

† T. J. Wertenbaker and Smith, D. E., *United States* (New York: Charles Scribner's Sons, 1931), pp. 18-19.

1. How do these accounts differ?
2. Speculate on the probable reasons as to WHY they differ.
3. Which account seems most reasonable to you?
4. How does one know what to believe?
5. Any implications here for your reading or believing?

Value Sheet 13

Copernicus

Some 400 years ago, a mathematician named Copernicus studied the earth and the heavens and concluded that the conception of the earth as the center of the universe was incorrect. Calculations showed him that it was more reasonable to see the sun as the center, and the earth as rotating around it. The German mathematician Johann Kepler confirmed and refined the findings of Copernicus; but this new idea was too revolutionary to be considered dispassionately, on its scientific merits.

"Because man is conservative, a creature of habit, and convinced of his own importance, the new theory was decidedly unwelcome. Moreover, the vested interests of well-entrenched scholars and religious leaders caused them to oppose it," writes Morris Kline in his *Mathematics in Western Culture.*°

Martin Luther called Copernicus an "upstart astrologer" and a "fool who wishes to reverse the entire science of astronomy." Calvin thundered: "Who will venture to place the authority of Copernicus above that of the Holy Spirit?" Do not Scriptures say that Joshua commanded the sun and not the earth to stand still? The inquisition condemned the new theory as "That false Pythagorean doctrine utterly contrary to the Holy Scriptures," and in 1616 the Index of Prohibited Books banned all publications dealing with the idea.

Galileo was thought to believe the new theory to have some merit, and was called by the Roman Inquisition and compelled on the threat of torture to declare: "The falsity of the Copernican system cannot be doubted, especially by us Catholics. . . . " Descartes, a nervous and timid individual, on hearing of Galileo's persecution, actually destroyed one of his own works on it.

Writes Kline: "Indeed, if the fury and high office of the opposition are a good indication of the importance of an idea no more valuable one was ever advanced."†

° This material comes from the work of Arnold Rothstein of Hofstra College.
† Morris Kline, *Mathematics in Western Culture* (New York: Oxford University Press, 1953).

1. Can you understand how people of good will might react violently to new ideas that they see as threatening some of their values?

2. Has there been another situation in history that you can recall in which the advance of knowledge was resisted by partisans with similar vigor?

3. Can you imagine something like that happening in the future in the United States if some new idea, say in sociology or some other discipline, were to seriously challenge the status quo?

4. What methods do you think might be used to fight new ideas?

5. What methods might be used to fight for the right to consider new ideas?

6. How receptive are *you* to new ideas, and how resistant are you? Can you think of conditions under which you would try to repress truth?

Value Sheets 6 through 13 provide examples that have been used by teachers both as "pure" value lessons and in relation to subject-matter units. They represent a few of the different forms that these sheets can take. Each of those sheets was written with a particular age of children in mind, but one can see how a simple modification of the language could adapt the sheet for students of other ages or for adults, for that matter.

Incidentally, any topic is suited to any grade level as long as the children have enough information, or can get enough information, to examine the alternatives intelligently. Most teachers are delighted by the surge of interest and intelligence shown by children when they are given important adult-sounding choices to reflect upon. The problem with most children is not that they face choices which they cannot handle, but that they are not given enough choices and the kind of help the value theory recommends to permit them to develop their choice-making abilities. We would encourage teachers to resist a temptation to keep young children away from "sophisticated" topics. Having seen primary grade children deal thoughtfully and seriously with racial prejudice and methods of teaching, intermediate children similarly deal with problems of war and peace and what makes for a successful marriage, junior high-school children reflect intelligently on matters of sex and on religion, and having seen high-school children of very average ability tackle with creativity and wisdom issues that deal with self-delusions, parent-grandparent relationships, and government policy in complex circumstances, we are convinced that many children wait only to have their minds and interests freed by teachers who dare trust them with important choices.

INCOMPLETE VALUE SHEETS

We said that value sheets can be built in many forms. The simplest form consists of a provocative and value-laden opening statement followed by a series of thought-provoking questions. Alternatively, one might prepare a list of questions for a reading the class has done, such as Value Sheet 4 on Silas Marner. Or one might simply have a series of questions on a concept, much like Value Sheet 6 on friendship. One can also present alternatives and ask a student to choose, such as sheet 5 on civil rights. Or one can construct sheets that add information and insights to the issue as one progresses through the questions, as demonstrated by sheet 2, "Illegal Behavior," and the "mind your own business" sheet 7. One can also use cartoons, poetry, music, and any other form that accomplishes the purpose of helping students to clarify their values.

Below are five possible openings for value sheets. The reader might want to use them to practice making value sheets.[2]

1.   "Merry-Go-Round"[*]
                    Where is the Jim Crow section
                    On this merry-go-round, Mister,
                    Cause I want to ride?
                    Down South where I come from
                    White and colored
                    Can't sit side by side.
                    Down South on the train
                    There's a Jim Crow car.
                    On the bus we're put in back—
                    But there ain't no back
                    To a merry-go-round!
                    Where's the horse
                    For a kid that's black?

---

[*] Langston Hughes, *Selected Poems* (New York: Alfred A. Knopf, Inc., 1959). Copyright © by Langston Hughes, 1959.

2.—The human being is made up of oxygen, nitrogen, phosphorus, hydrogen, carbon and calcium. There are also 12½ gallons of water, enough iron to make a small nail, about a salt-shaker full of salt, and enough sugar to make one small cube. If one were to put all of this together and try to sell it, the whole thing would be worth about one dollar.

3.—Louis Armstrong writing on his art: "I don't want a million dollars. See what I mean? No medals. I mean, I don't feel no different about the horn now than I did when I was playin' in the Tuxedo Band. That my livin' and my life. I love them notes. That why I try to make 'em right. See? And any part of the day, you liable to see me doing something toward it for the night.

"A lot of musicians, money make a damn fool out of them. They forget all about the life they love, standin' on the band-

---

[2] See Appendix A, p. 231–32 for value sheets based on these openings.

stand. They get famous and can't play no louder or no softer, and I ain't goin' play no less. I might play a little *more*, but always up to par."

4.—Shuttlesworth's civil-rights biography reads like something out of Horatio Alger: Christmas, 1956, Shuttlesworth home bombed and completely demolished; winter, 1957, his church dynamited by racists; late 1957, Shuttlesworth and wife, mobbed, beaten, and stabbed; jailed eight times—four times during the Freedom Rides; sued for three million dollars by state officials of Alabama; car and personal property sold at public auction; driver's license revoked for a whole year; the three Shuttlesworth children illegally arrested and beaten.

5.—"In Germany they first came for the Communists, and I didn't speak up because I wasn't a Communist. Then they came for the Jews, and I didn't speak up because I wasn't a Jew. Then they came for the trade unionists, and I didn't speak up because I wasn't a trade unionist. Then they came for the Catholics, and I didn't speak up because I was a Protestant. Then they came for me—and by that time no one was left to speak up."—Pastor Martin Niemoller.

THE VALUE SHEET: AN OUTLINE OF THE STRATEGY

Let us see if we can now succinctly outline the strategy that we call "value sheets."

As the clarifying response aims at a particular expression of a particular child, the value sheet aims at students in general and thus deals with ideas that are important for most students. Such ideas often emerge from topics related to:

1. *Money,* how it is apportioned and treated.
2. *Friendship,* how one relates to those around him.
3. *Love and sex,* how one deals with intimate relationships.
4. *Religion and morals,* what one holds as fundamental beliefs.
5. *Leisure,* how it is used.
6. *Politics and social organization,* especially as it affects the individual.

7. *Work,* vocational choices, attitudes toward work.

8. *Family,* and how one behaves within it.

9. *Maturity,* what one strives for.

10. *Character traits,* especially as they affect one's behavior.

Value sheets take different forms. Often they are based on a single provocative statement. Sometimes two or more divergent positions open a value sheet. Sometimes the questions and statements are woven together so that the value sheet has a dramatic development, with the student being increasingly involved in a complex issue. Sometimes value sheets consist of nothing more than a series of probing questions that are keyed to a common reading done from a text, a current events reading, or a piece of literature, or keyed to a common experience like an assembly program, a class problem, or a major public event. Cartoons, films, recordings, television shows, and other stimuli can also be used to begin a value sheet.

The questions on a value sheet are in the style of the valuing theory. That is, the questions do not try subtly to convince a student to believe what the adult believes, but rather the questions help the student take the issue at hand through the value criteria. The crucial elements, of course, are *choosing* (freely, thoughtfully, from alternatives), *prizing* and willingness to affirm, and *acting* (living one's choices in some pattern, not just talking about them). The thirty clarifying responses of the preceding chapter are illustrative of this style.

The value sheets are used in a variety of ways, the *least* effective of which is as discussion lessons. One does not get values in the busyness of a classroom discussion, especially a heated discussion. One needs quiet, hard thought and careful decisions if one is to have clear, persistent, and viable values. These do not easily come in the midst of a room full of talking.

A discussion is inappropriate for value lessons for the following reasons:

1. A value discussion tends to move toward argumentation, with participants becoming defensive of positions they may not exactly hold after the heat of the talk is finished. Values require a non-defensive, open, and thoughtful climate.

2. Participants in a discussion often perform in ways that are

partly motivated by factors irrelevant to the issue being discussed, such as desires to please other students and/or the teacher, and thus the thoughtful, deliberative aspects of valuing often become diluted with emotional considerations.

3. Valuing is an *individual* process; one cannot get values from a group consensus; one must *himself* choose, prize, and act; and this is difficult to do in a room in which a lot of talking is going on.

4. Although valuing is an active process, requiring much individual intellectual energy, most persons are passive most of the time in a discussion. In fact, many persons are passive almost *all* of the time in discussions. In most discussions, the bulk of the talking is done by a certain predictable few.

5. Finally, a discussion tends to generate pressure on individuals to accept the group consensus or the strong leader's arguments or the teacher's suggestions, and values cannot come from pressures to accept something. The free choice must, in this value theory, be truly free if it is to lead to a meaningful personal value.

For those reasons, we have found that the most effective ways to use value sheets begin with individuals responding to the questions privately and deliberately. Usually, we insist on written responses; writing elicits more careful thought than just speaking about something. Sometimes, however, the teacher will find it advisable to make the value sheets in whole or in part optional, or to permit students to write their responses anonymously. This is especially helpful when students might fear being completely candid in a certain area or when the teacher does not feel confident that he can insist that a student deliberate about certain ideas, such as religion. Each teacher will find his own way, but the following approaches are those we have found useful.

Students do value sheets for homework or during study times. They may even be handled as programmed instructional material. A number of teachers have found value sheets to be especially appropriate for weekend assignments, when students feel somewhat fewer pressures and have more time for unhurried thought. Then, several alternatives are possible:

1. Students discuss their written answers in small groups without the teacher's presence. This forces the students to think through issues without looking to the teacher for "the right way."

2. Students turn in their writings and the teacher later reads,

without comment or evaluation, selected viewpoints that raise interesting alternatives and/or nicely illuminate the issue. This is best done without the teacher identifying the writer, however with the writer having the opportunity to claim credit for what is read to the class if he so wishes. Discussion may follow.

3. Students turn in their writings and the teacher returns them with occasional comments in the margins. The comments should, of course, be in the style of the value theory and should ask further questions that help the student rethink certain aspects of what he has written. For example, asking students if something they wrote came after considering alternatives, or asking them to define a word or an idea, or asking them if they really live in ways consistent with what they write, these are all valuable comments to use in reacting to what a student writes for a value sheet. Naturally, the teacher does not evaluate the students' values. He may, however, evaluate the language usage, spelling, etc.

4. Students turn in their writings to a committee which selects representative ones to be read to the class or posted on the bulletin board.

5. Each student completes written answers and then the class has a general discussion about the topic. This is useful inasmuch as it raises for some students new alternatives and ideas. It is harmful inasmuch as pressures for conformity tend to develop. In any case, it is preferable for group discussion to *follow* individual thought on value sheets and the teacher should strive to protect the right of dissent and, in fact, himself should present alternative arguments when they are not forthcoming from the group. Without individual commitment to a position after full examination of the alternative arguments, no values can be very firm or intelligent.

6. After a while, the teacher may find that some students will want to make up value lessons for the class. This will occur after the sense of the value process is absorbed, and it is to be encouraged. We recommend, in fact, that students be taught the criteria for a value and how to make effective value sheets.

As was discussed earlier in the chapter, value sheets can be used apart from subject matter, or they can be used to initiate subject lessons, to close subject lessons, or in the midst and as a part of subject lessons. The *Silas Marner* sheet is an example of this last approach. More about the relationship between subject matter and value approaches appears in Chapter 9.

But, to close, ten do's and don'ts may help the teacher begin to develop his own value sheets and put them to use.[3]

DO try an adaptation of one of the sheets presented in this book for a starter, if you like.

DON'T moralize, no matter how subtly, when you make your own value sheets or during value discussions. It is contrary to the theory. An easy way to check yourself is by asking two questions of your sheets: (1) "Can the reader be fairly sure from this sheet what my position is?" If so, it is a sign that your beliefs are shining through and will affect those tractable children who need, more than the rest of the class, the experience of thinking things out for themselves. (2) "Are there any questions that have implicit in them 'right' answers?" Asking a question such as "Don't you think that it is good to be neat and clean?" is not asking a question at all for most students. Moralizing has not worked in the past; do not be afraid to abandon it as a classroom practice.

This does not mean that a teacher should never make his views known to students.[4] We think that a teacher should be quite candid about his viewpoints, although making it very clear that students are not to accept those viewpoints uncritically. For most classes, however, it may be wise for the teacher to conceal many of his viewpoints until such time as students realize that they will be expected to find their own values and not to mimic the positions of others, even of the teacher. And in all classes, it is wise to keep the questions section of the value sheets as neutral as possible. When the teacher is communicating his position, he should do so openly and forthrightly. "This is how *I* see the issue," he should declare. He should try not to let his viewpoints slant and load his value sheets, for that would make it more difficult for students to choose freely and intelligently and, thus, to obtain values.

---

[3] Appendix B, p. 233 contains a form useful for helping to predict the effectiveness of value sheets.

[4] Smith (p. 34, 1958) argues that it is not *possible* for a teacher to remain completely neutral in presenting issues.

DO avoid "yes-no" and "either-or" questions, for both limit value-related thinking. And avoid "why" questions for they push children who have no clear reasons for choices to make up reasons for the benefit of the question. Some substitutes for "why" questions are: "Do you *have* a reason for your choice? If so, please mention it." "What alternatives did you consider before you arrived at your choice?" "List the consequences that you desired from your choice and also the consequences from alternative choices that you rejected."

DON'T worry unnecessarily about parents. Experience tells us that most of them will respond to value sheets with feelings of relief that important issues are being raised in a non-directive, serious way. The user of value sheets will likely get many times more accolades than complaints.

DO get into sensitive areas, important areas, as soon as you dare. They are the ones students like to think about and need to think about.

DON'T ask too many questions. If there are more than three or four complex questions, permit students to answer only the ones that interest them or that they have time for. You don't want value sheets to be a chore or a bore.

DON'T try to give the students grades on the basis of what they say, for that will squelch honesty faster than almost anything. You can, naturally, grade the usage of language.

DO include many "you" questions on value sheets, for that is the essense of the value process.

DO make certain that every value sheet contains a choice to be made, alternatives to consider, and that the consequences of each alternative are pointed to. Sheets without choices, such as those that have students reflect on their feelings about situations, do little to advance value clarity. The purpose of the value theory, and the strategy of these value sheets, is to help children think through important areas of their lives and, eventually, to learn to respect their own decision-making abilities.

DO ask many questions about actual behavior, about what a person does or intends to do about his choice. So very many of us have learned to talk a good game, but to let it go at that. But, as Paul Goodman so aptly put it, "When we do nothing, we run the risk of becoming nothing."[5]

---

[5] See Appendix C, p. 237 for examples of other value sheets.

Chapter 7

Other Classroom
Methods

"No pleasure endures unseasoned by variety," said Syrus some two thousand years ago and there is plenty of variety for the teacher who would work at values. This chapter adds to the clarifying response and the value sheet nineteen other strategies that a classroom teacher, regardless of grade or subject specialty, can use to help children escape from value confusion. The reader will find some hints for the use of these strategies in the chapter following.

The first six methods below are concerned with the development of classroom discussions on value-related issues. Emphasis is placed on discussion techniques that are especially worthy of wider usage. Since these first six strategies lead into classroom discussions, they lead to the use of the clarifying response presented in Chapter 5. It may be helpful to review that chapter, for it sets the basic method a teacher must use in responding to a student in a value-clarifying situation, the method, not of moralizing, but of reflecting, questioning, challenging, and generally helping the student to look at what he is choosing, prizing, and doing. The list of thirty responses in that chapter may be especially helpful.

THE VALUE-CLARIFYING DISCUSSION

We must first differentiate between different kinds of discussions and point to a common pitfall in value-clarifying discussions. Some discussions have as their purpose the teaching or review of subject matter. In such discussions, the teacher can point to errors in data, make judgments about the adequacy of answers, and provide standards of rightness and wrongness. Other discussions have as their purpose the clarifying of student values. When the discussion has this purpose, the teacher must be non-judgmental and accepting. If the teacher—no matter how subtly—were to make judgments or provide standards in a value-clarifying discussion, he would be depriving students of the privilege of making their own decisions about the topic under consideration. Moreover, he would be implying that students cannot do their own thinking and their own valuing, an implication that, if frequently repeated, would tend to convince students that it is so. The result would be the conformity, apathy, indecisiveness, and overdissenting of which we spoke earlier. Value confusion, in short, cannot be cleared by a process of clever teacher direction.

The importance of this point cannot be overstressed. Many teachers habitually use leading questions in a discussion to help the student see, for example, that honesty is the best policy. This kind of "guided" discussion is well suited to the teaching of subject matter but disastrous for consideration of values. If the teacher thinks his students are not ready to judge the issue of honesty, to use the same example, he should not pretend that he permits them to do so. He should up and tell them, "Students, we cannot let you decide this for yourselves right now. This decision is one that is too complicated (or dangerous) to give you. Most adults around here believe that honesty is the best policy and you can expect to run into trouble if you behave in ways that contradict this. When you are older you will certainly have a chance to think this through for yourself. Any questions?" But when the teacher *does* intend to give students the choice, he must avoid leading the students to his values (or to any other values). Thus, a discussion in which the teacher is really concerned that the students move toward value clarity in the area of honesty should not contain such a leading question as, "Would you like *me* to be dishonest to *you?*" That question virtually demands one answer and reflects one position. When the teacher has one answer in mind for a question, it is unlikely to be a question that permits students to use the valuing process.

Below is an excerpt from a discussion between a class and a teacher who is concerned with value development but yet who will not permit dishonest behavior in his classroom. The problem here is to give students free choices while preventing unacceptable behavior. Note how this teacher attempts to do this.

TEACHER: So some of you think it is best to be honest on tests, is that right? (Some heads nod affirmatively.) And some of you think dishonesty is all right? (A few hesitant and slight nods.) And I guess some of you are not certain. (Heads nod.) Well, are there any other choices or is it just a matter of dishonesty *vs.* honesty?

SAM: You could be honest some of the time and dishonest some of the time.

TEACHER: Does that sound like a possible choice, class? (Heads nod.) Any other alternatives to choose from?

TRACY: You could be honest in some situations and not in others. For example, I am not honest when a friend asks about an ugly dress, at least sometimes. (Laughter.)

TEACHER: Is that a possible choice, class? (Heads nod again.) Any other alternatives?

SAM: It seems to me that you have to be all one way or all the other.

TEACHER: Just a minute, Sam. As usual we are first looking for the alternatives that there are in the issue. Later we'll try to look at any choice that you may have selected. Any other alternatives, class? (No response.) Well, then, let's list the four possibilities that we have on the board and I'm going to ask that each of you do two things for yourself: (1) see if you can identify any other choices in this issue of honesty and dishonesty, and (2) consider the consequences of each alternative and see which ones you prefer. Later, we will have buzz groups in which you can discuss this and see if you are able to make a choice and if you want to make your choice part of your actual behavior. That is something you must do for yourself.

GINGER: Does that mean that we can decide for ourselves whether we should be honest on tests here?

TEACHER: No, that means that you can decide on the value. I personally value honesty; and although you may choose to be dishonest, I shall insist that we be honest on our tests here. In other areas of your life, you may have more freedom to be dishonest, but one can't do *anything any time,* and in this class I shall expect honesty on tests.

GINGER: But then how can we decide for ourselves? Aren't you telling us what to value?

SAM: Sure, you're telling us what we should do and believe in.

TEACHER: Not exactly. I don't mean to tell you what you should value. That's up to you. But I do mean that in this class, not elsewhere necessarily, you have to be honest on tests or suffer certain consequences. I merely mean that I cannot give tests without the rule of honesty. All of you who choose dishonesty as a value may not practice it here, that's all I'm saying. Further questions anyone?"

Thus in this discussion a teacher who is concerned that students develop an intelligent and viable relationship with their worlds, that is, develop clear values, (1) helps them to examine alternatives and consequences in issues, (2) does not tell them, directly or indirectly, what is "right" for all persons and for all times, (3) is candid about his own values but insists that they not be blindly adopted by others, (4) sometimes limits behavior that he considers ill advised but never limits the right to believe or the right to behave differently in other circumstances, and (5) points to the importance of the individual making his own choices and considering the implications for his own life.

Value discussions do not end in ways similar to subject-matter discussions. There are no conclusions to draw, no consensus to identify, no test items to take. The teacher ends a value discussion merely by having somebody summarize what has gone on, or by pointing to some next steps, such as the setting-up of subgroups of those who are interested in talking further about the issue, or by offering an invitation to the class to raise the issue again at some appropriate time. We often close our value discussions with the simple comment, "Well, class, *so what?* What use has this discussion been? Has it helped you in any real way? Think about this for a moment." After a long moment's pause we are apt to add, "If any of you adjust your life on the basis of the thought generated by this discussion, if you really live differently, I'd like to hear about it and how things work out. Please give me a note sometime, and let me know if you would be willing for me to share it with the rest of the class."

Caution: many teachers do not end value-clarifying discussions soon enough. Cut them at the first sign of dullness. What is usually effective is a few sharp questions, some silence for students to use for private mulling, a few student comments, and then out. Let the issue hang in the air for a bit and move on. Those who want to clarify their thinking on the issue will think more about it later; those who do not need not sit through a lot of, to them, irrelevant chatter. Of course, a discussion that is rich and of wide interest need not be cut short. But do cut those discussions that touch just a few or that fail to catch fire; there will be other days and other ways to try again.

As for initiating value discussions, we need say very little. Subject-matter lessons will give many leads. The topics mentioned in the chapter on value sheets are suggestive (money, leisure, maturity, religions, politics, friendship, love, work and career, family, and character traits). And just plain teaching experience will uncover many ideas. A few special ways of initiating discussions may be worth noting.

1. Quotations

Write out a provocative quotation or read it to the class. For example, Gustave Flaubert said, "Nothing great is done without fanaticism. Fanaticism is religion; and the eighteenth century 'philosophers' who decried the former actually overthrew the latter. Fanaticism is faith, the essence of faith, burning faith, active faith, the faith that works miracles. . . ."

After making sure that the class understands the quotation, the teacher might proceed with some questions to spur the discussion on. These are suggestive:

A. Are *you* a fanatic about anything?

B. What groups of people in our society seem fanatical to you? Why would you or wouldn't you join them in their efforts? What is better about *your* alternative?

C. How did you arrive at your decision about what to do?

D. Have you done anything lately about what you believe?

Here are several other quotations which have brought about exciting discussions:

Thoreau: "The mass of men lead lives of quiet desperation. What is called resignation is confirmed desperation."

Confucius: "To see what is right and to do nothing, that is cowardice."

Hemingway: " . . . I know only that what is moral is what you feel good after and what is immoral is what you feel bad after. . . . "

A teacher's own portfolio of quotations will grow as he works at this. One warning we would make is that the teacher must be prepared to be disagreed with, to have, perhaps, his own understanding of his favorite quote vastly increased and, finally, he must realize deep down that there is no one right answer to how one lives by the words of another man.

2. The Picture without a Caption

The teacher brings in a picture which involves a story of some kind. It must be large enough to be seen from all parts of the room or the teacher must employ an opaque projector or transparency device. Students are asked to supply a caption describing what is going on. After various captions are examined in the light of the available evidence, an attempt is made to see what the students would have *done* in a similar situation. As examples, photographs of a street fight were used. In another case, photographs of a group of pickets provoked a heated discussion.

3. A Scene from a Play or a Movie

A teacher obtains the script from a play, TV show, or a movie and duplicates a small part of it. Students act it out, but it is cut off before there is any solution to the problem. The students then take over and discuss what *should* have been done, how this situation was like something in their own lives, etc. Showing films which are cut prematurely can also lead to interesting discussions. It is usually better to obtain excerpts from something students have *not* seen. Below we have an example, a brief scene from a play from the early 1940's, Maxwell Anderson's *High Tor*. A value-sensitive teacher will delight in the responses that an excerpt like this elicits.

The setting: A section of the broad flat traprock summit of High Tor, a mountain overlooking the Hudson River. Van, who lives by himself on the mountain, is having a picnic supper with his sweetheart, Judith, who has come to see him.

JUDITH: Van, I want to talk to you seriously.

VAN: Can't be done. Listen, things get serious enough without setting out to do it.

JUDITH: Van, this spring you had three weeks' work, laying dry well. You could have had more, but you didn't take it. You're an expert mason. . . .

VAN: I'm good at everything.

JUDITH: But you work three weeks in the year. . . .

VAN: That's all I need. . . .

JUDITH: And all the rest of the year you hunt or fish or sleep, or God knows what. . . .

VAN: Ain't it the truth?

JUDITH: Last fall I came looking for you once, and you were gone . . . gone to Port Jervis hunting . . . deer, you said on the postcard. . . .

VAN: Sure, I was hunting deer . . . didn't I bring you half a venison?

JUDITH: But not a word to me till I got the postcard ten days later. . . .

VAN: Didn't have a minute. . . .

JUDITH: Then last winter there's a note nailed to a tree and you're in Virginia, down in the Dismal Swamp tracking bear. Now, for God's sake, Van, it's no way to live.

VAN: Jeez, it's a lot of fun.

JUDITH: Maybe for you.

VAN: You want me to take the job?

JUDITH: Why don't you, Van?

VAN: Porter in a hotel, lugging up satchels, opening windows, maybe you get a dime, I'd choke to death.

JUDITH: I'd see you every day.

VAN: Yeah, I could see you on the mezzanine, taking dictation from the drummer boys, all about how they can't get home. You can stand it, a woman stands that stuff, but if you're a man I say it chokes you.

JUDITH: We can't live in your cabin and have no money, like the Jackson Whites over at Suffern.

VAN: Hell, you don't need money. Pap worked that out. All you need's a place to sleep and something to eat. I've never seen the time I couldn't find a meal on the mountain here, rainbow trout, jugged hare, something in season right around the zodiac.

JUDITH: You didn't like the Chevrolet factory, either?

VAN: (walking toward the cliff edge). Look at it, Judy. That's the Chevrolet factory. Four miles down, and straight across, that's Sing Sing. Right from here you can't tell one from another; get inside and what's the difference? If you're in the factory you buy a car, and then you put in your time to pay for the thing. If you get in a hurry and steal a car, they put you in Sing Sing first, and then you work out your time. They graduate from one to the other, back and forth, those guys, paying for cars both ways. But I was smart. I parked at a police station and rung the bell and took to the woods. Not for your Uncle Dudley. They plugged the dice.

JUDITH: But one has to have a car.

VAN: Honest to God now, Judy, what's the hurry? Where are we going?

JUDITH: If a man works hard, and has ability, as you have, Van, he takes a place among them, saves his money, works right out of the ruck and gets above, where he's safe and secure.

VAN: I wouldn't bet on it much. But suppose it's true. Suppose a man saves money all his life, and works like hell about forty years, till he can say: goodby, I'm going, I'm on easy street from now on. What's he do? Goes fishing maybe? I'm on vacation now. Why should I work forty years to earn time off when I've got it?*

---

* *High Tor*, Copyright 1937 by Maxwell Anderson. Copyright renewed 1964 by Gilda Anderson, Alan Anderson, Terence Anderson, Quentin Anderson, and Hesper A. Levenstein. All rights reserved. Reprinted by permission of Anderson House, Hinsdale, N.Y.

The purpose of this discussion technique is that it allows the teacher to elicit values in a very systematic way. He does not wait, as the teacher does in the "responding" phase of the value-clarification methodology, for the students to bring up values issues, although he does that, too. As an initiator of issues, the teacher is always keeping his eyes and ears open to provocative material which could start a clarifying discussion in class.

4. Provocative Questions

Provocative questions, such as the following, often stimulate rich discussions.

A. How often do you consider the consequences of what you do before acting?

B. How do you know when something is good or right?

C. Why should we give high salaries to some and low salaries to others?

D. How come so many of us want to get ahead and are never satisfied?

E. Consider examples, such as honest journalism or local democracy, in which a discrepancy exists between reality and what people say is supposed to be.

F. Should one do what one likes to do? When and when not?

G. When, if at all, is it right to tattle?

H. When, if at all, is it right to take dares?

I. What is *good* about teasing, war, thievery, prejudice, etc.?

J. Should the majority of the people be able to do *anything* with society?

K. What is *not* good about being law-abiding, generous, confident, obedient, wise, etc.?

L. How often do you do things of which you are not proud?

M. How often do you do things just because others expect you to do them that way?

5. Other Idea Sources

Briefly, here are other suggestions for sources of materials to spur discussion having a value-clarification focus.

A. Editorials

B. Letters to the editor

C. Literature passed around at election time

D. Popular song lyrics

E. Tape recordings of news broadcasts and other programs

F. Tape recordings of interviews students have obtained from various persons in the community with strong viewpoints

G. Excerpts from speeches

H. Materials from embassies of foreign countries

I. Advertising

J. Cartoons, comic strips, etc.

K. Films

The list is endless, for the teacher will soon be deluged with materials which students begin to bring in because they know that discussion in their class often leads to an examination of things which are terribly important. If he so desires, the teacher can select from the items brought in by students those which fit most fully into the plan he has for subject-matter lessons and then relate the two. We have also seen that discussions have very valuable contributions to make toward motivating a study of a unit. For example, the *High Tor* discussion was used by a teacher to motivate a unit on "Mass Production and Automation." An English teacher made use of the Confucius quote, and the discussion which followed, to lead her students toward both a unit on biography and an examination of the opportunities in men's lives to turn their backs upon the wrongs they have witnessed.

ROLE-PLAYING

Worthy of a special category is role-playing, or sociodrama, or dramatic improvisation, as it is variously called. The delight most students take in play-acting makes this an important value-eliciting strategy. Students seem to welcome the chance to take on a new identity in a temporary and protected situation and a flush of real feelings and penetrating insights—fuel for productive value thinking—often emerges.

Sometimes the teacher sets up role-playing situations with much structure, selecting the participants and outlining their initial stances. For example:

"Bill, you play a counterman at a lunch counter in the South that has never served Negroes. You be behind the counter attending to some washing. Chuck and Mary, you be Negro teenagers who have come to demand service." (After they have proceeded a bit.) "Fred, you be a white person who enters the lunch room and helps with the argument on the side that seems to be getting the worst of it."

"You three be students selected by your class to protest the lunchroom conditions in the school cafeteria. You want to be forthright but polite. Sally, you be the principal, who thinks the students have no right to complain." (After a while.) "Bert, you and Sally change places. You be the principal now and let Sally be the group leader."

"Rick, you are the leader of a union. You walk up to Jim, who is a worker in the plant, and you tell him that you heard a rumor that he has been criticizing you for illegal use of union funds. After you have spoken for a while, either of you can call other members of the class to join in the discussion. Simply say something like, 'Come over here Florence and tell him how we all know he's a crook, he's a liar, he's a nice guy, or something.' You can use others in any way you want. But, Jim and Rick, you two start by yourselves."

Situations need not be so carefully structured, and, after students get the hang of things, they can take off from the least bit of preplanning. For example:

Who will be three family members? One be the child and the other two be parents. The child comes with a request that the parents think is unreasonable. Take it from there.

Who will be three friends arguing on a street corner?

Who wants to be a girl approaching her parents for advice on dating a boy of another religion?

You three want something badly, but she stands in the way. Act something out.

Any kind of potential or real conflict situation is useful for role-playing, or any situation in which real feelings are often concealed. Consider situations in school, in the family, on the playground, at work, or in politics or government.

Start with a lot of structure and the most secure and out-going students. Later use less structure and involve less out-spoken students. Do not permit acts to drag; cut them short rather than let them become silly or a bore. One way to liven things is to add characters while the play is in process ("Jean, you be the secretary that overhears the scheme and interrupts with a protest") or permit the actors to add characters as they see the need for it. The latter approach permits the scene to develop more in the control of the actors and is, usually, preferable. Or change roles in the middle of the play for an injection of life and a taste of what the other person feels ("Now the high-school dropout and the employer switch roles").

Following a role-playing situation, a discussion in large or small groups is valuable. Questions that often click are: (1) How did you as actors feel? (2) How would you observers have done things differently? (3) Would things work out that way in real life? (4) What might we learn from this situation?

Of course, the teacher would make good use of clarifying responses, such as those in the list of thirty, when a student expresses a belief, attitude, interest, aspiration, feeling, etc. The wise teacher, also, makes good use of passivity and often lets the discussion take care of itself.

THE CONTRIVED INCIDENT

Sometimes a teacher has to contrive a situation in order to get students beyond the level of mere verbal responses. Occasionally, we need to shock our students into an awareness of what they are for and against.

1. Many teachers have used the experiment reported in Asch's *Social Psychology* (1952) involving the discrimination between two drawn lines. One by one students are asked to say out loud which line is longer. Almost all of the students are in on the ruse and say that the *shorter* line is the *longer one*. After hearing one after another say this, it takes a rare student to avoid twisting his visual perception. When the ruse is revealed, the teacher discusses with the students who mistrusted their own eyes the feelings and ideas that went into their decision. This then can be used to look at other "blind spots" we may have in our lives and to examine issues such as "de facto" segregation, conformity, success, organization men, etc.

2. A teacher found his class discussing rigged TV quiz shows in a desultory manner. The class concluded that no one had really done anything wrong by giving some of the contestants the answers beforehand. Concocting a very difficult test, the teacher hinted to a few of the students that he wouldn't mind if they looked at the answers on his desk. After the quiz, in which the students who had the answers got perfect scores and everyone else in the class failed, the class was told what had happened. They all protested violently and complained bitterly about the unfairness of the situation. When the teacher reopened the discussion on the quiz scandals, the value indicators which emerged seemed to have been much more painfully considered.

3. A teacher had a friend come into class billed as a famous expert

on a topic the class had just studied. In order to draw out the value inclinations related to his topic, the speaker took a completely opposite view to the one which the class had come to understand. The confusion and doubt thus generated tended to foster clarification inquiry. Of course, they were let into the plot and used this, too, for examining such things as the adoration of authority, definition of expertise, etc.

4. Prior to studying the novel *1984*, the teacher came into class one day and said that he was sick and tired of the way the class had been behaving. He set up new rules, which were strikingly similar to the ones in the book, for controlling the class. The outrage this turned loose was handled via the clarifying operations and much insight into totalitarianism was gained through this direct, if contrived, experience.

5. The students in one particular class became rather overimpressed with their academic superiority. It was a college-bound class and had in it some particularly gifted students. The rest of the school was often held in tacit contempt.

The teacher set up a field trip as part of a study of simple machines in their physics class. They went to a vocational high school. There each of the students from the so-called academically superior class was placed with a student from the vocational school. The vocational-school student had been asked to explain to the student assigned to him the most complex of his mechanical skills. The auto-repair student proceeded to reassemble a carburetor, the sheet metal student with deft skill completed a complicated soldering operation, and the machinist did a lathe set-up and machined a part to a special clamp he had devised.

When the students returned to their own school, the teacher opened up topics having important values implications: What is success? What is dependence and independence? Who is a leader and who is a follower?

What is the formula for a contrived incident? We doubt that there can be one, but a few general observations are possible. The contrived incident's purpose is to simulate as closely and as dramatically as possible something that will give students a real feeling or experience or understanding. It cuts through the easy level of words. It is like the difference between saying that war is hell and spending a few weeks in the middle of the stench, exhaustion, and desperation of a kill-or-be-killed situation. Since schools have a tendency to fill themselves with easy intellectualizations, it is often very useful for the teacher to identify the feelings or understandings involved and contrive something that will permit the student to taste them more directly than words permit. After the incident, an acknowledgment of the purpose of the incident and a discussion about what emerged from it are almost always in order.

Teachers who have used contrived incidents quickly recognize their importance. They produce learnings that are sharper and are longer retained than does almost any other strategy. The next time a class is talking about fear, or prejudice, or fulfilment, or tedious work, or job insecurity, or the importance of precise communication, or any number of other things that are easier to talk about than to understand and feel, try contriving a situation that will dramatize the topic being discussed. Then, of course, use the clarifying responses to aid students in digesting that experience. Students usually are enthusiastic about learning from contrived incidents.

THE ZIG-ZAG LESSON

What we call a zig-zag lesson is less dramatic than a contrived incident, but it has a special flavor that adds interest to discussions. What the teacher does is identify a value area that he thinks the students have not clarified sufficiently, such as the idea in the first example below of what pride in work consists of. Then he prefaces an introduction of the idea with some innocuous questions which have the result of piquing students' interests and setting them to wondering what the lesson is all about. The confrontation with the central idea, then, is often startling as it contrasts with the very mild questions that preceded it.

The teacher asks some quick questions, not dwelling long on any of them: "How many of you can tell which shoe you put on first this morning? Do any of you tie double knots in your laces? How many have heels which wear out unevenly? How often do you look closely at a shoe, noting how it is stitched and cut?" Then the teacher pauses and asks: "Did you ever think what it must be like to sit at a workbench and plan, cut, and sew a pair of shoes?" After that question settles and perhaps after some discussion, the teacher might continue to stimulate the valuing process with such questions as: "Can a person be proud of producing a good pair of shoes? Are you proud of the jobs you do? When is a job something to be proud of and something to get out of the way the easiest way possible?"

Here are three other lesson outlines that first zig along innocently enough and then abruptly zag to the heart of a value issue.

Discrimination

1. Make a list of all the persons who come to your house to visit or to eat. Make a second list of all those whose homes you visit on occasion.

2. Note how many in each list are relatives, how many are beyond walking distance, and how many you really are very happy to visit with.

3. Calculate the proportion of your lists made up of relatives, etc.

4. Look at your lists again. If you are, say, white, Protestant, and middle class, how many on your lists are white, Protestant, and middle class? If you are Negro and working class, how many on your list are Negro and working class? If you are Irish, how many on your list are Irish? That is, how many on your lists are in much the same groups as you are in?

5. What is the difference between segregation and integration?

6. Would you like your lives to be more integrated? If so, what can you do about it?

7. Will you do anything? Can I help? Will you let us know?

Migrant workers

1. How many had orange juice for breakfast this morning?

2. What other juices, if any, did any of you have?

3. Anybody squeeze his own juice this morning?

4. How heavy would you say one orange would be? How many would it take to make a pound?

5. Anyone think this morning how the oranges that produced juice for some of us got off the tree? How was it done? Who did it? (The teacher fills in information until the role of the migrant worker is clearly delineated.)

6. What do you think it is like to pick fruit and vegetables for a living? How would you like it?

7. We noted the working, living, and health conditions of migrant workers; what would be some of the important things to change in these conditions?

8. Where should the money come from to help migrant workers? Would *you* be willing to pay more for your fruit and vegetables? What would you be willing to give up if prices were to be raised for the benefit of migrant workers?

9. Is there anything any of us can do about this situation? Want to? Individually? As a group?

Polio vaccine

1. Please make a list of everything you did yesterday which made you use your legs.

2. Check the items which would have been difficult if one of your legs was not in perfect shape.

3. How many of you have had full protection against polio either through Salk Vaccine or Sabin Vaccine?

4. Is there anyone we can help get such protection? Want to write a note to your family right now?

DEVIL'S ADVOCATE

Too many discussions in value-related areas suffer from having only two positions in the room: a consensus and a "don't care" position. Especially in certain political and social topics, dissension is often absent. What often is needed is persuasive argument *against* civil rights, *for* the use of profanity, *against* respect for elders, *for* revolution, *against* patriotism, and so on. At least such dissension is needed if the alternatives to many issues are to be fairly treated. And since the value theory sits squarely on the need for an examination of alternatives, the use of the devil's advocate is often a very productive strategy.

If someone has to advocate the unpopular side of issues, why not let it be a friend of the devil? The devil's advocate role lets the unconsidered alternative come in with full force. It helps prevent passive drift toward unconsidered consensus. For example, look how this fourth-grade teacher launched into a discussion of the first heroes of the space age:

> I want to play the devil with you. I'll screw on my horns and get ready to jab you with my pitchfork. Watch out.
>
> You know all of that stuff you've been reading about these heroes who go up in space ships? Well, this devil thinks they're not heroes at all. What's so heroic about going up in a space ship? Why they have those things so carefully figured out that nothing can go wrong. With all of those movie cameras grinding and all of those TV cameras focused on them, you don't think our government could afford to have the bad publicity of anything going wrong do you? This devil thinks that your walk to school every morning has about as much danger in it as the danger those so-called heroes had to risk. And to ride in a car without seat belts is twice as dangerous as that. But no one calls you a hero when you do that.
>
> Anyhow, if there is such risk, what kind of man would leave his wife and children to do something a monkey could have done? Finally, you foolish children, this devil wants to raise the question about all that money that goes into this man-on-the-moon project. Did you know that we spend over a billion bucks a year, and that money could easily wipe out the slums, build new colleges, work productively on cancer and mental illness research.
>
> So spoke the devil.

What a lively class session followed the devil's discourse. Few students take that kind of confrontation lying down, and the alternatives to consider filled the room. It was value clarifying on a high level, for students were forced to examine what they prized and cherished, to affirm it in front of the entire class, and, of course, to be willing to be examined in terms of whether or not they had indeed made choices from among alternatives which they fully understood.

There was no right answer with which even the devil wanted each student to agree. But the teacher, not the devil, wanted to make sure that students considered alternatives to the popular notions that are so easy to leave unexamined, thus encouraging misunderstandings and lazy thinking habits.

Each teacher does well to announce to the class that, from time to time, he will play a role that is not his real one, that he will do it merely to present a position that has not otherwise arisen. It is often fun to label this role as that of the devil's advocate and to announce what one is doing when it is played, but usually that is unnecessary.

The extreme and dogmatic statements that characterize the devil's advocate signal that something is afoot. And those statements also ignite interests, challenge thinking, and, thereby, help children move toward deeper understanding and clearer values.

The next strategy, the value continuum, is designed for very similar purposes.

THE VALUE CONTINUUM

We have observed that one of the main planks of clear values rests on a consideration of alternatives. The devil's advocate role is often useful for presenting one divergent viewpoint, but most issues are not a simple matter of black or white, and therefore a method is needed to get at the full range of possibilities in issues. In an era of avoidance of controversy, centralization of news services, and pressures for conformity, the provision of the full range of alternatives in some issues is perhaps particularly urgent. We have devised a strategy we call the value continuum for this purpose.

It works like this: The class or the teacher identifies an issue to be discussed in class. It could be federal control of education, interscholastic sports, religious tolerance, censorship, socialized medicine, birth control, or anything else. Then two polar positions are identified, e.g., the federal government should control virtually everything a school does and the federal government should have no influence in what a school does. These two positions, sometimes captured in argument from two newspapers or magazines, one reactionary and one radical, are placed at opposite ends of a line on the board, and the continuum is born. The task of the class, then, is to identify other positions in the issue and try to place them on the continuum, both in relationship to the poles and to positions already placed.

Sometimes issues will be found which are multidimensional and therefore more than one long line is needed, but usually this is unnecessary. In any case, the importance of the value continuum is not in giving visual representation to an issue but in showing the class that most issues have a wealth of possible alternatives, each of which has particular consequences.

The value continuum is especially useful in the initial stages of a discussion on a controversial issue, before the consequences of any one alternative are examined so thoroughly that students begin pre-maturely to take positions. It is, of course, best if minds remain open until the variety of possibilities that usually exist is developed. One thing the value continuum, or "value line," as some younger children like to call it, does well is to permit the teacher to introduce alterna-tives into an issue without having to appear to favor one or the other. There is some tendency for students to believe that, because Miss Jones suggested that consideration be given a certain alternative, she favors that choice. This method affords an easy way to get alterna-tives opened up before heated discussion closes minds.

The method can also be used without discussion. An effective assignment is to state an issue, such as the extent to which one should conform, and ask each student to identify as many positions that deal with the issue as he can and to place them on a value continuum. Even without discussion or teacher comment, such an assignment pays high dividends. It forces students to think deeply and, to some extent, non-judgmentally.

Thus the value continuum demonstrates the complexity of thinking that most issues deserve and offers a method of simplifying the identification of alternatives. It helps overcome either-or thinking: either this is right *or* the other is right. Finally, it helps the teacher deal with the most controversial issues without appearing as if he is indoctrinating. It is a most useful value-clarifying tool.

The preceding six teaching methods develop value-clarifying dis-cussions. Those discussions could, in turn, lead into written assign-ments for students, assignments that might encourage deeper and more personal thought. The following five strategies lead directly to written work, however. In that sense, they resemble the previously-presented value sheet.

THOUGHT SHEETS

When we enter into value clarification, we need always to be on the lookout for ways to elicit values in a consistent way, and to do it without building an atmosphere marked by students giving the teacher what he wants to hear. The moralizing disease sits just below the surface in students, too. One of the most effective techniques involves giving students the opportunity to write freely about anything that has occupied their attention during the week. Unlike most of the preceding strategies, this gets directly at the concerns of the students. It does not rely upon topics initiated by the teacher.

It works this way. Each week a student turns in a single sheet or perhaps a four-by-six inch card upon which he has written some thought of importance to *him*. It is written after due reflection and indicates something of the quality of living or thinking in the preceding week. These are called "thought sheets." To introduce them, the teacher may say something like this:

1. A thought sheet is due every week on Monday. It is to be your ticket of admission to class on that day.

2. Thought sheets may be of any length, any style, any form. Prose, poetry, skit, drawing, etc.—all are acceptable. However, a few words are enough. Long statements are not necessary.

3. A thought sheet may be on *any* topic as long as it relates to *your* values.

4. Your thought sheets will not be graded or "corrected' in any way. They are treated as sincere expressions of some of your deepest concerns and are not to be written as "compositions" to impress the teacher. They are yours.

5. Although usually I prefer to have one thought on each sheet each week, this first week, to get us started, you may include *three* thoughts or ideas or observations, or anything else that is important to you on your sheet.

Students are also told that from time to time excerpts from the thought sheets will be read to the class anonymously. And the first week the teacher is careful to read a selection of them to illustrate the different forms and styles and kinds of topics that are possible. This is healthy stimulation to those students who wait cautiously to see if the teacher is kidding when he says that students are to write what is important *to them*.

Here are some excerpts from thought sheets that students have written:

I can see why you brought up the point yesterday about whether feeling alone in the world might be a horrible experience or an exhilarating one. Now that I think about it. . . .

. . . A bright flash emanated from the object in the shop. The watchman lay dead. Another tape clicked from the computer, "IT'S

ALL RIGHT. THE HUMAN IS DEAD. COMMENCE WORK."
The shop came to life again.

Exams to me are a waste of time. After all, what is an exam? What
does it show? Nothing! It doesn't prove whether I have learned anything over the year, because I could study before the test and probably a few days later I wouldn't remember a thing. If a final is given,
it might not be a bad idea to give it unannounced without letting
the students "prepare" for it.

   . . . As I watch the space up high
In my mind I wonder why
I ever thought big was I
For if big am I what is the sky?

The other day, coming home from school, I saw a very bad fight.
I wanted to stop it, but I didn't know what to do. I didn't do anything and I am ashamed.

When thought sheets are read, the classroom usually comes to a
most respectful hush. Students like to hear the thoughts—honest
thoughts—of fellow students. Comments following the reading are
usually lively and direct. The unidentified author frequently takes
part in the verbal exchange. One listens to and experiences contact
with students who may be doing exciting and important things. We
hear of alternatives or consequences in life we had never considered.
It is a mirror held up to our own lives. A thought-sheet reading day
is one of the most vibrant of schoolroom activities, and one of the
most productive in terms of value clarification.

Notes are frequently sent by the teacher to the authors of the
sheets. The teacher may include a question which he hopes advances
clarification. He may simply commend the writer on his thoughtfulness. He may suggest something else to read on the topic, something
which may be in direct opposition to the student's expression. He
does this because he knows that a value must be chosen from among
alternatives and that one must be able to stand up and affirm his
position, even in the face of another strong opinion in opposition.
Sometimes the teacher's reading of a thought sheet gives him an important contact for a brief one-legged conference with a student.

Sometimes the thought sheets are not returned until midway in
the term, when a summary series of questions are posed, for
example:

1. Which of your sheets (list the titles) reflect your most cherished beliefs or attitudes?

2. Which sheets would you drastically rewrite at this point?

3. Can you spot a pattern to the things you stand for as they are revealed in your thought sheets?

4. Which of your sheets would make worthy "editorials" for the school paper?

5. Pick the one sheet which you would most like the class to know you wrote.

6. If your thought sheets have not yet made you proud, what can you do about it?

7. Pick one sheet in which you expressed a very strong, positive opinion. Have you done anything about it?

8. Why do you or do you not like to write thought sheets?

One English teacher, William Dell, whose students wrote the above-quoted excerpts, used thought sheets as a means not only to value thinking but to more formal writing practice. Figure 1 shows an assignment sheet he distributed to his classes.

Thought sheets are usually returned again at the end of the term. They often are an amazingly accurate gauge of how intent has been the search for values in an individual classroom. One of the most rewarding things to a teacher is to see how many students continue to write thought sheets, on their own, beyond the time when they have ceased to be an assignment. Indeed, some teachers have discontinued the requirement that thought sheets be written as soon as the idea is grasped, which usually takes at least four weeks. Making the writing optional greatly reduces the number that is written, but insures that those that are written are truly thoughtful, deeply and personally. Try thought sheets several ways and see which approach suits you best.[1]

FIGURE 1

Thought Sheet Theme Assignment

Read over *all* of the thought sheets that you have written so far. Then write a theme on *one* of the following topics.

---

[1] For a more detailed discussion on thought sheets and their uses, read Phyllis Lieberman and Sidney Simon, "Values and Student Writings," *Educational Leadership*, April, 1965.

1. Summarize what you seem to be saying in your thought sheets. What seems to be the direction or trend of your thinking and feelings? You may find that you might be concerned with one or more of the following questions.

A. What is my outlook on life?
B. What do I value in life?
C. What are my goals and purposes?
D. What do I believe in?
E. What are my problems?
F. What things am I interested in?
G. How do I spend my time?
H. What do I think about?

2. Take one or more of your thought sheets and compare it in terms of style, form, and content to one or more of the rest of your thought sheets. Be thorough.

3. Take one or more of your thought sheets and expand the content into a theme, story, or poem.

4. Sort through your thought sheets and notice if they seem to classify themselves into certain groups. What headings would you give to these groups? Discuss what these headings tell you about your life, such as, your thoughts, feelings, concerns, observations, awareness, etc.

5. Select your *best* thought sheet and your *worst* thought sheet. What is good about your best? What is bad about your worst?

WEEKLY REACTION SHEETS

A time to sit down and look back very systematically at the week just lived is helpful to value growth. Many youngsters are surprised to see the absence of activities which are personally selected and satisfying over the seven-day span, and some may come to question just how many weeks have passed in this manner.

To supplement the non-directive thought sheet, sometimes a weekly reaction sheet is introduced about midway in the term. Five copies are passed out to each student, and he is asked to fill out one for each of the next five weeks, sometimes in substitution for the thought sheet. Among the questions which we have included on weekly reaction sheets are:

1. Did you act on any of your values this week? What did you do?

2. Did you do anything this week which required more than three solid hours?

3. What, if anything, did you do this week of which you are proud?

4. Did you work on any plans this week for some future experience you hope to have?

5. List one or two ways in which the week could have been better.

6. Were you in emphatic agreement or disagreement with anyone this week?

7. What did you learn this week, in or out of school, that you are likely to use in your later life?

8. What did you do this week that made you very happy?

9. What was the best day of the past week? What made it the best?

10. Are you happy with the way you spend your weekends? How could you improve them?

11. Identify three choices you made during the week.

12. Were there important contradictions or inconsistencies in your week?

13. How was this week different from the previous week?

A teacher would need to select from among this list and, of course, include other questions he feels would encourage the process of value clarification; one would not use thirteen questions at one time.

The idea of the weekly reaction sheet is to promote value thinking, and thus useful questions are those that touch on choosing freely, choosing from alternatives, and choosing after consideration of consequences; prizing choices and being willing to affirm them; and acting on choices, and acting in some pattern of living. One can perhaps sense how regular attention to questions such as those above would encourage persons to take hold of their lives and live them more positively, enthusiastically, purposefully, and proudly.

A variation on the weekly reaction sheet is the *daily reaction sheet*. For this, the teacher poses one question every day or every other day and each student takes a moment or two of class time to write a response to it. For example, one fifth-grade teacher asked students every morning to complete a sheet headed, "Things I did since yesterday morning of which I am proud." After a few weeks of this, the teacher noted new awareness of behavior among children.

It is important to realize that there will be some resistance from some students who feel that this kind of questioning borders on prying or invading privacy. We inform each student that he has the right to leave any questions blank any time. (However, to leave any particular question blank for three or more times may also bring forth a gentle "why" from the teacher.)

Now, what does the teacher do with these reaction sheets as they come in? Although the main purpose of the reaction sheets is served when the student thinks about the questions and answers them, they become even more valuable (and motivation to do them thoughtfully is increased) when the teacher uses them in some way. Here are three ideas:

1. The teacher may simply read them to look for any pleas for help or guidance. He may comment on some of the points made. He may ask questions, either directly of the student or in the margins of the student's paper. He may call a conference if one seems to be wanted or needed.

2. He may mimeograph several student responses to one particular question or read them aloud and give the class an opportunity to discuss these responses.

3. He may have the students examine one another's reaction sheets and thus interview one another as to how life goes and how each one's values are growing.

Whatever the teacher does with these reaction sheets, there is enough evidence to indicate that they are one of the important ways we have of helping students to examine in some consistent manner the relationship between thoughts and the ways in which we spend our hours of the week.

OPEN-ENDED QUESTIONS

The two preceding strategies—the thought sheet and the weekly reaction sheet—are best used regularly, in a patterned way. On the other hand, open-ended questions give the teacher a method of getting the students to reveal some of their attitudes, beliefs, activities, and other "value indicators" on an irregular basis or in a one-shot effort.

An open-ended question is dictated or written on the board and students are asked to write responses either in class or at home. For example, "If I had twenty-four hours to live. . . ." or "The purposes of my life are. . . ." What comes out of such writing, usually, is a rather fruitful list of some of the child's interests, hopes, fears, the people he likes the most, and some things in his life which he considers worthy or unworthy.

The teacher then can write a simple, single question on each paper. It takes very little time. Naturally, it would be a question which helps the student reflect on his writings. The teacher may also read several papers anonymously to the class and ask any class members if they have any questions, and it must be limited to *questions*, that they would recommend to this anonymous author. (This is one of the ways we have of teaching our students the value-clarification process. Besides, their questions often reveal more sensitivity than the teacher's.)

A familiar subject-matter unit might grow out of such writings. A rich lesson for students who are studying a person's life or reading literature is to ask them to try to deduce how that person might answer certain open-ended questions. A comparison of results and the justification of answers provides depth understanding and exciting thinking.

Here are some other open-ended questions which have been productive:

1. With a gift of $100, I would. . . .
2. If this next weekend were a three-day weekend, I would want to. . . .
3. My best friend can be counted on to. . . .
4. My bluest days are. . . .
5. I can hardly wait to be able to. . . .
6. *My* children won't have to. . . . Because. . . .
7. People can hurt my feelings the most by. . . .
8. If I had a car of my own. . . .
9. I've made up my mind to finally learn how to. . . .
10. If I could get a free subscription to two magazines, I would select. . . . Because. . . .
11. Some people seem to want only to. . . .
12. The night I stayed up later than ever before I. . . .
13. If I could have seven wishes. . . .

14. I believe. . . .
15. Secretly I wish. . . .
16. My advice to the world would be. . . .

CODED STUDENT PAPERS

All of us are familiar with the ways in which teachers "go over" students' papers for grammar, spelling, and other errors in expression. Some teachers have also become adept at examining papers for the clarity of thinking and for errors in fact. These are important, but it also seems important to help a student see the nature of the values he expresses. Coding student papers for values does this.

First, the teacher asks students to do writing which is apt to elicit value-related expressions. Papers on controversial topics, thought sheets, weekly reaction sheets, or open-ended questions can, of course, be used for this. The teacher then marks a "plus" sign over those expressions the student writes which indicate something he seems to be *for* and a "minus" sign over that which he seems to be *against*. It is a simple enough process. A teacher comes to do it with great speed. For the student there often is quiet impact. For the first time he may become aware of what he says he is for and against.

When the paper is returned, the student is asked to change any statements he has made and wishes to change. He is also asked to rewrite any parts so that they more fully say what he really wants them to say. Furthermore, he is asked to comment on any grouping, pattern, or, as the case may be, any serious inconsistency which emerges from the things he seems to be for and against.

The teacher may choose also to read the paper in a search for statements which reveal one of the value indicators: interests, activities, purposes, beliefs, attitudes, aspirations, and so on. The student may be asked a question in the margin which attempts to clarify the value indicator. For example, "Have you *done* anything about this?" or "Where did you first get this idea?"

Since critical thinking is such an important part of the clarification process, the teacher may also, on some papers, call attention to students' statements which reveal that a serious *assumption* is made, or that the student has used *extreme* statements, or that he has made use of *either-or* thinking, and so on.

The student has the option of answering or not answering the questions posed. He may or may not arrange for a conference to talk further about them. A short correspondence may result between the teacher and student. No one can *make* a student value, but a teacher can stimulate clarification.

It may seem that the teacher's volume of work would get to be overwhelming once he begins this paper-coding routine.* We have found, however, that the coding adds very little time compared to the usual comments teachers make on student papers, while the growth which sometimes takes place as a result of this clarification process makes it seem very worthwhile.

TIME DIARY

We already alluded to the complexity of decisions regarding the use of one's time, how one spends each day's twenty-four hours and each years' 365¼ days. At the highest level, the use of time is consistent with one's values. In effect, the person does what he values and values what he does. But all lives are not at this level. For many of us, there is a terribly visible gap between our use of time and what we claim to cherish.

This gap is illuminated and often at least partially closed for students by keeping a time diary. A time diary is simply a chart of one week's activities broken down into, perhaps, half-hour segments. In each half-hour block, each student records what happened to his life. The teacher does not ask to see this, for time diaries are often very personal. But the teacher does ask each student to analyze his completed diary with questions like these in mind:

1. How do you feel about how you spent your time?

2. What proportion of your time represents your life at a truly gratifying level?

3. What inconsistencies, if any, are there in the week's activities?

4. What proportion of time was used for things that you do not value highly?

5. When you are older, do you think that you will be proud of having used that week in your life in that way?

---

* See Appendix D, p. 247 for a list of symbols to be used in coding student papers.

After individuals have examined their diaries from the perspective of questions such as those, a discussion that shares insights is useful, although not necessary. More important would be for the student to summarize what he has learned from the study of his time diary and give that summary, *not* the answers to the questions above, to the teacher for comment or simple recognition. Also very useful is a repeat of the time diary assignment after some weeks, with the added assignment that a comparison be made of the weeks recorded.

AUTOBIOGRAPHICAL QUESTIONNAIRE

Early in the term a teacher can take a step to find out as much as he can, short of prying, about his students. A rather lengthy autobiographical questionnaire can be distributed. Students have the right not to answer any question, but again the tone is one of encouragement, support, and acceptance. The data that comes in can be reviewed or can be filed until such time as information about a particular student is desired, perhaps when one needs value indicators in order to work with a particular student.

Some sample questions for an autobiographical questionnaire are below, but each teacher should adapt, add to, and eliminate questions from this list to suit his particular class.

1. Name
2. Birth date   Age in years
3. Address   Phone number
4. What other schools did you go to? Tell me something about them.
5. Who are the people in your family? If you had to use two sentences to describe each person, what would you say about each member of your family?
6. Have you ideas about what you would like to do when you grow up?
7. What possibilities have you talked over with your parents?
8. What does your father do for a living?
9. What are some of his interests, hobbies, etc.? What does he do when he isn't working?
10. Does your mother work?
11. What are her interests, hobbies, etc.?
12. How do you spend your time after school?
13. Of all the things you do in your free time, which do you like most?

14. Which do you like least?
15. What does your family usually do for Thanksgiving? Christmas?
16. What have you done the last two summers?
17. What have you done the last two Christmas vacations?
18. What magazines do you read regularly?
19. Do you subscribe to any yourself?
20. What are your favorite TV shows?
21. Have you seen any movies in the last few months which you particularly liked?
22. Tell me a sentence or two about each movie and why you liked it.
23. What are your favorite sports, if any?
24. If I were to ask you what books you've read which you've liked the best, what would you answer?
25. Do you work after school or on Saturdays? Where? What are you using the money for?
26. What do you like best about school?
27. What do you like least about school?
28. If you could change some part of your educational program, what would it be?
29. If you were a teacher, how would you teach your classes?
30. Have you a hobby which takes up a lot of your time? What is it?
31. How did you get interested in it?
32. Which of your friends are interested in it with you?
33. Who are some of your friends who aren't interested in this activity?
34. Is there an adult outside of school whom you dislike intensely? Why?
35. Are there some adults outside of school whom you admire intensely? Why?
36. Do you have some good ideas about things which you might like to mention?
37. Have you ever invented anything? What?
38. What is there about you which makes your friends like you?
39. Is there something you want badly but can't quite afford right now? What?
40. Of all the people you know who have helped you, who has helped the most? How did they go about it?

The preceding classroom methods are easily classifiable; the first group (value-clarifying discussions, role-playing, contrived incidents, zig-zag lessons, devil's advocate, and value continuum) deals mainly with discussions, and the second group (thought sheets, weekly reaction sheets, open-ended questions, coded student papers, time diaries, and autobiographical questionnaires) with student writings. Along another dimension, the first group (plus the value-sheet technique) is concerned mainly with issues that the teacher identifies as likely for the value-clarifying process; the second group (plus the clarifying-response technique) generates ideas and issues which students identify as important to them. The third group of methods, following, is hardly a group. Its only common denominator seems to be power in a classroom.

THE PUBLIC INTERVIEW

One of the more dramatic value techniques is called the public interview. Let's look at one which took place in an elementary school class and see how it develops.

TEACHER: Today, class, I would like to introduce the public interview. For this we need a volunteer, someone willing to be interviewed publicly, in front of the whole class.

The person interviewed comes up and sits here at my desk, in front of the room. I will go to his seat and interview him from there. The spotlight, you see, is on the person being interviewed.

Now, what I will do first is ask what topic the interviewee wants to talk about. He can choose one of the topics on our list of value areas,* or any other topic, even a very particular topic, like what he did over the weekend, or an idea he has, or a problem or decision he is facing. Anything he chooses.

Then I will ask him clarifying questions, questions that may help *him* get clearer on the topic of the interview, or questions that I think may help the class to get clearer on what he is saying.

By the way, if you volunteer and pick "smorgasbord," then I choose the topic. You can always veto my choice, however.

And if you volunteer, relax, you always have an "out." If I ask you any question that is too personal or that you would rather not answer here in front of everyone, you just say, "I pass," and I will go right on to another question.

---

* On the wall may be posted a list of significant value areas, such as friendship, use of time, use of money, love, morals, freedom, responsibility, politics, occupational choice, family, etc.

And if you want to end the interview, you just say, "Thank you for your questions." That's the signal for you to take your own seat and for the interview to terminate.

Got it? The volunteer picks the topics, or can pick dealer's choice. He can say "I pass," whenever he wants to pass a question. And say "Thank you for your questions," if he wants to terminate the interview before time runs out.

Now who will be a brave soul and be the first to take the interview seat?

(There is a pause as, one by one, five or six hands emerge from laps. The teacher waits, finally selecting Paul, a rather secure boy, a safe bet for such a new venture.)

All right, Paul, you be the first. Others may have a chance another time. Take my seat, Paul. I'll sit in the back. How do you feel, Paul?

PAUL: (In the teacher's chair.) O.K., I guess.

TEACHER: Do you recall what you say if you would rather not answer a particular question? (Making certain the safeguards are understood.)

PAUL: I pass.

TEACHER: And if you want to end the interview before time runs out?

PAUL: I say, "Thank you for your questions."

TEACHER: Fine, Paul, now on what topic would you like to be interviewed?

PAUL: My sister.

TEACHER: Would you care to tell us something about your sister, Paul?

PAUL: Not especially. Except that we hate each other. I want to be interviewed, asked questions, rather than just to say something.

TEACHER: O.K., Paul. What do you hate about your sister?

PAUL: Well, she is two years younger than I am, and she always is in the way. Like she argues about what TV program to watch, and she hangs around me when I'm playing, and she . . . she is just a nuisance.

TEACHER: Are there sometimes when you *like* having her around?

PAUL: No, absolutely not. (Laughter.)

TEACHER: How do you define hate? What do you mean by that word?

PAUL: Terrible. Like I want to murder her. She should go away.

TEACHER: What's the difference between hate and dislike?

PAUL: One is stronger. Hate is stronger.

TEACHER: What is the difference between hating someone and hating things that the person does?

PAUL: Hmm. I just thought of a time when I didn't hate my sister. Once we were walking along and someone said how nice we looked together, we were younger and were walking hand in hand. It was a good feeling. But, I don't know. If you hate enough things a person does I guess you end up hating the person. Is that right?

TEACHER: What do you think?

PAUL: I don't know.

TEACHER: Paul, what are you going to do about the situation between you and your sister? Apparently you don't like things the way they are.

PAUL: What can I do? I know what I'd *like* to do . . . (Laughter.)

TEACHER: Well, one thing you can do is keep away from her. Another is try to work things out so that there is less argument and conflict between you. What other alternatives are there?

PAUL: I don't know. I don't know. But thank you for your questions. Can I go now?

TEACHER: Certainly, Paul. That's the rule. Whenever you want. Thank you. (Moving to the front of the class.) Maybe we'll ask for another volunteer for a public interview tomorrow, but now let's get ready for our arithmetic work.

The purpose of the public interview is twofold: first, it gives one person the satisfaction and feeling of importance that comes from being the main attraction in a relatively dramatic situation, and second, and more importantly, it gives the classroom teacher a vehicle for getting lives revealed to each other in more than a superficial what-did-you-do-over-the-weekend fashion.

The assumption here is that it is often useful for us to share our thoughts and ideas with others. Sometimes a view of another's life opens up ideas and actions that are worth considering for our own lives. It gives us alternatives to consider. Sometimes the public interview increases understandings of others, leading to increased empathy and appreciation of the complexity of their lives. Sometimes a view of another's life removes guilt from one's own life; this happens when we find that what one thinks or does is not so terrible or so unusual.

Furthermore, the public interview always demonstrates that one can talk honestly about one's thoughts and experiences, even deeply personal ones, with a group that is supportive and nonjudgmental.

The need for denial and suppression of feelings and concerns is reduced within the group and may well be reduced within each individual.

There is also, especially for the person being interviewed, the clarifying experience that may be stimulated by the teacher's questions. Paul, for example, may be stimulated to consider whether he hates his sister, the things his sister does, or something else, whether "hate" is what he really feels, and what, if anything, he might do about it. At the very least, Paul has now had an opportunity to get a bothersome issue off his chest. One can imagine how other students might also find food for thought in that interview.

Needless to say, a public interview must be carried out in a classroom in which there is acceptance, security, and warmth. There can be no judging, certainly no ridicule. What we get is a glimpse of a real life, a life that must be respected. All our lives have both beauty and blemishes, and we use the public interview to raise some of this to the surface, to look at it, to understand it, to learn from it. The public interview is an effective technique for bringing more humanness into the classroom.

Public interviews are not everyday events. They are too potent for that. They are used on occasion, to fill a loose ten minutes, to give a spurt to a dull afternoon, or to recognize a person who has something to share with the class.

One finds students selecting topics for such things as unusual experiences they have had, problems they face, plans for the future, and, among older students, topics as profound as the use of nonviolent resistance, the role of revolution in the future, defects in ideal democracy, and the purpose of life. Many students will select "smorgasbord" and then a good part of the excitement is to see what topics the teacher may hit upon. Often it is lively when the teacher flits from topic to topic, always, of course, giving the student being interviewed the opportunity to say either "I pass," or "Thank you for your questions." Some questions that have proven provocative are:

A. Are there things you would not tell even best friends? What kinds of things, and why?

B. Would you bring up your children differently from the way you are being brought up? How and why?

C. How do you feel about going steady?

D. Do you do things to make your parents feel good without them asking? What? When?

E. How do you feel about the mixing of different racial or ethnic groups? How about you, personally?

F. What do you see yourself as doing five years from now? Twenty years?

G. Did you ever steal something? Recently? How come?

H. Do you receive an allowance? How do you budget it?

I. Anything you would like to change about yourself that you would care to talk about in public?

J. Ever get teased? Ever tease others?

K. What does "love" mean to you?

L. How has school been for you over the years?

M. Can you think of something that you would be willing to say to the class and that you think might be good for them to hear?

The careful structure of the public interview also makes it useful for dealing with heated or emotional classroom issues. The teacher facing two fighting angry children finds it helpful sometimes to say, "Let's have a public interview about this. Who would be willing to take the interview seat?" Neither of the combatants would need to volunteer, and it might be best to start with someone else until they cool off. An onlooker or someone who participated in a similar fight in the past would be likely ones to start, perhaps, a series of interviews. The purpose, of course, is to understand the issue and help the children deal with it intelligently. The public interview is a convenient way to begin the process and to give the teacher control over the situation. (Note: One must be careful when dealing with an emotional situation such as two students fighting *not* to try to settle the quarrel, for example, by finding out who is to blame for starting it. One does better to let cooler feelings and understanding settle the quarrel and to work at *general* ideas: the nature of disputes, the use of force, the role of self-control, the difficulty of placing blame, the way feelings color our perceptions, the way one felt in the midst of a dispute and afterwards, etc.)

As to the mechanics of the public interview, a few points may be helpful.

1. Although usually students will choose the topic for an interview, sometimes, as in the case of the quarrel discussed above, the

teacher may select the topic and ask for volunteers to talk about their experiences, perceptions, or ideas about it. Thus the public interview can be used not only to look more closely at one person's life, but to look steadily at one issue. As different students talk about the same issue, alternative ideas and understandings are evoked and the issue becomes more fully understood.

2. One might well have two or three interviews, each of a few minutes, at one time. Or one interview might extend for as long as thirty minutes, if the interest held. Some students have rich lives that are delightful and fascinating to look at.

3. Sometimes the interviewee is told in the middle of the interview that he may ask the teacher or any one member of the class a question on the topic under discussion, with the opportunity for the person to avoid answering by saying, "I pass." If it seems to be working out well, the student in front of the room might be permitted to ask another question or several more, thus temporarily turning the questionee into the questioner. Children like this opportunity for turn-about.

4. Another way to add variety and strength to the public interview is occasionally to ask if another student has a question for the person being interviewed. Take care not to permit another student to make a speech or embarrass the person up front; if a member of the class has something he feels he must contribute to the interview topic, permit *him* to be interviewed publicly later. But let students occasionally practice the art of questioning and clarifying.

5. Usually students will not terminate interviews with a "Thank you for your questions," and teachers will find it wise to tie things up with something like, "That's all we have time for now," or "Let's see if someone else is willing to take the interview chair." And sometimes a topic chosen by the student does not lend itself to many questions of much interest and then the teacher might ask that the student being interviewed select another topic on which to continue the interview or to give someone else a chance. There certainly is no reason to stick with one topic throughout one interview if it does not go any place.

6. Repeat the rules of the game frequently enough, especially in the beginning, so that the public interview keeps its structure and identity intact. Much of the structure, of course, is designed to make the interview dramatic and psychologically safe for the interviewee.

7. Naturally, the teacher does not moralize or take issue with the student being interviewed. The questions can be like those from the list of thirty clarifying responses earlier presented. And simple acknowledgment of answers is sufficient: "I see," "Uh, huh," or "I understand you better now. Thank you."

8. The public interview is not the sole teaching strategy available to deal with an issue, of course, and teachers might do well to try not to settle complex matters merely through one or several public interviews. Often a teacher will find it useful to give a brief lecture to a class about some aspects of a topic, to increase their understandings of the alternatives or the consequences of alternatives. This need not be done right after the interview, and perhaps should not be done so promptly, lest the interviewed students feel as if they have merely been used to get at a lesson the teacher has in mind for the class. Note that the teacher interviewing Paul above did not immediately carry the sibling rivalry issue further, either through discussion, lecture, or any other technique. Here the emphasis was on Paul and his life. Thus, unless there is a pressing, general concern for an issue in the class, it is probably better to work at complex matters gradually, and later. Sometimes a public interview will lead to readings for some students. And sometimes other value strategies are called for: discussions, thought sheets, value sheets, open-ended questions, etc. A teacher has many available tools and usually sufficient time. There is almost always another day and another way for a teacher to deal with a topic.

Thus, public interviews are open dialogues usually built around a student's interests, activities, ideas or feelings. Sometimes, however, they are built around a particular topic or issue. In both cases, they open up lives and share insights and perceptions. They inform, they illuminate alternatives, they deepen understandings of one another.

The teacher with an accepting classroom climate need not fear, as may seem possible, that the public interview will get out of hand and lead to dangerous revelations. Students thirst to talk about deep, personal things in their lives if they can only do so without getting hurt. And the teacher, through mood setting and control, can minimize possibilities of hurt and maximize possibilities of education. If there is some danger that someone will say something that would better be left unsaid, there is much more danger, it seems to us, that the important things in life go unsaid and unexamined, all too often to fester inside. If our experience is any guide, the teacher who would consider using public interviews may be reassured. If the mood is right, students will enjoy them, ask for more, volunteer freely, and find them useful and exciting.

DECISION-MAKING INTERVIEW

Teachers engage in several kinds of interviews in their professional lives. What we call the *public interview* was discussed above. In Chapter 5, "The Clarifying Response," we described the use of brief exchanges initiated to stimulate a student to clarify something he has said or done; we sometimes refer to such an exchange as a *one-legged conference.* Also, there is the familiar *data-gathering interview,* used to gain information from a student about his life; the *parent interview,* used to exchange information about a child; and the *instructional interview,* used to test or tutor a child in some subject area. These last three interview situations might well make use of some clarifying responses and techniques, but one additional interview form—the *decision-making interview*—is ideally suited to such an approach.

A student who has a decision to make and who comes to the teacher for help and advice enters a decision-making interview. Except for those extremely rare circumstances when the decision to be made is beyond the abilities of the student, the consequences involved might be dangerous, *and* there is an alternative to the student making the decision for himself, the value theory offers an ideal tactic for such interviews.

The theory outlines a role for the teacher that is characterized by the following.

1. Unconditional acceptance of the student and problem

Neither delight nor horror can be expressed at the issue or the student if the teacher is to help. Even when a young girl talks about a decision that involves sexual activity that terrifies the teacher, the teacher must accept the issue, as calmly and seriously as possible, as one that is real and important to the student involved. Expressions of distaste or amazement—"You shouldn't be involved in things like that!"—only serve to disqualify the teacher as a helper. We may earnestly desire that the student would not be faced with the existing circumstances, but if the facts of the matter are such that those circumstances *do* exist, all the teacher can do is help the best way he can at that point.

2. No advice-giving, even when that is requested, but many clarifying questions and comments

The role of the teacher is to help the student better understand the ramifications of the issue, the whole array of alternatives that are available, and the consequences that are likely to be attached to each alternative. Then the teacher must hold himself back, restrain himself from suggesting—however subtly—which alternative the student would be wise to select. The purpose of the decision-making interview is not only to help a student make a perfect decision in the one particular instance, but to teach him a process for weighing such decisions in the future and to give him the experience that can be obtained only from making the choice himself.

3. Looking at the issue from the vantage point of the values of the student and not of the teacher

A student says, "I can't decide whether or not to go away for a long weekend, skipping school on Friday, or to stay home and study for Monday's big test." The temptation for the teacher to think and talk in terms of the importance of the school work can be overwhelming, but must be contained. After all, it is very possible that, in a given circumstance and for a given student, the weekend away will be more valuable than the weekend of school and study. Another student says, "The gang wants me to go stealing with them. What should I do?" Again, the teacher must refrain from placing his values against the issue, but must instead ask such questions as, "What are the alternatives? What might happen if you do this and then if you do that? Of what will you be most proud? Of what will you be least sorry? Did you forget that so-and-so is a factor? It sometimes is difficult to decide in such issues, but you must do it; can I help further?"

If the relationship between the teacher and the student is honest enough that the student knows the teacher is not trying to manipulate matters, the teacher is justified in saying something like this, "I don't know what I would do if I were you, but if that happened to me, I would probably choose so-and-so because of so-and-so. I mention this to give you some idea of how one person might react, but you have to choose for yourself, based on your feelings and your values."

What kinds of decisions are suited to this approach? Here are some common ones.

A. Whether to spend saved money on a model airplane or to wait longer and use it for a bicycle.
B. Whether to drop out of high school or not.
C. Whether or not to take on an after-school job.
D. Which role to try out for in the class play.
E. Whether to run for class office or not.
F. Picking from among the various opportunities for a summer experience.
G. Advantages and disadvantages of buying a car.
H. What to do for a friend who is sick in the hospital.
I. How to handle a situation in which the student has had a serious argument with his best friend.
J. What to do when a student knows another student has not read the book for which he did a book report.

In summary, the decision-making interview grows out of the value-clarification process. The teacher resists leaning toward one choice over another. He asks questions, instead, and gives no advice. Such a procedure is consistent with the value theory, which stresses that, ultimately, all decisions, if they are truly to reflect values, must be made freely, after due reflection, and from an adequate exploration of all the available alternatives. It is such decisions of which we are proud, which we are apt to affirm, and which, certainly, we will act upon.

An interesting self-test for the teacher is how often students come to him for help with personal decisions. The teacher who is quick to advise and judge, and who thereby restricts the opportunity students have to learn to think things through for themselves, would not, we

would guess, have many students approaching him for help in decision-making situations. The teacher who listens respectfully, who
asks questions designed to help the student to understand better,
who respects student judgments even when they differ from his own,
and who is reluctant to decide what is good for another person's life
is likely to get many such invitations to help. Students seem to appreciate *help*, not dictation, when they face personal decision, and to
respect the teacher who is willing to let them learn from mistakes, as
well as from triumphs—as long as the teacher's knowledge of
alternatives and consequences has been honestly and openly shared
with them. In short, the teacher has an obligation to point out what
he considers an impending mistake, but an equal obligation to
permit the student to learn from it.

Because of the large number of students in our schools who assert
that they have no one with whom they can really share their problems—least of all the busy school counselor—and in view of the
many perplexing decisions which trouble today's children, the
importance of the decision-making interview here described may
well be substantial.

VOTING

Here we refer not to the usual occasions in the classroom in which
a vote is taken, but to a special technique, much like the public
interview, that brings to the verbal level issues and ideas that might
otherwise be difficult to make public.

To use the voting strategy, the teacher poses a list of questions,
such as those used in the public interview, and students state a position by a show of hands. For example, the teacher might ask the
following sequence of questions, pausing after each for a vote, the
recording of the vote on the board, and a moment to reflect on the
ideas generated by the question:

1. How many of you have ever been seriously burned?

2. Anyone here ever own a horse?

3. How many think sometimes of dying or what death might be
like?

4. I'd like to see how much loneliness is in this group. Vote either that you feel lonely often, sometimes, or seldom. How many feel lonely often? Sometimes? Seldom?

5. How many have a favorite political party? How many have no clear political ideas?

6. How many feel strongly about some religion or religious beliefs?

7. Who here watches television more than four hours a day on the average?

8. How many would want to be told if they had bad breath that was annoying to others?

9. How many of you have no fathers living in your home?

The teacher may conclude such a voting session with something as innocuous as a "thank you, that was very interesting," and go on to a subject-matter lesson without fear that the time was wasted. Performed sensitively and paced evenly, the teacher can be assured that some students will for the first time understand how many of his peers have no fathers and perhaps think a bit about what it must be like to live in a fatherless home. Some students will note with relief that death is a topic that others think about and that it is possible to talk about it. Some will be reminded of the seriousness of playing with matches: serious burns might result. Some will consider how they feel about political matters, religious matters, how much time they want to use for television, and so on. A simple vote, with no one talking but the teacher, can lead to a lot of clarifying thinking.

Sometimes the teacher will ask three students to prepare a voting list for use at some future break in the proceedings. Sometimes the voting will lead to other value strategies, such as a discussion. Sometimes the teacher will merely say, "There were things to think about in today's vote. Anyone who wants to may write me a note sometime about things you thought about. I'd be happy to see that and maybe I'll make a little comment back, and you can reply to my comment, if you like. Do this anytime." Sometimes the vote will lead to a subject-matter lesson and votes can be prepared, of course, with that in mind. One arithmetic teacher held such votes regularly and used the numbers that came out for all kinds of problems and examples. But, all the time, a vote is permissive and not mandatory;

one may raise his hand for any position but one may abstain whenever one wishes, with no questions asked.

Sometimes votings will be focused on a single issue. Here, for example, is a sequence used by a sixth-grade teacher:

1. How many people feel that a child in the sixth grade should get an allowance?

2. How many of you believe that there should be some work, some doing of chores, before a child gets an allowance?

3. How many of you believe that chores are something you should do anyhow, and that any money you get from your parents should come from special work, work beyond mere chores?

4. If you voted for allowances, how many think that a sixth grader should get more than one dollar a week?
How many say between fifty cents and one dollar a week?
How many vote for a number between twenty-five cents and fifty cents a week?
How many think the allowance should be less than twenty-five cents?

5. How many think that every child in the family should get the same allowance?

6. How many people would be willing to buy their own clothes if their allowance were doubled?

7. Do you think an allowance should be for:
A. recreation
B. food
C. saving for big things, like an archery set, etc.
D. whatever you want
E. school supplies

This voting technique is like the public interview in that it opens up issues and questions nicely and often dramatically. It is less personal and therefore less threatening, and therefore perhaps something to use before introducing the public interview.

FIVE-MINUTE QUOTE WITHOUT COMMENT

After a teacher has been working with value-clarification techniques for some time, a climate grows in which the pursuit for clear values becomes more and more important. Students are taught the seven criteria for a value, how to recognize value indicators and the questions which help to advance clarification. There is room, also, for a technique which we call the "five-minute quote without comment."

What happens is that, whenever a student requests it, he is given up to five minutes to make a statement to the class. The time can come from any place where there is a spare five minutes; between lessons, after homework is collected, etc. The statement reflects something important to the student, something he would like to say to others. Often it is something connected deeply with his value system. Sometimes it is a critical comment. Often it is strongly affirmative. It may be emotional. But it is distinctively the student's, and not in any way censored by the teacher, of course.

No comment is permitted at that time. What is sought is demonstrated free speech with brave talk removed, at least temporarily, from the need to defend itself. The statement should reach undisturbed to the four corners of the room. People need, if their values are to grow, to publicly state what they believe in.

What often happens, if the statement has been particularly provocative, is that a rash of thought sheets will talk to the points raised. Students may well talk individually with the student who made the five-minute quote. There may be a movement to look at a values issue further, via a dittoed value sheet, a values continuum lesson, etc. Another way a student has of dealing with an issue is to ask for five-minute quote time for himself. Naturally, we are not encouraging a debating society; the emphasis is upon affirmation of one's own values, not upon finding holes in or taking pot shots at someone else's.

Occasionally, the five-minute quotes are read to the class by a student. This is, of course, acceptable and may provide a useful record in instances in which review of the quote is helpful. Some teachers may tape record the quotes, and these can be played back later in the term, used to lend importance to the statement, or used for absent students. A teacher may also ask a student to duplicate his statement so all can examine it more closely.

To summarize, the "five-minute quote without comment" is designed to help implement one more criterion for a value: "to affirm publicly what one values." Students are told that they may have, time permitting, a maximum of five minutes to make a statement to the class. No comment is permitted. It is a chance for any student to have five minutes of control of the class ears. It is his few moments to affirm something important to him. And, among its other benefits, it clearly demonstrates that the teacher respects student ideas.

STUDENT REPORTS

Few activities thirst for improvement more than the tired old student report, book report, research report, or term paper. They are dull enough to read, but to suffer through a session of oral reports can be devastating. And when this chore is multiplied by the chores of the many students preparing the many reports, which is virtually synonymous with copying from the encyclopedia or book jacket, the combined agony and the small educative result must be classical in its failure.

The value theory suggests a way to bring new life and real education to these student reports through the simple device of having those reports focus on personal choosing, prizing, and acting. Take the book report, for example. Compare the usual bland directions to summarize and evaluate the book with the following suggestive questions:

1. Which character is most like you? What did he do which you would like to do some day? What did he need to do to get ready? What will you need to do?

2. What forces in life did he attempt to shape? What help did he seek and how did he use that help?

3. In what ways would he have made a good parent? A good teacher?

4. In what ways does the author's understanding of love differ from yours?

5. Describe how the major characters viewed money? Contrast and compare their views of money with your own.

6. Project how the hero of the book would have stood in terms of some political strife now occurring in your own community. Where do you stand?

7. Who was the hero's most important human obstacle? How did he deal with this obstacle? Were there any other alternatives open to him? What would you have done? Are there any human obstacles in your life? How do you live with these?

8. Which of the clichés of our culture does the hero affirm or refute? Are there some clichés which you no longer believe in?

9. What things did the hero do for leisure which appeal to you? How can you get started in that activity?

10. What are some things which the hero might have done *himself* to make his life a richer and fuller one?

For the social studies, sense how the seventh-grade unit introduced through the sheet reproduced below differs in pertinence to life and thought from that of the more common assignment, "pick a man and a country and report on them in six hundred words."

We are starting an important unit on South America. You will be asked to work on an individual as well as a group project. During the course of this unit, I hope to bring you into contact with the people of South America. You will be dealing with those people who are living, working, and struggling today as well as with those who lived and worked and struggled in the past.

You will be getting information from books, pamphlets, and articles which will enable you to answer the questions raised below. This should prove an interesting and rewarding experience if you will make it so.

Individual Report

For your individual report, choose one of the following great men who fought to free South America from foreign rule: Jose De San Martin, Bernardo O'Higgins, Antonio Jose De Sucre, Francisco De Miranda, Simon Bolivar.

Your individual reports should consider the following: What was there in the life of the man you have chosen that interested you? Are there any things in your own life which are similar to his? For what things did you admire him most? Have you known any other adults who have these qualifications? What exactly did he achieve? Were his goals or aims at all like any you have dreamed up for yourself? What difficulties did he have to undergo to achieve his goals? In what ways was he weak? How did this hurt him? How would he have made out in our world? Explain.

Where did his life seem less fulfilled or satisfying? Do most great men have large areas of their lives which are not fulfilled? Explain. What did his friends feel about him? How important were their feelings to him? In what ways were his friends' feelings influential upon him? Where did he display his greatest courage? Where did he display his greatest wisdom? Where did he make his greatest contribution? Who benefited from this contribution? Are there any ways he lived which would be good for people to follow today?

Group Report

For your group report, choose one of the following countries that Bolivar helped to make free: Colombia, Venezuela, Peru, Bolivia, Equador.

Deal with the following questions as part of your group report: What does the farmer want in the country you have chosen? What stands in his way of getting it? How does he go about getting what he wants? What help does he have? What hopes do his children have? What do they know of their own country? Of ours? What do they think and know about politics or their government? What is their day like? Where do they sleep? How many in a bed? What do they fear? When do they marry? What do they do for recreation? What part does religion play in their lives? What is their idea of a good life? How does it compare with yours? (Discuss this last question with your group and come up with some ideas.)

Answer these same questions for an industrial worker and a wealthy landowner. Are your answers the same for all of these people? If not, why not? Are any answers you have the same or similar to those of another group? Which ones? (Find this out by reading and discussing work of other groups.) If your answers are similar, why do you think this is so?

Finally, note the research report assignment given by a high-school English teacher in Figure 2. The learning produced by that assignment was far different from the transporting of irrelevant information from a source book or magazine to some blank sheets of paper. Students were *educated* by that assignment. They better understood themselves and part of the world around them. And those reports were exciting to read!

No, student reports need not be dull and uninspiring. They can deepen insights into subjects being studied and exercise writing and research skills while at the same time being interesting and promoting clearer values. We can replace the hack work and the plagiarisms with creative and educative thinking if we make efforts to help students see reports as a chance to look searchingly at some alternatives for living and the consequences of those alternatives, and all in the framework of the feelings and beliefs and actions of the student doing the report.[2]

FIGURE 2

Research Paper

On May 1, you will all be required to hand in a research paper; papers will not be accepted after that date unless you are absent. The paper should include an outline, footnotes, and a bibliography. You will be given more information on the format of the paper later. As for the content of the paper, choose one of the following types of persons and answer the following kinds of questions about that type of person:

A. What specific problems does this person have? What has caused these problems? Has he himself caused some of these problems? Which of his problems have been caused by things or people outside himself? Are any of his problems similar to yours? Is there anything in his life similar to yours? What is the average day of this person like? Where does this person usually sleep? What does he usually eat? What are his fears? Is anybody against him? Why? Are the problems of this person unknown or misunderstood by most people? Why? What do this person's problems do to his body? What do they do to his mind or personality? What do you admire or hate in this person? Why? How is his family affected by his problems?

B. What can be done to help this person? Who is trying to help him? How? What are his hopes and goals? How is this person better

---

[2] For a further discussion of student reports, see Lieberman and Simon (1964).

off today than he would have been fifty years ago? Can the government change old laws or make new ones to help this person? Explain. Will changing people's attitudes toward this person help him? Which attitudes? How can they be changed? What do your parents or friends think about this person and his problems? Do you agree with them? Why or why not? Can you do anything to help this person? What have you done or plan to do?

1. Alcoholic
2. Juvenile delinquent
3. Narcotics addict
4. Migrant worker
5. Cuban peasant
6. Cypriot Turk
7. Berlin citizen (East and West)
8. Southern Negro
9. New York tenement dweller
10. Sufferer of mental illness
11. Person in prison
12. Man or woman seeking divorce, before and after divorce
13. Beatnik
14. Algerian Frenchman
15. Gabonese
16. Indian Untouchable

17. Compulsive gambler
18. Union man on strike for extended period of time
19. American soldier in Viet Nam
20. Man facing capital punishment
21. Boxer getting too old to fight
22. Peasant in Red China
23. Coal miner
24. Unemployed man
25. Person over 70
26. Derelict
27. Pacifist
28. Physically disabled
29. Mentally retarded
30. Polio victim
31. Member of a mixed marriage
32. Orphan

ACTION PROJECTS

Occasionally, a teacher can talk about values too much. The words begin to sound hollow. Some highly verbal students become adept at saying the right things but change little, especially on the behavior front. It may be time for a teacher to recommend an action project.

For example, students may have talked, complete with shocked and passionate reactions, of slaughter on the highways. There comes a time to turn their talk into action. With this challenge, one teacher prompted a class to start a poster campaign about seat belts. Other students made an arrangement with a supermarket, roped off a section of the parking lot and, supervised by a mechanic, they installed *gratis* seat belts for car owners who were willing to pay for them. Here safety was closer to becoming a value than talk alone would permit.

Another class, after soul-searching about race relations, arranged to work with a neighborhood group in a slum ghetto in an effort to make a filthy, rubble-piled empty lot into a children's playground. Students, teacher, neighborhood mothers and fathers, and children, kindergarteners to high-schoolers, worked side-by-side. The talk was about the work and the life people led in the ghetto. The students took home more than they may have left. It was a way of closing the gap between what they said and what they did. It was an action project with value implications.

There are other examples. Students have worked for the political party of their choice, in campaign headquarters, during an election. They have organized and carried out letter-writing campaigns. They have conducted surveys to gather and disseminate information. They have read to older and infirm citizens. They have worked together to produce a show which they have taken to the children's wards of public hospitals. The motivation is the same, to put one's money where his mouth is and learn in the process.

If there is an injustice or some need, students can take action to help, individually or, if there is consensus, collectively. As they do, they learn and become clearer about what their values are.

It is important to note here that some students come back from an experience such as working on a playground with prejudices and stereotypes which are reinforced. This is a risk, and consistent with the value theory. We do not undertake an action project to have everyone come out with the same answer, but we go there in order to get more data, both on reality and on our own feelings, with which to make the decisions which we must make if we are to have values.

The form any action project takes is determined by particular situations, but three bits of advice may be helpful. (1) Encourage students to see that they have power. Children's collective and concentrated power, politically, physically, morally, can often be enough to make a real and lasting difference. Students often fail to see this and, much too often, become so accustomed to not seeing it that they slip into an adulthood that neither recognizes nor uses its potential power.

(2) Permit the students to select or reject any action project. When a teacher imposes action upon a group, he leaves himself open to all sorts of criticism, especially in these days when the value of field projects is not yet fully appreciated. Too many students, administrators, parents, and teachers see schools as places only to *talk* about things. Make certain that the students understand the kind of idea or understanding that needs more concrete representation, or the kind of purpose they want to support, and explore with them, openly and creatively, possible alternatives to action. It is entirely possible, and not at all undesirable, for different action projects to work simultaneously at different and incompatible ends. Projects, of course, must be appropriate to the needs or values of the participating *individual,* not necessarily the class as a whole.

(3) Finally, do not insist that every student participate in every action project. Some projects may contradict a student's values, may threaten his security, or otherwise result in more grief than education. Besides, permitting any student to abstain from action projects at any time provides a relief valve that forestalls much criticism, both from within and without the school.

Part Four

Using the Value Theory

Chapter 8

Getting Started:
Guidelines and Problems

A long time ago Confucius noted that ideas have to be turned into action if they are to be of any worth. The purpose of this chapter is to help the reader take some of the ideas of this book and turn them into action in the classroom.

Those who have worked with children in ways roughly analogous to those recommended by the value theory may merely want to use these approaches more systematically or extensively. Those readers might skip the next part of this chapter and move directly into the discussion of guidelines for classroom use of the value strategies.

Others may feel as if the value theory requires a substantial change in attitudes and operating procedures, and they might do well to consider some of the real difficulties in changing one's ways, briefly considered below.

TAKING A NEW ROAD

Getting started with a new approach is at best difficult. Even more difficult, perhaps, is avoiding giving up when the going gets tough, when the newness of the approach runs into the inevitable problems and confusion and resistances. Our old ways are so comfortable. Often we are not even expected to take new paths, so external motivation is missing. Sometimes we are even pressured *against* taking new paths, so why fight it? Why, indeed?

Because students will benefit? Well, yes, although we really cannot be certain of this until *after* we have suffered the trials of getting the new method to work.

Because it makes it easier for us to educate students who are so confused by values as to be apathetic, very uncertain, conforming, or irrational in the classroom? Again, yes, *but*, we will not know about this until after we give it a try. Besides, it might be easier to suffer the apathetic, uncertain conformists, and the others than to try to change teaching ways.

Because, if it does work, children will like us more and we all like to be liked? Perhaps.

Because, again assuming it works, parents and other teachers and school administrators will have more respect for our talents? Sure, why not?

But there is another reason: This new method offers the opportunity to move to richer levels of teacher satisfaction. It adds another, and, according to the evidence so far, very potent tool to the teacher's resource kit, and, like the expert use of any effective tool, it gives immense satisfaction when it is well handled. To see children move from apathy or confusion toward positive, purposeful, proud living and learning—and to know that one is partially responsible for this— is to experience something deeply satisfying, both professionally and personally.

Why then do we emphasize the trouble of getting started? Because it *is* difficult, *not* easy to do. Few teachers appreciate how much of their professional behavior is a subconscious result of their past experiences, not the result of conscious decision. A number of us lecture because our experiences have associated lecturing with security or success or power or fame or something else personally meaningful. Some of us are lenient with students because *we* feel better when we are that way. Some history teachers are history teachers because *they* enjoyed history when they were in school— and they tend to teach it the way they remember that it provided enjoyment, even when it is quite clear that many of their students are not finding the same pleasure. And so it goes. There are foreign language enthusiasts who are "convinced" that foreign languages are good for students. Teachers who found more satisfaction in the woodshop, however, will not easily be convinced that woodshop is not much more valuable than foreign languages. And the sad part is that, like many a political and religious discussion, one can consider these things at great length without ever getting at the "real" reasons. The logic behind arguments for foreign languages, woodshop, the lecture method, leniency, academic history, and so on is often rationalization for the less understood need to defend one's subconscious heritage.

These reasons help explain why education courses have not had much effect on teacher behavior. One just cannot argue away many teachers' needs to relive their past positive experiences. Thus, there is the seemingly absurd difficulty of getting educational innovations that are demonstrably superior adopted by school people. Their satisfactions may just float in another sea.

There is a somewhat special obstacle for many teachers in a method, such as the value theory, that aims at developing the student's independence and self-responsibility. As Peck and Havighurst (1960, p. 193) put it:

> . . . a good many Americans either do not really want children to become independently responsible beings, or they will not tolerate the frequent frustrations of selfish impulse which are required to treat a child in an ethical manner. This is true of a good many teachers and preachers, just as it is true of many millions of American parents. The millennium in human ethics will not come by wishing; it is a far-distant goal that must be arduously worked for, on a personal scale, day to day.

Of course, none of this is meant to imply that all teachers resist all change. Regarding children suffering from value confusion, many, many teachers are seriously concerned about the disinterested, conforming, and uncertain child and are not only willing but anxious to find some workable approach to such children. There are other teachers who see the unhappy results of moralizing—humans without the self-confidence and skills to guide other lives—and want to avoid that. Other teachers find pleasure in striking out and trying potentially more effective teaching approaches, sometimes because they recall with dismay and regret school days of their own that were frustrating or empty. But for all, the willing and the hesitant, developing new styles of behavior is not easy. Perhaps to be forewarned is to be forearmed. For the hesitant, also, perhaps awareness of some of the common reasons that tie us to older practices will help overcome resistance.

GUIDELINES FOR GETTING STARTED

How, then, might one begin? What problems can we point to that might help a teacher minimize difficulties? Generally, we would suggest a two-stage approach. The first stage would have the teacher give some strategies of the value theory a preliminary test, with the object of perfecting them and getting subjective impressions of their effect. The second stage would involve a more systematic test of the theory, and might follow several months of the more informal trial. A way of systematically evaluating the value theory in the classroom is outlined later in the chapter. First, eight general guidelines and problems to avoid for those who would give the theory even a preliminary field test are discussed.

1. Work Toward a Psychologically Safe Classroom Climate

Many kinds of student growth flourish in a schoolroom in which the student feels accepted, supported, relaxed, and generally unthreatened. Value growth is probably in this category. Therefore, it is wise for the teacher working for value development to also work for the proper classroom climate and, in particular, to try to have students feel safe and secure enough to think logically and express themselves honestly. To do this, students will have to perceive that the teacher basically likes and respects them and that they will not be punished in some way, overtly or covertly, if they make a mistake in judgment, look foolish as they search for clarity, or adopt a value that contradicts one of the teacher's or the school's.

This does *not* mean that the teacher must be extremely permissive, although it probably does rule out an arbitrary or autocratic climate. More important than permissiveness is respect and concern. Students must feel that, even though rules exist and there is teacher direction, the teacher respects the values of the student and is concerned that the student works at those values in his own way. Indeed, we have seen teachers develop an *unsafe* classroom climate by rapidly removing controls and direction in the mistaken belief that permissiveness was necessary for value development. As a result, the students' need for security was so threatened that neither values nor much of anything else was attended to.

This does not mean students should not have freedom. Students need freedom if they are to practice directing their lives, and it is only through such practice that viable values develop. But freedom must be won gradually and, usually, giving a whole class freedom quickly is giving more than can be handled. The problem of group decision-making and group self-control is so complex, even for many adults, that it is more likely to swamp than to nourish efforts at self-direction.

In summary, try not to confuse a lack of controls, the teacher's by abdication and the students' by lack of development, with the climate necessary for value clarifying. The required climate is related more to respect and acceptance of students than to freedom for students.

2. Work at Eliminating Tendencies to Moralize

This is very hard for many people. Whether we consider ourselves so wise, or because we cannot easily entertain the idea that our values might not be ideal, or for whatever reason, the tendency to try to persuade children to accept *our* values is controlled only with great effort. Most of us all too easily judge others. We apply our standards to all sorts of actions for which those standards may not really apply. We assume that persons who have not had our experiences should nevertheless have our understanding. We lecture about righteousness. We bribe and punish behavior to mold it to what we consider acceptable. We complain when children do not follow our excellent models. We preach, we nag, we cajole, we do many things to bring about *our* values. We are delighted when students accept them, and we consider it a failure, sometimes a personally threatening failure, when they reject them.

But, as discussed in Chapter 3, this moralizing, directly or indirectly, has not worked very well. And it has robbed children of the privilege of thinking value-related issues out for themselves. The results are the value confusion, the apathy, the conformity, the uncertainty, and the irrational behavior of so many children and adults today.

We must learn that we cannot foster the ability to think critically in value-related issues at the same time that we demand, even subtly, that the outcome of that thinking must conform to what we believe. If we are to inculcate values, we cannot expect that they will be thoughtfully adopted and freely lived. If we want children to really live what they believe and believe what they live, we must give them the opportunity to do so. When we restrict beliefs or actions, we restrict this opportunity. The argument against "guiding" value decisions of children is strong even if the failure of that approach has not sobered us to the need for an alternative.

The assertion here is that values, defined as freely and thoughtfully chosen, prized, and acted upon, do _not_ come from a process of adult manipulation. The definition says that they _cannot_ come except by free, open, intelligent, informed choice. This does _not_ mean that teachers accept any kind of behavior. Children have to be protected—not from erroneous beliefs, those will be exploded in the process of free and thoughtful development of ideas—but they have to be protected from any actions that will restrict their development in the future. Even adults have limits to their freedom to act. No adult may kill whomever he wishes. Children, generally, have more limits than adults. They may not quit school before a certain age; they may not contract to buy merchandise; they may not marry; they may not continually disrupt a classroom; etc. But we assert that there is a difference between limiting a child's behavior and respecting his right to his own opinions, beliefs, and values. It might be a very healthy thing if everytime an adult made a judgment that limited a child's actions or was in opposition to the child's ideas, that adult were to say something like, "But everyone may not agree," or "We have to do this for so-and-so reasons, but some people think that those and other reasons lead to different conclusions," or "You may campaign for your way, but for now . . . ," or "Although my idea is so-and-so, you should have your own ideas, whether they agree or disagree," or in some similar way make clear that even while we limit behavior we want children to think and value thoughtfully and individually.

In terms of classroom behavior, this suggests that a teacher may limit behavior that he judges to be detrimental to students, explaining the reasons whenever possible, but a teacher should not try to influence the values of students in any arbitrary, non-rational, or covert manner. He may argue for a particular value, but he makes certain that alternative arguments are presented, and he respects the students' rights to adopt an alternative. A values teacher is modest when it comes to his own values. He is proud of them, clear about them, but not certain that they are the last word for him or anyone else.

Six ideas to help oneself work toward the elimination of moralizing:

A. With value issues, avoid questions to which you already have an answer in mind, such as, "Would you like me to do that to *you*?", after Jim socks Phyllis. Use open-ended questions, such as, "What else might have been done?", and the list of thirty clarifying responses in Chapter 5.

B. Avoid "why" questions, "yes-or-no" questions, "either-or" questions, or questions that tend to make a student defensive, ready to rationalize his position, or that limit his choices.

C. Begin with written value lessons, such as value sheets and thought sheets, so that you can reread your responses before the student sees them and so that you can have time to think carefully before you respond.

D. Ask a friend to listen to your classroom responses or to read your written comments in value issues and to note moralizing tendencies.

E. Ask students if they feel as if you are loading the dice about issues that you believe are not being loaded and if you are accepting alternative values in cases in which you make your position clear.

F. Most importantly, begin the use of value strategies with topics in which you have no strong feelings one way or the other, such as how children should spend leisure time or what occupation they should choose. When the teacher has no position, he is less likely to unconsciously try to sway the beliefs of the students.

3. Start Slowly, but Not Too Slowly

Do not try the whole array of strategies suggested in this book the first week. It is probably wise to go slow at first, feeling your way and letting the students become accustomed to any departure from what they are accustomed to. Do not go so slow, however, that any method gets lost in the shuffle. It is probably wise to proceed fast enough so that the teacher does not forget the feeling of one technique by the time he gets to the next, and slow enough so that the boat does not rock everyone overboard.

Of course, begin with the strategies that are most comfortable to you and the students. Value sheets and written comments on student papers are often an easy way to get going.

Many teachers have found it useful to make a list of those clarifying responses of the thirty in Chapter 5 that suit them most and to keep it on their desks or at some place, as on a seating chart, where it can be glanced at during a class. This may be a helpful aid while learning to respond to students in a non-judgmental, value-clarifying manner.

4. Keep Administrators and Other Teachers Informed

Some teachers have added to the difficulties of making innovations by waiting for a student or a parent to let administrators and other teachers know what is going on in the teacher's classroom, and thus raising unnecessary envy and feelings of being slighted. Even though it is within the professional responsibility of teachers to use methods such as those of the value theory, it is wise to keep the lines of communication open between oneself and others on the school staff. It is often helpful to offer to explain what one is attempting to the P.T.A., a student assembly, and, especially, a faculty meeting. This is not asking permission to teach as one sees fit but notifying others of ideas that may be new and interesting to others on the professional team.

5. Talk About the Value-Clarifying Process in Tentative Terms

Until one has worked with the value theory enough to obtain the kind of results desired, it is probably wise to talk about it in tentative terms: "I'm trying this approach," not "I'm adopting this approach." This will help others understand that you are open-minded about it, and that you will need time to avoid the blunders that accompany all new ventures of this type. Then, when you do err as you work to perfect the methods, other teachers and administrators are less likely to judge you harshly. There will be enough difficulties while learning this or any new teaching approach to make the addition of harshness unnecessary.

It is perhaps wisest, in fact, to label your venture "an experiment" and, until you have become somewhat skillful with the valuing strategies, to use the experimental approach recommended below. Certainly do not insist that other teachers use your methods. One may champion them and help others understand their advantages, but one will only increase resistance by moralizing about the value theory, to say nothing about inviting questions about the consistency between what you say and the theory itself.

6. Prepare for Some Conflict

Some teachers think that they can always avoid antagonism and conflict with others. It is perhaps possible, but probably only by doing nothing. Anything as "different" as many of the suggestions in this book will threaten some teachers, and they will not want to see those suggestions successfully working in their schools. Prepare to defend your right to try those suggestions, but be careful to speak only for yourself; do not insist others do as you do. And do not wilt under the first conflict, or you forego your chance of doing many things beyond the ordinary.

7. Make the Ideas Fit You

Don't try the ideas of this book without adapting them to your personality and situation. You may find that you will have to revise some of the techniques and discard others. Some things just do not work well for some people and in some situations. There should be enough in the present volume to provide most teachers with a great variety of workable methods, however, and the teacher who gets the "feel" of this approach will doubtless create more.

8. Encourage Several Colleagues to Join You

Without insisting, try to get at least one or two others to join you in your experiment. This will give you added support and will provide some exchange of experience and opinion. It might be possible, if there is enough interest in one school system, to invite someone who has successfully worked the value theory to come to consult with and advise you. It may even be possible, of course, for one or more who have worked it through in a school system to act as resource persons for others who might want to learn it, as in an in-service workshop. It is not only extremely helpful to work with other teachers, but it is a professional responsibility that is often not fully recognized.

AN EXPERIMENTAL DESIGN

This teaching theory is based on a testable hypothesis, and it is recommended that a teacher, after he has become skillful with at least some of the teaching strategies recommended by the theory, put it to the test. The experiment is not at all difficult, although it demands more rigor than merely gathering results subjectively. But the pay-off is likely to be worth the added effort. The teacher will know more positively what has been accomplished, without fearing that personal desires are coloring interpretations of the outcome, and will more easily be able to communicate findings convincingly to others.

The steps are three: (1) measure the degree of value-related behavior among students, (2) use the value-clarifying process, and (3) again measure the degree of value-related behavior. The hypothesis is that, as students have opportunities to become clearer about their values, they will behave differently: more purposefully, positively, proudly, and enthusiastically.

Of course, this is not likely to be so for students who are *already* purposeful, positive, proud, and enthusiastic; and thus it is suggested that teachers focus their experiments and their value-clarifying experiences on those who need them most. Some student types that seem especially in need of valuing experiences, what we call value-related behavioral types, are noted below. These types of behavior, of course, occasionally typify most students, but some students seem to be almost chronically so typified. This latter group, we believe, might well be provided special help in clarifying their values.

Value-Related Behavioral Types

1. The apathetic, listless, disinterested child

This child lacks interest in almost everything. He often goes through the motions expected of him, but he just doesn't care. He is passive and indifferent. He looks out windows, fools with things in his pockets, daydreams frequently, and gets excited about almost nothing. He is difficult to motivate and often a school drop-out. The words "apathetic" and "disinterested" suit him well.

2. The flighty child

This child is interested in almost everything, but just for a fleeting moment. The flighty child is characterized by quickly shifting interests. He wants to be the star in the play, soon changes to the person in charge of scenery, but before work is begun asks for the job of publicity director and, promptly, leaves that for the make-up kit. He flits from this to that. He seems to have no stable interests. His attention span is short, and he rarely follows through with something begun.

3. The very uncertain child

Some children seem unable to make up their minds, not sometimes, but almost always. Simple choices throw such a child into a quandary. He takes a long time with decisions. He seems to be in doubt about what he wants and what he likes. He often prefers that others make decisions for him and he almost always is reluctant to be involved in decision-making situations.

4. The very inconsistent child

This type of child supports one thing today and supports just the opposite tomorrow. Now he is for integration; later he will likely be for segregation. Or he talks for peace in this context and war in that context. He blows hot and cold. He seems regularly and persistently to take positions and engage in behavior that is inconsistent. Sometimes he says this but does that. Sometimes it is just that nothing is repeated.

5. The drifting child

Some people seem to drift through life. No purposes seem to guide them. They seem not even bothered by worries. Nothing seems very important. They take what comes without trying to change things or themselves. They respond, but not with gusto. They almost never get deeply involved. They don't seem to expect much and they don't seem to give much. Their manner is typically lackadaisical and it seems appropriate to refer to them as "drifters."

6. The overconforming child

This type of child will expend great efforts in trying to conform to what he perceives as the norm or the power position. Sometimes he will say or write what the teacher or other grownups want him to say or write, but sometimes he does just the opposite when the peer group is perceived as dominant. The overconforming child seems to have no positions or ideas of his own. He takes his cue from others. Left alone, he often feels lost and anxious. He needs to get direction from others.

7. The overdissenting child

Most children dissent sometimes, but some children seem to be persistent, nagging dissenters, finding fault whenever they can, picking and complaining at all but invisible stimuli. This type of child does not seem to be a rational dissenter, although he will oftentimes be very skillful at making up arguments when he needs them. The dissension seems irrational. It almost seems as if he likes to be different and thrives on contention. It's as if, not having a value pattern of his own, he gets his identity by opposing others, and especially those in authority. This kind of nagging dissenter is not a very pleasant person with whom to deal.

8. The role-playing child

Finally we note the poseur, the child who searches for his identity by pretending to be someone else. He may be the class fool. He may be the stoic, or the romantic lover, or use an ever-changing variety of roles. He often seems to be acting, and in an unreal and immature way. His roles seem contrived, not really him at all. We call this type of child a poseur or a role-player.

Now we do not assert that these are the only types of behavior patterns that identify children with very unclear sets of values. We have reason to believe, for example, that the chronic underachieving child is often in this category, although underachievement can also result from other causes. Nor do we assert that the above types *necessarily* represent value confusion. Each individual case would have to be studied to see if there were physical or emotional factors that were motivating the behavior pattern. But, lacking such other causal factors, we would say that a diagnosis of value confusion is at least preliminarily warranted. Our experience says, further, that the majority of students whom teachers would classify as apathetic, flighty, very uncertain, very inconsistent, drifters, overconformers, overdissenters, or role-players would respond very positively to a program of value-clarifying experiences.

Measuring the Degree of Value-Related Behavior

The hypothesis of the teacher's experiment can now be restated more precisely, as follows: *As students who present problems in their value-related behavior are provided value-clarifying opportunities, those behavior patterns will become less frequent and/or acute.*

What the teacher, or group of teachers, does is measure the degree of value-related behavior problems (apathy, flightiness, etc.) before applying the value theory and afterwards, and compare the two measurements to see if there has been any change. It is very useful when doing this to include measurements of a group of children who are not exposed to the value theory, as a control, to see if any changes might have occurred even with no special value experiences, perhaps just because of maturation.

There are several ways that one might go about measuring the degree of value-related behavior. The simplest way is for the teacher to identify those children in his class who have problems in their value-related behavior, as in the list above, and to make some informal notes for each student on the extent and the acuteness of that behavior for, perhaps, one week. Figure 3 shows a sample form that might be used to record this data. If this is done early in the year and again after the value experiences have been provided, a comparison of the before-and-after notes will give evidence as to whether the value experiences were effective. If there are other students, either in the experimental teacher's class or in other classes, who have been typed as value-related problem cases and who have not been provided value-clarifying experiences, data collected before and after the experiment on these students can be used to indicate whether any change can really be attributed to the value experiences, for one would expect less of a positive change in this group than in the experimental group.

FIGURE 3

Form for Measuring the Degree of Value-Related Behavior Problems

Student name _____

DIRECTIONS: Please rate the above student on the frequency and acuteness with which he exhibits each of the eight types of behaviors listed below. Use the scale provided for your ratings. An elaboration of the meaning of each type of behavior is available if you would like.

Apathetic: frequency this student exhibits this trait._____
               acuteness of this behavior for this student_____

Flightiness: frequency_____   *Frequency Scale*
               acuteness_____   0 — Never
Uncertainty: frequency_____   1 — Almost never
               acuteness_____   2 — Perhaps every few months
                                       3 — Monthly, on the average
Inconsistency: frequency_____   4 — Several times monthly
               acuteness_____   5 — Weekly
                                       6 — Several times weekly
                                       7 — Daily
                                       8 — Several times daily
                                       9 — Hourly
                                       10 — Constantly

Drifting: frequency_____   *Acuteness Scale*
               acuteness_____
                                       0 — Not at all
Conformity: frequency_____   1 — Extremely mild
               acuteness_____   2 — Mild
Dissension: frequency_____   3 — Medium
               acuteness_____   4 — Relatively acute
                                       5 — Acute
Role-playing: frequency_____   6 — Extremely acute
               acuteness_____

One need not rely upon such informal measures. Indeed, it is recommended that whenever possible more precise and systematic measures of value-related behaviors be made. One way to do this is through a simple sociometric device. One duplicates a sheet that lists all the value-related behavior types, such as in Figure 4. After students have been together long enough to know one another, each student is then given a copy of that list, together with a name list of all those in the class. Students are then asked to fill in the form with whatever names apply.

Figure 4 includes two non-value-related types—good-looking and well-co-ordinated—as control items and to disguise the nature of the instrument somewhat. One could use such an instrument before and after the experiment and compare results—see how many names were left off the sheets that were originally on them. Of course, one would expect less change in the two non-value-related types—good-looking and well-co-ordinated—than in the other eight types. If the instrument was given to other classes as well, further controls would be available with which to compare experimental results. And if value experiences were focused on only some of the value-related types in the experimental classroom, one would expect them to change more than their counterparts not so treated. (Some teachers have used clarifying responses with only a part of their students to test the effectiveness of the theory.)

FIGURE 4

Who Is Like This?

1. I do not seem to be interested in anything. I sit quietly, dully, passively, bored much of the time in school and out of school. I don't care one way or the other. I am apathetic, *disinterested.*
   a. What students are VERY MUCH like this?
   b. What students are SOMEWHAT like this?

2. I am *flighty.* I am interested in a lot of things, but only for fleeting moments, then I get interested in something entirely different. I can get started, but I don't seem to follow through. I am attracted to a million things, but I don't stick with anything long enough to do something about it. I fly rapidly from this to that.
   a. What students are VERY MUCH like this?
   b. What students are SOMEWHAT like this?

3. I am considered *good-looking*. I look like people in movies or in pictures. Some people might call me handsome or beautiful.
   a. What students are VERY MUCH like this?
   b. What students are SOMEWHAT like this?

4. It's hard for me to make up my mind. I take a long time to make decisions. I am full of doubts. I am often *very uncertain*.
   a. What students are VERY MUCH like this?
   b. What students are SOMEWHAT like this?

5. I am *very inconsistent*. Today I may be for something, but tomorrow I may be against it. It's hard to tell what side I will be on. I say this, but I do that. Or sometimes I say one thing and then, later, say just the opposite.
   a. What students are VERY MUCH like this?
   b. What students are SOMEWHAT like this?

6. I just seem to drift. I go from here to there without having much to do with it. And I don't care much. I go the way events take me. I don't struggle. Some people might call me a *drifter*.
   a. What students are VERY MUCH like this?
   b. What students are SOMEWHAT like this?

7. I am *well-co-ordinated*. I may not be strong, but I can control my motions and can play sports very well. Some people say I am graceful. I am not at all clumsy.
   a. What students are VERY MUCH like this?
   b. What students are SOMEWHAT like this?

8. I like to *conform* to what is expected of me. I may conform to what a grown-up wants. I may conform to what other kids want. I may have one person to follow and I do whatever that person wants. But I don't much want to be independent. I like to follow someone else's lead.
   a. What students are VERY MUCH like this?
   b. What students are SOMEWHAT like this?

9. I am just the opposite of a conformer—I like to dissent, to argue with anyone and everyone, to take the opposite point of view. I seem to be against most everything. I like to argue, complain, *dissent*.
   a. What students are VERY MUCH like this?
   b. What students are SOMEWHAT like this?

10. I like to make believe that I am somebody else. I often *play*

roles, pretending that I am somebody different, right in the classroom
or outside. I like to act even when there is no play.
   a. What students are VERY MUCH like this?
   b. What students are SOMEWHAT like this?

It is also often possible to have other teachers contribute to measures of the kinds of behavior noted above. One might start by making
a tentative list of those characteristics. One might, then, watch those
children for a week or so, revising the original list if necessary. Then
one could gather data from others to see if those students are chronically and generally representative of value types. Former teachers
could be asked how they saw those students on the list. (To do this,
it is better not to ask if the child is like this or that, but to ask an
open-ended question, "What were some outstanding characteristics
of this child last year?" And it is better, too, to add a few extra
names to the list, to conceal a bit what is sought.) Students who are
currently apathetic, for example, but who were not at all apathetic
the previous spring might well be excluded from the value list. Their
apathy may be too situational or temporary to qualify them for cate-
gorization as a value "case." Something other than value confusion
is probably causing that apathy.

One could also go to school records and see if related data are
available. And one could go to other teachers who currently come
into contact with the children being studied. In a departmentalized
curriculum there will be several such teachers; but even with a
self-contained classroom, often there is an art teacher, a music
teacher, a physical-education teacher, or an administrator who will
know some of the children well enough to venture a judgment. A
form, such as in Figure 3 or Figure 4, may facilitate the gathering
of these data. Be sure to add some extra names to the list, so that
respondents do not get the idea that all children deserve extreme
ratings on the scale.

Some teachers have even gathered information from parents, and
a form for that purpose could easily be devised. It is even possible
to ask students to rate themselves. To do this, a sheet might be
developed that described the eight characteristics in a paragraph or
so and each student asked how much he is like each of those de-
scriptions, or he could be asked to rank the eight paragraphs and
perhaps a few extra ones in order of their accuracy as a self-descrip-

tion. Parent information and student self-ratings would not be the only data available, but it could provide an interesting bit of supplementary information.

Of course, not all of these sources of data need be used. Generally, the more the better, but each teacher need strive for no more completeness than he needs. Use whatever is appropriate for the situation.

It is important, regardless of what measuring system is used, to eliminate from the list of value-related behavioral problem cases all those who suffer from physical or emotional disturbances, for those disturbances need treatment other than value clarifying. Raths and Burrell (1962) offer a convenient way to identify children suffering from unmet emotional needs. The school nurse, the student personnel services staff, parents, and the students' permanent record folders offer sources for finding such information. Children in need of physical or emotional treatment should be helped to get those first. Until a child feels emotionally secure, for instance, value-clarifying experiences are probably of little benefit and may even add to his disturbances.

The above procedures are for identifying children whose behavior classifies them as suffering from rather extreme value confusion. The teacher could, after identifying them, work mainly with those, for example, by focusing value responses such as those in Chapter 5 on them. However, the teacher could work with the class as a whole, using any number of the value strategies, but directing the experiment toward those whose need is greatest.

One could also get measures on all class members, from zero to maximum, on behavior associated with value confusion and test for change in every student. This is usually unnecessary because a student who shows no tendency toward being flighty, for example, has little room to grow in that dimension. He cannot be significantly less flighty at the end of the experiment. It is certain that not all students suffer from value confusion. Many homes and situations that students find themselves in have been helpful for them in the area of values. Therefore, general class measures of value growth are as inappropriate as general class measures of improvement in physical health, for example. For some children, there is not much room for improvement.

However, it is possible to measure, not changes away from apathy, flightiness, and so on, but changes in general patterns of behavior. For example, J. Raths (1962a) reports an experiment in which all children were exposed to value-clarifying experiences and changes on all children were measured in terms of: (1) positiveness of attitudes toward learning, (2) activity in raising questions and alternatives, (3) initiation and self-direction in classroom activity, (4) perseverance, and (5) active participation. In this experiment, discussed more fully in Chapter 10, several auxiliary teachers (art, music, library, etc.) completed a form for each student at the beginning and at the end of the year, and comparisons were made between pre- and post-scores. If there were classes not exposed to the value processes, comparisons could also be made with such groups. The assumption in this type of measurement is that the clarifying experiences have a positive effect on the kind of learning behavior for which most teachers strive.

Some teachers who wanted to obtain general classroom measurements, not measurements of value-related behavior problems, but in positive characteristics associated with clear values, such as degree of enthusiasm, positiveness, pride, and purposefulness have measured those dimensions. Figures 5 and 6 show forms prepared for four characteristics: interest and involvement, independence, enjoyment of learning, and perseverance. Note that those forms, one for teachers and one for parents, include three dummy or control characteristics not believed to be particularly responsive to value experiences: neatness and cleanliness, contentment and stability, and friendliness. These control items would be expected to change *less* than the value-related items in response to a value-clarifying experience.

FIGURE 5

DEAR PARENT:

A small but important research project is underway in your child's school. The project is seeking more effective ways of helping children.

It would be very helpful for this project if we could have some idea of how some parents in this community see their children. For this, we ask your help.

Would you be kind enough to complete the form below for your child _____. You need only put a check on each line at the point that shows how you see the child (outside of school) and fill the dotted line below.

Then seal this sheet in the envelope provided and have your child return it to school. It will be sent directly to the research staff for analysis with other sheets. No one in the school system sees these sheets.

Thank you for your valuable co-operation.

always active	INTERESTED AND INVOLVED IN NON-SCHOOL ACTIVITIES	always passive
always	NEAT AND CLEAN IN APPEARANCE	never
always	INDEPENDENT—WILLING TO ACT WITHOUT DETAILED DIRECTIONS	never
always	SEEMS CONTENT AND PLEASED	never
always	SEEMS TO ENJOY SCHOOL	never
always	FRIENDLY AND KINDLY WITH OTHERS	never
extremely persistent	STICKS TO ACTIVITIES	gives up extremely easily

How are you related to the child? _____

(father, mother, older brother, etc.)

FIGURE 6

Student _____

We need some confidential information about some students, for a research project underway here. Please make a check (✔) on each of the lines at a point that best describes the above student.

always	INTERESTED AND INVOLVED IN CLASSROOM WORK	never
always	NEAT AND CLEAN IN APPEARANCE	never
always	INDEPENDENT—WILLING TO ACT WITHOUT DETAILED DIRECTIONS	never
always	APPEARS STABLE AND SECURE	never
always	ENJOYS LEARNING	never
always	FRIENDLY AND KINDLY WITH OTHERS	never
extremely persistent	STICKS TO ACTIVITIES	gives up extremely easily

Rater: _____ Date: _____ Co-ordinating teacher: _____

Treating the Data

It appears as if at least half a school year should intervene between the "before" and "after" measurements, that is, the experiment should continue for at least three or four months. This, of course, is all *after* the teacher has worked through the value strategies in a preliminary trial lasting several months. It would not be reasonable to expect students to change in response to poorly used techniques.

Then a simple comparison of before and after measurement might be made with the data prepared in a table of some sort. If control students were used, these data could be placed in the table for comparison. If there were control dimensions in the measuring instruments (such as "good-looking"), measures on those should also be placed in the table. A simple statistical technique might be applied if one wanted to determine if the data vary markedly from mathematical expectation. The appropriate way to handle results will depend on the purposes for which the experiment was designed. Most basic research books, such as Selltiz *et al.* (1961) and Best (1959), offer more elaborate discussions of ways to analyze and treat such data.

SOME COMMON QUESTIONS TEACHERS ASK

As we have spoken to others about the value theory and the effectiveness of it, many teachers and teachers-to-be have reacted with an anxiety born of conflict between attraction to the ideas and some real hesitations. As we speak to such persons, these hesitations often come out in the form of questions: What do I do about subject matter? What if I lose control of the class? How can I do some of this without adding to my already overloaded-schedule? And more. We conclude this chapter by looking at fourteen such questions. The reader will note that some of these questions have been touched upon in the preceding pages and occasionally reference will be made to those sections instead of reporting that material here.

1. What do I do about subject matter?

Some teachers may want to push some subject matter aside to make a little room for something the schools have long recognized as important but were heretofore unable to effectively work on: *value development*. A case could probably be made for the position that, if something has to give way, a certain amount of subject matter is less important than is value clarity. See Raup (1950). Edgar Dale (1963) reminds us that "the critical choices of individuals are not *chiefly* mathematical, linguistic, scientific, or historial. Rather, they are choices of values, of the use of time, energy and money, choices of friends or of a mate, choices in receiving and expressing ideas." But we believe that subject matter need not give way to values; they can be worked at contemporaneously, each supporting and enriching the other.

Indeed, there is no such thing as values without understanding, without knowledge, without subject matter. One of the criteria of a value is that it be thoughtfully chosen, with awareness of the alternatives and the consequences associated with each. This obviously requires information, and thus values require subject matter.

To work the opposite road for a minute, one might inquire what the purpose of information is. If one were to think of the word etymologically, one might say that information is to inform. To inform what? At least in part, to inform our decisions, our choices of what to do with our time and space. And thus subject matter can lead to values. We believe that both subject matter and values must be the concern of schools. As was said once in another context, you can't have one without the other.

In Chapter 6 we discussed how values and subject matter can be wedded. As noted, one could use a value issue to *introduce* a subject-matter unit, and one could also use a value issue to *culminate* a subject-matter unit. For example, a unit on health could end with consideration of the issue of poverty in the local community and, especially, what each student's values are vis à vis that issue. And value clarifying can *penetrate* a unit, as when a unit on immigration includes consideration of how each student feels about pulling up roots and making major changes in what he feels is his responsibility, if any, toward recent immigrants. One could occasionally use sentences for a spelling quiz that were value laden and that might provoke productive thought. (Not something as neutral as, "Winter. The snow falls in winter. Winter.", but something to stimulate thought, as, "Winter. A mother warms a child in winter.

Winter." Also consider, "Father. A boy has no father. Father."
"Orange. A student painted his walls orange. Orange." "Terrible. I
feel terrible when I act cowardly. Terrible.") One could use value
issues in mathematics' problems, in foreign language lessons, in
vocabulary units, in book reviews, and in many, many kinds of
"purely" subject-matter units. See "Subject Matter and Value
Sheets" in Chapter 6.

But note that the clarifying response described in Chapter 5 need
not take any time at all from subject-matter lessons. Clarifying responses fit in the day without disruption to other plans.

Several of the value strategies, such as the thought sheet and the
public interview, take very little time; and some other strategies,
such as the value approach to student reports and the contrived
lessons, sufficiently enliven subject-matter units so that even the
most dedicated subject specialist is likely to find that more is gained
than lost by their use.

Another idea occurs to us. Would it be possible to identify a
series of value issues that are so common in today's world and so
important for most lives that they could be considered as "required"
subject matter? Some such issues might be:

Relationships between men and women
Relationships between work and leisure
Change vs. stability in life and society
The meaning of friendship and love
The relationship between science and humanism
Relationships between self interest and social welfare
Acting on insufficient evidence vs. inaction
Material vs. aesthetic satisfactions
Social planning vs. individual freedom

These could then be handled in several ways. Each teacher could
touch on them when convenient and appropriate. Certain teachers
could be asked to take major responsibility for certain issues.
Science teachers, for example, might deal with the issue of the scientist and the uses of his work (should scientists work to develop new
human poisons or products that appear to be substantial but which
will wear out faster?). Or perhaps special value courses could be
designed. In secondary schools, home-room teachers might take this
responsibility, or group guidance teachers, or we could set up small

group-discussion classes (see Wiles, 1963). In any case, it may be profitable to consider values as worthy as other academic or vocational subjects currently taught in schools.

It may even be that value issues could act as the co-ordinating concepts for most subject matter taught in schools. Education has had difficulty in finding ways of relating the various kinds of topics and courses to which students are exposed. The idea of a fusion of courses, a problems approach, and a core curriculum have been proposed but not widely accepted. Could it be that the way each student uses subject matter to illuminate issues important to him in his efforts to make sense out of life might be the way to integrate dissimilar subject matter?

2. What if I lose control of the class?

Many teachers see value approaches as implying so much permissiveness as to raise discipline and, perhaps, safety problems. This implication is not intended. As was discussed earlier (see the section on the value-clarifying discussion in Chapter 7 and the first two guidelines in this chapter), the requirements for value clarifying are not lack of control or permissiveness. The teacher may limit behavior in any reasonable way, it seems to us, and still maintain an atmosphere conducive to value clarifying. What is needed, however, is *intellectual* permissiveness backed by an honest respect for the experiences, thought processes, and values of students. A teacher can limit classroom behavior, and be consistent with this value theory, as long as he does not limit choices, prizings, and action in the larger, total-life sense.

3. How can I do this with my already overworked schedule?

This is a common response to a challenging educational idea. The problem is that teachers *do* have more than they can handle and it is unfair to ask them to do more. It is even more unfair to make them feel guilty as they struggle with a task that is too large and with aid that is too inadequate. Until schools can be organized more effectively and until educational understandings reach the point where aid more viable than the tired old clichés can be provided teachers, we humbly suggest that each teacher do the best he can. Do just a bit, if that is all that is reasonable. Some strategies, of course, take less time than others and are easier to get started. Teachers may be heartened to know, however, that in many cases the value approaches of this book, once mastered, make teaching *easier*, more enjoyable, and more effective. Squeezing value approaches into a crowded schedule may be the large investment that has even larger dividends.

4. I already use these approaches. What's so new about them?

For many teachers, the value theory will be nothing more than a confirmation and an extension of what they already, often only intuitively, know and do. Such teachers, and we hope there is a large number of them, may only use this book to identify some new ideas and techniques and to learn a framework for focusing their clarifying work on students who need it most. Such teachers may also find the book useful in interpreting to others what it is that they have been doing.

5. It's too complicated. I don't know where to begin.

For teachers who have not worked in ways similar to these approaches, it may seem as if the recommended strategies are forbiddingly different. For such teachers we would recommend an easy, slow start, perhaps with value sheets adapted from those in this book and occasional clarifying responses, perhaps in written form, in the margins of student papers. Also consider some other strategies easy to get going: thought sheets, weekly reaction sheets, open-ended questions, coded student papers, time diaries, and student reports. But the main recommendation here is to take it slow without dismissing the ideas entirely. Choose a few techniques and work with them. The larger ideas and commitment may come later, especially, as is very possible, if the initial trials prove rewarding to the students and the teacher. Few teachers, and we hope this is reassuring, fall flat on their faces with the value theory. About the worst that can happen is that there will be no change. (But be cautious in attributing no change to the theory or one's use of it; it may be nothing more than insufficient dosage.)

6. What will people say if I start raising unusual and controversial issues in my classroom?

Some will say how delighted they are that someone is finally helping children think through these complex and important ideas. Some may recognize the degree of conformity and passivity that surrounds most of us and will compliment you on the courage it takes to face these ideas. Some may complain that you are permitting students to think about ideas that they would prefer to try to indoctrinate. Some may wonder why you try to do such difficult things and why you do not stick with the routine subject matter, so easy to drill and test.

What you might tell persons who inquire is:

You only raise issues about which you believe students are old enough and wise enough to make at least preliminary judgments.

You insist that consideration of all ideas—those raised by you or students—be thoughtful, informed, and deliberate. You consider that an important goal of a person's education is to learn to think critically about complex and controversial ideas.

You do not permit students to indoctrinate one another nor will you do this. You are not trying to change the ideas of students but to help them learn a process of thinking and valuing, so that they are less likely in the future to follow any persuasive leader blindly, to settle important ideas only on the basis of emotional preference, or to confuse thought with irrational approaches to vital issues.

Children are exposed to most of these ideas anyhow. Your job is to insure that the exposure is intelligent and balanced.

One of the reasons such ideas are considered touchy or controversial is that many persons avoid them, do not deal with them squarely and forthrightly.

Such issues are too important to avoid.

For a related discussion, see "The Crucial Criterion of Choice" in Chapter 3. Also of interest might be the arguments of Hunt and Metcalf (1955) for helping students explore six areas of culture that remain largely closed to intelligent consideration and thus prey to all forms of myths and fears and irrational beliefs: economics (capitalism, socialism, colonialism, etc.); minority group relations (Jews, Negroes, American Indians, de facto segregation, etc.); social class (success and failure in a class society, etc.); sex, courtship, and marriage; religion and morality; and nationalism and patriotism (local allegiance vs. world allegiance, etc.)

7. Will this value theory work with my children?

This theory will probably not help children suffering from more fundamental problems, such as physical or emotional illnesses. It may even add to the difficulties of some emotionally disturbed children, although more evidence is needed on this point. But it is applicable to other children. It is especially useful for students who are difficult to motivate and are sometimes called slow learners. As reported below, the value strategies have been found effective in moving underachievers to normal work levels.

We would not recommend the dismissal of these approaches before a trial. And after a fair chance, those situations in which the value theory does not work will clearly show themselves. Like many another educational approach that has not worked, teachers will know when that is happening.

8. Can very young children work on values?

We are not certain about this. Little work has been done with primary-age children, but what evidence there is suggests that it has some benefits and few detriments. Teachers of young children have been successful in setting clarifying climates that students have carried with them to the playground and later grades, and some simple issues can, of course, be dealt with even by preschool children. We would recommend caution in the issues used for clarifying responses. If students can make reasonably intelligent choices in the issue, clarifying efforts seem warranted. At least the non-moralizing value approach probably can show children at an early age that they are expected to think for themselves, be proud of themselves, and use their intelligence to guide their own behavior. But more research is needed.

9. I don't have any clear values myself. How can I help others?

A confused teacher can help confused students in the same way that a physician with a heart condition can help patients with heart trouble: by doing what has to be done. There are some advantages, of course, for children to deal with teachers who have clear values, but a teacher who can operate in the style of this value theory can help children, and we see no reason why teachers with less than clear values cannot do this. The crux of the issue is whether or not the teacher can control his behavior enough to give his students what *they* need, and not what the teacher thinks they need or would like to give them. This is a function of understanding and self-control, functions that can be performed even by someone whose own values are still being clarified.

10. Should we not moralize about anything? How about God, patriotism, love, values themselves—may we not moralize about them?

We would say, one would be advised not to moralize about anything if one could help oneself. Moralizing does not have much of an effect, if experience is any guide, except to encourage persons not to think for themselves and to accept uncritically what the persons with power or status happen to be telling them at the time. Even with the valuing process, we do not argue that it is good for all persons and for all situations. Our purpose is to describe this method of dealing with such matters and to encourage others to see if it works for them. Moreover, when a teacher asks a value-clarifying question, he is not insisting that the student do any clarifying. He is encouraging it, but the student who would rather not do so would hopefully feel the freedom and security to reject the opportunity. And he might just as well do this; for if one is not of a mind to clarify, it seems unlikely that someone can force him to make a free choice, prize, and act in accordance with the valuing definition.

In short, if one wants citizens who freely choose, prize, and act, one defeats himself by moralizing about anything.

11. Somehow I do not feel as if I am making progress when I attempt to work with values. Is there something wrong?

With value clarifying there is a different feeling of progress than with filling children with facts and understandings. It is less tangible, less testable, less quick. It is more like the progress that comes with teaching a complex skill. The sense of progress comes from identifying behavioral change, and it is sometimes as difficult to see this as to be aware of the changes in a child's height. As a consequence, several teachers have complained that with values there is no feeling of accomplishment. Nothing seems to change. For this reason we would recommend the collecting of behavior profiles from time to time, much like a mother marks the height of her children on the back of a door. Occasional checking of such profiles, perhaps using forms as in the preceding section, will provide not only evidence for others but evidence for one's own sense of accomplishment.

12. Can the teacher express his own values in the classroom or must he remain forever neutral?

Our position is that, ideally, the teacher should be able to be quite candid about his points of view and values. By so being, and by being accepting and respectful of students, students are reassured that square talk is permissible. Also, students have a real position to look at, to cross-examine, and to measure against their own ideas. The teacher, of course, would make it very clear that an expression of his position is not an indication of what would be desirable for others. We all have different experiences and outlooks, and we should all select values that are individually suitable.

Sometimes, however, we find it desirable to compromise with the ideal. Sometimes, for example, children are too accustomed to following what an adult says, even when the adult cautions them not to do so. And sometimes a teacher may want to keep his values hidden for more personal reasons; neither he nor the students will be well served to hear them. And sometimes a teacher will purposely play a devil's advocate role to bring a special point of view into a classroom in a dramatic fashion. Consequently, although we generally find it advisable for teachers to be as honest and open as they hope students will be, for immature students, whatever their ages, and for other special reasons, we sometimes recommend that a teacher be wary about revealing his position. Of course, even with immature students, after they understand the difference between revealing one's own position and proselytizing, candor can replace concealment.

Incidentally, it is useful for those same reasons for teachers to reveal their lack of clear values. This shows students how difficult it is sometimes to be certain about some issues and underlines the importance of candor and honesty on all sides.

See the second of the "Do's and Don'ts" in Chapter 6 for further discussion of this point.

13. Is it "bad" not to have values?

It depends upon what one means by "bad." For a person in a period of great change, as in adolescence or in the midst of a major life readjustment, few values may exist. For those in a more stable portion of life, one might expect some patterns of life to have been worked out based on free choice, understanding, and pride. If this has not happened, one would suspect that such a person is operating at a lower level of life than need be.

But, especially for children, the crucial question is not how many values one has or what those values are, but what *process* a person uses when faced with value-related decisions. Does he acquiesce readily? Does he act impulsively? Does he choose things of which he is not proud? Does he do one thing and say another?

We would be inclined to say that, from *our* set of values, it is "bad" not to use the valuing process. More objectively, we would say that a person who does not use that process is likely to live a less rich life than one who does. That is, he is likely to live a life which does not make use of the full human potential for intelligent existence.

14. Upon what topics should clarifying efforts be focused? How do I know what issues to introduce for value purposes?

The reader might review the section, "Topics Ripe for Value-Clarifying Responses" in Chapter 5. There we noted some common indicators of values: attitudes, aspirations, purposes, interests, and activities. Others are beliefs, convictions, opinions, feelings, and worries. When a student expresses one of these and receives a clarifying response, he is often helped to examine his life in helpful ways. Thus we would say that such value indicators are worth clarifying efforts. Since often a particular attitude, activity, purpose, etc. will be common to many students, such indicators often lead to issues of interest to many persons.

But then some issues are not readily indicated by students; or sometimes, as with a new class, there has not been time enough to elicit value indicators. In any case, we have identified some criteria for judging what is worth clarifying.

A. Things most worth clarifying are of *concern to the individual*. There needs to be sufficient involvement to permit the lifting of an issue to the level where it may be prized and cherished. In short, there must be personal meaning for the students.
Examples: Problems of life and death, love, money, family.

B. Things worth clarifying involve a *variety of alternatives*. In other words, there has to be about the issues no universal agreement, otherwise there would be little room for choice. On the other hand, there may *seem* to be agreement when in reality there are unconsidered or suppressed alternatives.
Examples: In the first group, issues about urban renewal, about teen-age marriages. In the second group, comments on the equality of all men, the right of the government to tax income.

C. Things most worth clarifying are *significant for many lives*, for substantial groups of people, as opposed to issues which touch upon just a very few lives.
Example: The issue in a particular trial is less important than the principle underlying the trial.

D. Things most worth clarifying affect *large areas of life*.
Example: Choosing friends is more pervasive than choosing a pair of shoes.

E. To be worth clarifying something must be *open to control*, there must be something that can be done about the issue.
Examples: War, not earthquakes. For young children, what should be done to make school better, not whether or not one should go to school.

F. Things most worth clarifying are *related or joined to other issues*. It is most useful to work on issues that help illuminate other issues.

Examples: The role of women in society touches upon marriage, working mothers, dating behavior, etc.

G. Things most worth clarifying *recur* as opposed to being transient.

Example: Sensational topical issues are less useful than persistent issues such as independence and dependence, courage, appropriate male and female role behavior, and graft.

Another point is germane here. Oftentimes a "small" values issue will grow from the interests or attitudes of students but can be extended to more profitable issues by the alert teacher. So, for example, a consideration of the wisdom of purchasing automobile seat belts can lead to considerations of how much of life's risks are worth controlling, what is the role of one person (such as an automobile manufacturer) regarding the safety of another (such as the automobile purchaser), and the uses to which we put our money.

Of course, even consideration of "small" issues is useful to the extent that it sharpens the skills of the valuing process and makes those skills more available for student use when other issues arise. Whether or not to teach for value clarification must be decided by each teacher who considers using this theory in his classroom. In making this decision, the problems that will be encountered must be considered and all aspects of possible difficulties carefully thought about.

Guidelines have been presented in this chapter, but not *all* problems can be anticipated. An attempt has been made to answer important questions that are frequently raised about this theory. In addition, some problems often encountered when beginning the use of this theory in the classroom are discussed. Methods of coping with or preventing early difficulties are also considered. Although there are many other effective teaching approaches, when the value theory is effectively used, the results can be distinctly rewarding as clearer values and the often accompanying scholastic improvement of students are measured and observed.

Chapter 9

Emotional Needs, Thinking, and Valuing

In the beginning of this book we commented upon the tendency among teachers to attribute every problem a child has to some imbalance in his emotional make-up or in his I.Q. score. As we have already emphasized, not every behavior problem is to be viewed as resulting from a confusion of values. We must try to make clear distinctions between the various behavioral symptoms children reveal; and, as a first step, we look more closely at differences between children with unmet emotional needs and children with unclear values.

EMOTIONAL NEEDS[1] AND VALUES

There is a great deal of confusion over the interpretation of what is meant by needs and what is meant by values and, unfortunately, no research evidence clearly establishes this distinction. What follows are distinctions made by the writers in terms of their definition

---

[1] The emotional needs theory is fully elaborated in Raths and Burrell (1962).

of "value" and in terms of their experience with children and with those who teach children. There is research bearing upon this, but it has not been decisive in fully justifying what will be said. What follows, therefore, is a statement of position. Others will see these matters differently and it may be a long time before we can assert with confidence that what follows establishes the ways in which needs and values have to be distinguished.

Age at Which They Appear

Emotional needs reveal themselves in the first years of life. Such needs as those for affection, security, achievement, and freedom from fear and guilt come very early. Values tend to come much later. The French writer Beauvoir suggests that when a child becomes conscious that he is now different from what he was, when he does not like what he used to like, and so on, he is ready for the clarifying of values. In other words, when a *self* is recognized, values can develop.

Shame and Pride

There is something about emotional needs which are a source of shame. If we are in great need of praise or attention, we tend to apologize for it. If we are extremely fearful or feel deeply guilty, we are somewhat ashamed of the situation and do things to hide the facts. On the other hand, when we have values, we are genuinely proud of them; we cherish and esteem them and hold them dear.

Pervasiveness and Selectivity

Behavior which is associated with our emotional needs tends to be pervasive. When we need friendship, we search for it in all situations, in school, on the playground, at home, and in our work. It pervades our life. Values, on the other hand, are selective. We choose what we prefer and what we like. We budget our time and money to accomplish what we prize. We can control value types of behavior under certain circumstances. This is not true with the behavior associated with needs that are blocked, for such behavior surges forth with a will of its own.

Visceral and Cerebral

This may be only another way of saying what has just been said. Our needs grow out of the emotional side of our life. Although values also have some of this component, they lean more heavily toward the intellectual side; there is deliberation, assessment, a looking at alternatives, and a choosing. The visceral reaction associated with needs is more explosive in character, more impulsive. Value activity is more reflective.

Push and Pull

Values seem somehow to be out in front of us. They represent the carrot. They tend to lead us or to pull us. We are attracted and we tend to organize our activities in such a way as to go toward values. With respect to needs, they seem instead to push us into forms of behavior that are not necessarily rewarding. If we are aggressive, for example, we are pushed into doing things which often make the condition worse. We are not choosing and controlling. We are being pushed into things that we probably will be sorry that we did.

Self-Help and Outside Help

If we are in great need of praise and recognition, we must get it from others. We cannot pat ourselves on the back and get a feeling of recognition. If we deeply need love and affection, we cannot love ourselves and be happier. Emotional requirements must come from outside. In terms of values, however, we must do the valuing by ourselves. Each must do it for himself. If someone else tells us what to value and how to value it, it is not our value until we ourselves go through the processes of prizing, choosing, etc. A teacher can help a child by setting up chances for him to examine his values, but each person must develop his own values or be without them. The meeting of needs is done *to* you, but valuing is done by you.

Needs Behavior and Value Behavior

When we speak of value-related behavior we think of apathy, flightiness, overconforming, overdissenting, great uncertainty when faced with decisions, wide swings in mood, role-playing and pretending, and a tendency to achieve much lower than one is capable of. When we speak of behavior patterns that are associated with the blocking of emotional needs, we usually think of: (1) a consistent tendency to be unusually *aggressive;* (2) a consistent tendency to be unusually *withdrawn* or isolated; (3) a consistent tendency to have *symptoms of psychosomatic illness;* (4) a consistent tendency to display *submissiveness,* obsequiousness, or subservience; and (5) tendencies toward behavior which *regresses toward earlier ages.* Thus, the behavior patterns associated with unmet needs are usually distinguishable from those associated with unclear values.

Working with a Needs Child and Working with a Values Child

When working with needs cases, we put a great emphasis upon what the teacher does to lead a child toward emotional security. See Raths & Burrell (1962). In working with a values child, we tend to assume that the emotional security is there, that his needs for the most part have already been met. Or we try to meet a child's needs first and then move on to values, although with many children we would meet needs and clarify values together. One takes precedent over the other but does not exclude the other. It is important to be clear, also, that as we go ahead with the idea of asking questions to which only the individual child has the answer, i.e., value questions, we become somewhat threatening. Such questions call for facing up to one's self. A child carrying a heavy burden of unmet emotional needs can rarely handle very many such trenchant questions.

THINKING AND VALUES

Let us now attempt to make a distinction between the value theory and another theory we have considered, a thinking theory. We are confronted here with the fact that the major objectives of education overlap considerably. As we stated earlier, we are not always able to distinguish between the emotional needs and the values of children. With thinking theory as well, although we make distinctions, a lot of confusion remains. This is particularly so in the case of values and thinking because our definition of valuing included such a large component of intellectuality.

Thinking may be understood as a method of inquiry which is directed toward understanding. In the valuing process there is an added factor, that of making a decision. Thinking may help us to see the alternatives which are relevant, and valuing helps us in the process of choosing from among these alternatives. Thinking may help us to anticipate a variety of consequences associated with the alternatives, but valuing leads us to make a choice from among the weighted consequences.

Thinking appears much earlier in life than valuing. Certain relationships between means and ends are discerned before realization of a self is attained. Very early in life children fathom the relationship between the stable position of an object at some height and the idea of its falling to the floor, for example. They also see very soon that the relationship of the movement of a tricycle's handle bars to the direction that the tricycle takes is constant and predictable. Hundreds of examples may be gathered which indicate the ability of little children to think. The idea of self and the recognition of changes in one's self come much later. For many children this does not emerge clearly until age seven or thereabouts.

There is a greater quality of uncertainty about the thinking process when compared with valuing. In the thinking process, to comprehend meanings and possible relationships, it is often necessary to recognize assumptions. Many times one has to make a judgment as to whether an assumption is probably true or probably false, and very often the data are inadequate to make the judgment. One is aware of how important the assumption is and one is often very uncertain about its reasonableness. Yet after a decision about a course of action has been made, one becomes more certain however uncertain one was in previous moments. The decision-making factor itself seems to give an air of greater certainty to the process. Feelings of confusion seem to diminish with a resolution that ends in a choice.

In many situations a problem can be solved through a variety of ways. If one were to stop for a moment and ask, "No matter how this problem is finally solved, what values do I wish to protect?", it would suggest that one wanted to bring thinking to the defense of values. We recognize a difference between the two operations. Often, thinking is in the service of values. Thinking may take on the dimensions of a machine while valuing takes on the dimensions of the power behind the machine.

In terms of behavior there are some striking differences between those associated with poor thinking, and those associated with lack of valuing. With an absence of thinking or with poor thinking we often recognize:

1. *Impulsiveness* in actions, jumping the gun, going off half-cocked.

2. *Being stuck,* overdependence upon adults, seemingly blocked even at the start of a situation which requires thinking.

3. *Missing the meaning,* not understanding what has gone on, not getting the point of a story, losing sight of the connection between means and ends.

4. *Inflexibility of thought,* rigid adherence to previous ways of doing things, anxiety in the face of alternatives, a wish for simplicity.

5. *Dogmatic statements,* loudness, name calling, assertiveness.

6. *Fearfulness about thinking,* lack of faith in one's own ideas, timidity about sharing thoughts.

7. *Wishful thinking* in which the wish is father to the thought, where the conclusion comes first and one later seeks evidence to prove one's point. There is often the associated tendency of not wanting to think, to have a wish and let it go at that.

Compare such behavioral symptoms with those typically associated with the lack of values or the absence of valuing: apathy, indifference, listlessness; flightiness, a wish for everything for just a little while; great uncertainty when a choice has to be made; wide swings in attitudes, feelings, purposes, and aspirations, general inconsistency; drift, lack of purpose; great overconformity; a tendency to nag, carp, dissent; and the aping and mimicking of others, of role-playing, of pretending that one is somebody else.

There are also differences associated with the methods that we recommend in working with children suffering from thinking "problems." Where we are trying to emphasize thinking, we usually involve the children in processes like these: (1) observing and reporting what is observed; (2) comparing and contrasting; (3) summarizing; (4) interpreting; (5) classifying and sorting; (6) imagining; (7) planning and executing; (8) outlining; (9) criticizing; (10) analyzing; (11) looking for assumptions; (12) discovering; and (13) problem-solving. These processes, the reader will note, are different from those discussed as relevant for children with value confusion.[2]

NEEDS, THINKING, AND VALUES

We have, therefore, these three relatively distinct theories, each with its own procedures and each with its own set of symptoms to signal that help is needed. In deciding which procedures to use, one judges whether a certain child's behavior seems to signal a problem with thinking, an unmet emotional need, or a confusion in values. Values and thinking problems also usually have nuances of unmet emotional needs, but there is typically a dominant type of behavior and that reflects the kind of treatment that is most needed. Each theory's techniques, and the techniques associated with needs and thinking have only been very briefly mentioned in this book, are geared to a specific behavior change the teacher may desire.

It may be appropriate to close with some comments about the ways in which needs and thinking and values are alike. We should notice, first of all, that the behavior associated with frustrated needs, with poor thinking, and with the lack of value development is of a negative sort. In other words, the consequences of unsatisfactory development in these areas are usually considered undesirable. Few teachers are happy to have a child who is apathetic, or impulsive, or aggressive—three typical "types" in those theories.

Still another way in which these three large areas are alike is that the consequences of unsatisfactory development tend to defeat the goals which gave rise to those consequences. For example, if a child needs love and affection and—in not getting it—becomes aggressive, he is even less likely to get love and affection. The behavior is self-

---

[2] See Louis E. Raths (1966).

defeating. A child who is impulsive impedes, by that very act, his own opportunities to arrive at thoughtful solutions to problems. The child who is apathetic or listless is by this very behavior less likely to become involved in choices and less likely to develop values.

These three general areas are alike in still another very important way. When children show these negative behaviors, adults tend to pay exclusive attention to the behavior and not to the probable underlying causes. If a child is aggressive because he needs love, we are *less* apt to give him love; we are concerned with stopping his aggression, and our first efforts are usually directed to some form of unloving coercion. If a child is listless and apathetic, we are apt to tell him that he should be different; we are less inclined to take time to help him clarify the ideas that led him to be apathetic. When a child is dogmatic, we are more inclined to tell him about his behavior than to accept the hypothesis that as he learns to think for himself he will modify this behavior.

The common element that is important for teachers should be clear by now. Problems in all three areas make teaching and learning more difficult. The three approaches, then, provide ways to help remove blocks to learning in the classroom.

There may be another factor which is common to all three areas. It may be that as adults we really don't want our children to feel secure; we don't want our children to have values; we don't want our children to be good thinkers. Perhaps such children constitute a threat to us. Many of us are not very secure. Many of us do not have clear values. Some of us are not very good at thinking. We do, however, have power. We are able to coerce and to dominate children. With greater feelings of security, with values of their own, with skill and practice and confidence in their thinking processes, children might threaten some of the power that we have. Is it possible that we are fearful of possible consequences if children were to develop in these ways?[3]

---

[3] See Appendix E, p. 249 for guidance in the use of the emotional needs theory.

Chapter 10

Research Completed
and Needed

Educational research has been the subject of much criticism, a good deal of it decrying the failure of most of the research to lead anywhere, to permit useful generalizations. See Conant (1961), Carroll (1961), Joncich (1962), and Elliott and Foshay (1963). Tyler (1962) asks especially for more research that serves to guide the development of effective educational practices and materials. It may be that research on this value theory can meet this condition, for the theory talks of what teachers might do to get certain specified results.

Only very preliminary research has been done thus far on this theory. And, unfortunately, research done on other approaches to values are of little use to this approach. Most other value research has used pencil-and-paper tests to get at the values a person holds. See, for example, the well-known study of changes in college students' values by Jacobs (1957) and the manual to the frequently used test by Allport, Vernon, and Lindzey, *Study of Values* (1960). What these studies obtain, of course, is pencil-and-paper values: what persons *say* that they value. For our purposes, this falls short on at least two grounds. First, we want to know how students *behave,* not only what they say. Putting choices into action is a major criterion for a value as we define it. Second, and more fundamentally, we are primarily concerned with the *process* that a person uses to get at a value, not with what value he chooses at any one time and place—we are concerned with the process of valuing and not particularly with the product. In this way, we are squarely with the instrumentalists, those who see values not as eternal truths, institutionalized and stable, but as instruments that help one relate to the surrounding world of people, things, and ideas. For us, it is less important to know that a person values something than it is to know *how* he arrived at that "value." Did he arrive there thoughtfully, proudly, actively, or is he thoughtlessly mimicking a current style, reacting to a momentary impulse, or whatever? See Dewey (1939).

Twelve research projects, however, have been completed relative to this value theory, and they are summarized below.[1] They give some preliminary evidence of the worth of the theory. They also illustrate some of the research difficulties and some of the theory's implications for education.

Klevan's College Study

Klevan (1957) studied the effects of the value clarification techniques on a group of college students, mostly sophomores, taking a course in education at New York University. He was particularly concerned with (1) changes in consistency of attitudes, (2) expressions of purposefulness, and (3) expressions of friendliness among class members. Since this was an exploratory study and lacked the controls required of careful experimentation, the findings are suggestive only.

The instructor of the course focused on a series of issues in education, selected by himself and the students, and stimulated thinking on those issues. Careful effort was made to insure that *critical thinking* took place. There was a systematic attempt to help students see the importance of such things as defining terms clearly, identify-

---

[1] Two other studies that deal with this approach to values are not summarized here. They are by Olmo (1964), whose findings were ambiguous, and by Gagnon (1965), whose findings were not available at the time of writing.

ing assumptions in thinking, searching for alternatives, and keeping an open mind. In general, the value-clarification method of discussion was utilized. Paramount was the desire to keep the atmosphere permissive and accepting while stimulating individual thought. One clever way the instructor stimulated thought was by having each student write opinions, by filing those writings, and by later returning them to the student if conflicts and inconsistencies arose among a student's papers.

There were two comparison groups, taught by a different instructor and *not* matched in any substantial way with the experimental group. These were given the same before-and-after measures as was the experimental group.

Klevan found that during the experimental period (one term) students in the experimental class did develop significantly more consistent attitudes and did express more personal purposes than the students in the comparison classes. He found, however, that growth in friendliness was not different among the groups.

Because of the many uncontrolled factors, it is not possible to attribute any of these results to the experimental method alone. Nevertheless, Klevan's personal observations were that many students in the experimental group became much clearer about what they believed and showed substantial increases in educational commitment and personal spirit.

Simon's Study with High-School Teachers

Simon (1958) reported a study in which ten high-school teachers were taught to use the value-clarifying processes. Each teacher was asked to choose a student who seemed to have a pattern of "non-value-based" behavior, specifically, who was apathetic, flighty, indecisive, inconsistent, overconforming, a nagging dissenter, or posing in various roles. Through an in-service program, teachers were to learn the techniques and apply them to the selected child.

The report indicated that most teachers did not seem to use the techniques effectively and consistently and that most children did not change their behavior. For a number of reasons, some teachers did not master the theory; and among those that did, some did not implement it.

One of the most interesting aspects of the report deals with the materials developed to help the teachers work with values. Another was the revelation of the difficulties high-school teachers had in learning and using the theory. Simon suggests that it might be easier for elementary teachers or for teachers accustomed to more personal contacts with students. The subject-matter orientation of secondary teachers seemed to be a substantial block to the development of interest in values.

Brown's Study with Elementary Teachers

Georgia Brown did a study (not yet reported) that paralleled Simon's study with high-school teachers. Using the same plan, she asked a group of sixteen elementary teachers (K-6) who were taking a college education course to respond with value-clarifying questions to a child who seemed to have unclear values (who was very apathetic, dissenting, etc.) and to keep records of what happened. Each teacher also identified a second child in each class that was similarly a value "case" to act as a control. Control students received no special attention.

The experiment continued for fifteen weeks and included children who were overconformers, dissenters, apathetic, underachievers, indecisive, flighty, and poseurs.

Unlike Simon's high-school teachers, all but one of these elementary-school teachers did master techniques of responding to students so as to clarify values. Excluding the teacher who did not learn the techniques, *all* experimental children were reported to have improved markedly while *none* of the control children so changed. Teacher after teacher wrote that whereas a student was not purposefully and constructively involved in schoolwork before the experiment, he was very much more so involved afterwards.

An incidental finding of this study was that teachers and children enjoyed the process, and teachers themselves seemed to become much clearer about their personal values and, in many cases, more dedicated teachers. Brown says that teachers with whom she had been in contact after the experiment continued to use the techniques.

Although this study was informal and used imprecise and subjective measures, the reports of the teachers involved in this experiment indicate that the value theory seemed to work well for them.

Three Elementary-School Experiments

A most significant series of studies with the value theory was carried out in one suburban elementary school. Three investigators who taught in the school, one each in grades three, four, and five, carried out identical designs to test the value theory and two other teaching theories developed by Louis E. Raths, theories dealing with emotional needs and thinking. These studies are reported by Jonas (1960), Machnits (1960), and Martin (1960). Only the portion of the studies dealing with values is discussed here.

Each investigator identified children in his class who fell into the categories that we suggest are likely to be related to a lack of value clarity. In the third-grade class there was a child who was a nagging dissenter and very flighty. In the fourth-grade class there was a very flighty child and one who regularly took on "artificial" roles to play. In the fifth-grade class there was a child who was extremely over-conforming and a child who was very apathetic.

Value-related behavioral types were similarly identified in different third-, fourth-, and fifth-grade classes that were not taught by the investigators and that were not part of the experiment. These children were used as a comparison group. They were not matched to the experimental children in any way other than representing the same types of behavior patterns, and received no treatment other than that usually provided in the classroom.

These children, both in the experimental and comparison classes, were rated as showing the behavior patterns for which they were chosen *very frequently* and *very acutely,* and were judged to be children who would be unlikely to change those patterns in the normal course of school instruction. These ratings were made not by the classroom teachers involved in these experiments but by teachers of music, art, library, and physical education and by previous teachers of those children, none of whom were told the nature of the experiment.

After initial measures were made of these children's behavior using the ratings noted above, the investigators began to try to clarify the values of the six in the experimental classes. They worked from October to February, carefully recording and reporting what they did for each child. An attempt was made to have one brief encounter that would be of a value-clarifying nature with each child each day. Because these were teachers of self-contained classes who had substantial flexibility in their programs, they managed to do this on most days.

The process they used was that of encouraging the child to look at himself and his behavior, examine alternatives in his life, consider what he prized and was important to him, and make choices for himself. This was done persistently, but gently. The details of the encounters are instructive, and three sample encounters are reported in their entirety from the work of Jonas (1960), pp. 162, 164, 167:

> TEACHER: As I see it, you have done a lot of thinking about hamsters and you really like them.
> STUDENT: Yes, I love Alvin.
> TEACHER: Do you think more people should own hamsters?
> STUDENT: Yes. They're wonderful pets.
>
> TEACHER: Would you like to be in a play?
> STUDENT: Yes, I guess so.
> TEACHER: What can we do to get you into a play?
> STUDENT: I don't know.
>
> STUDENT: (Says that she planned to go swimming at the "Y" after school.)
> TEACHER: Is that something you like to do?
> STUDENT: Yes.
> TEACHER: Would you recommend swimming as a sport?
> STUDENT: I sure would.
> TEACHER: Do you swim often?
> STUDENT: I hope to once a week.

If the above dialogues sound innocuous, or even silly, the effect of the series of them is that much more dramatic. The findings of the three studies were similar: the behavior patterns of the children in the experimental groups were reported by the art, music, and other teachers—and often spontaneously by parents as well—to have improved significantly. No such change was reported for the comparison group.

One exception was the third-grade child who was a chronic dissenter. He improved somewhat, but not enough to be included as a "success" case. The investigator (Martin) suggests that his limited success with the dissenting boy may have resulted from the difficulty he had in developing enough rapport with him to communicate effectively. Martin wonders if the value theory can work as easily with students who typically react to teachers in a rejecting fashion.

James Raths on Underachievers

James Raths (1960) reported on a careful study of the effect of the value-clarification techniques on high-school underachievers, defined as students with high measured scholastic potential but low scholastic performance. In this study, thirteen matched pairs of underachievers were formed on the basis of grade level in school, sex, I.Q., socio-economic class, and rank in class. From these matched pairs, six were randomly chosen to be in the experiment. From each of the six pairs, one was randomly chosen to be in the experiment and one was left as a control.

J. Raths met with each of the six students in the experimental group during study period or before or after school once a week for fifteen weeks in private conversations of some twenty minutes or so. Each student was asked to meet with the investigator to help him "understand the thinking and values of teenagers nowadays." All agreed to do so, apparently without understanding that the study was focused on something quite different. In fact, what J. Raths attempted to do was to clarify the values of the students to test the hypothesis that this would help them find more purpose in their lives and thus make their schoolwork more effective.

The research report includes details of Raths' procedures. In effect what he did was to ask questions, and occasionally get student reaction to written paragraphs of one sort or another, that elicited statements of student beliefs, attitudes, interests, problems, and aspirations. In some instances he was able to have students give him written work that they had done and that contained such personal statements. Then he responded to those statements with the clarifying techniques. For example, he would ask students how they had chosen something, if they were *glad* they had chosen it, if they had considered alternatives, etc. Sometimes he would merely repeat back what the student had said. Throughout, the mood seemed to be permissive and accepting. The investigator's goal was to prod six students to think about their beliefs, attitudes, etc. without threatening them or promoting any values of his own. From the sample conversations reported in the study reports, it would seem that this was accomplished. The fact that the students continued to attend the conferences willingly attests to the satisfactions that students seemed to find in the process.

J. Raths found that during the one semester of the experiment five of the six experimental students did better than their matched controls, as measured by improvement in grades and rank in the class. This was reported as being significant at the .109 level, using the nonparametric sign test. As with Martin, Raths also found it difficult to develop rapport with one student; this was the one student who failed to do better than his control.

In discussing the findings, Raths noted that a few chance occurrences had disrupted the experiment and said that an experiment with a larger sample would provide a better test of his hypothesis. A more significant weakness is probably the failure to give the control group special attention, thus permitting to stand the contention that it might have been the *amount* of attention, not the *kind* of attention, that made the difference.

Lang on Underachievers, Dissenters, and Apathetic Students

Lang (1962) designed a study that faced the issue that the study above left unresolved. His study took place at the college level and included along with underachievers some apathetic students and some nagging dissenters of the campus. Like J. Raths, he had matched pairs, with one of each pair receiving the value-clarification approach in private conferences. But Lang took the precaution of having each of the control students receive an equivalent amount of attention. In this case, each had meetings with college faculty members who used, compared to the value-clarification approach that Lang used, relatively directive counseling techniques.

Lang had sixteen meetings of approximately fifteen minutes with each student in the experimental group. His sample included seven underachievers with seven controls matched for age, sex, residency (on or off campus), marital status, I.Q., and cumulative grade average. A few underachievers who were found to have unusual physical or emotional problems were excluded from the samples on the grounds that their problems were more deep-seated than values problems and that, therefore, they would not be expected to respond to value-clarification techniques. Also in the experimental sample were five apathetic students and one dissenting student, with matched controls. None of the students or faculty members who worked with the control students knew of the hypotheses under study.

Before-and-after measures were taken on experimental and control students. For the underachievers, grade-point averages were collected. For the apathetic and dissenting students, ratings on the severity of the identified behavior were collected from each of the four or five instructors who had the students during the semester of the experiment.

Lang's findings were mixed; the clarification techniques worked well with the underachievers but not so well with the apathetic or dissenting students. For the underachievers, six out of seven experimental students improved more than did their controls. For the apathetic and dissenting students, only four of six experimental students did better than their controls. (Three of six would be expected on the basis of chance alone.)

Lang did a follow-up study after two years. He found that the advantage shown by the experimental underachievers in grade-point average had evaporated. He concluded that more than sixteen exposures to the value strategies are necessary for long-term effect.

A Study at a Campus Elementary School

James Raths (1962) reported on a study at the Campus Elementary School of the University of Wisconsin (Milwaukee). At that school, the four teachers of grades five through eight were concerned with the frivolous and superficial way with which students approached their learning and because school activities seemed to rank low in the hierarchy of student interests. The assumption was made that because the students were confused about their own purposes, beliefs, attitudes, goals and interests, they failed to identify with the purposes of the school. Accordingly, a program was initiated to help students become clearer about their own purposes. The hypothesis was that they would, in turn, become more active and purposeful learners.

All one hundred students in the four grades were placed in the study. First, a beginning evaluation of each student was made by the teachers of art, music, library, and physical education. Each of those teachers evaluated each student on a seven-point scale (i.e., *very often* to *almost never*) along the following dimensions:

Raising of questions and alternatives
Initiation and self-direction of classroom activity
Perseverance
Active participation
Attitudes toward learning

Then the four classroom teachers initiated a program that contained three essential elements: (1) an atmosphere in which students could express their real feelings without fear of harsh judgments or ridicule by others, (2) efforts to elicit attitudinal statements from students, and (3) the raising of questions with students that would help them think about their attitudes. To elicit student attitudes, teachers used free writings, writings in response to provocative issues, and role-playing in which students had to make choices about issues, such as breaking in on a lunchroom line.

At the end of the year, a final rating on the same five dimensions was made of each student by the art, music, physical education, and library teachers, who had no access to the original ratings and who did not know the nature of the study in progress.

Raths reports that 88 of the 100 students made gains on all five rating dimensions. Of the twelve that did not, *all* were found to suffer from patterns of unmet emotional needs. (It has earlier been suggested that children with unmet emotional needs may not be able to develop values in the same way that they are unable to learn other things very well.)

Weintraub's Study

Herbert Weintraub carried out a small and unpublished, but interesting, study. Reminded that many students do not behave in ways of which they are proud and that being proud of one's behavior, happy with what one does, is one of the criteria for a value, Weintraub wondered what would happen if he encouraged children to consider just that one aspect of life: being proud of what one does.

The experimenter randomly selected a fifth-grade class and had the teacher of that class instruct the students to write on a sheet of paper "those things that they said or did in the last twenty-four hours of which they were proud or happy." Students were asked to do this anonymously, with no identifying material on the papers, and were told that the papers would not be read by the teacher (unless they were marked with a large "R"). The directions were generally accepted by the students and they wrote rather freely.

Students were also asked to write, on the back of the sheet, those things that they did or said in the preceding twenty-four hours of which they were not proud. (This part of the exercise was later questioned as being potentially guilt-arousing and unnecessary for the purposes of the experiment and the value theory.)

This procedure, writing what one was proud of or not proud of, was repeated the first ten minutes of every day, for six weeks.

There was also a control group of five similar classes. For all six classes, teachers, who were unaware of the nature of the experiment, rated each student on eight scales that were presumed to be related to value clarity (from "always" to "never"):

1. Interested and involved in classroom work.
2. Independent—willing to act without detailed directions.
3. Assumes responsibility for his own actions.
4. Listens and shows respect for the ideas and experiences of others.
5. Sticks to activities, shows persistence.
6. Gets enjoyment from his own activities.
7. Interested and involved in non-school activities.
8. Works well by himself.

Teachers also rated each student on two scales that were embedded in the rating sheet but that were presumed unrelated (at least directly) to value clarity:

1. Participates and shows enthusiasm for music-related activities.
2. Participates and shows enthusiasm for art-related activities.

These latter two dimensions were called "placebo" scales.

All teachers completed a rating sheet on each student before the six-week experimental variable was used and after it. Comparison was made of the growth of the experimental students and the control students.

Weintraub found that on all eight value-related scales the experimental group was superior to the control group (all at the .01 level except for the scale number eight, which was at the .05 level). There was no difference between the groups on the first non-value or placebo scale, suggesting that the growth in the experimental group was not caused by any bias in the completion of the rating sheets, but the second placebo scale (art) did show a significant difference favoring the experimental group, raising the above interpretation into question. The fact that the experimental group had an art teacher that was not shared by the other groups might account for this finding, however.

In an analysis of the writings themselves, Weintraub found that students tended to write less toward the end of the experiment, supporting the observation that boredom set in and that once or twice a week (for a greater number of weeks) might have been better than every day for this kind of an exercise. Even more preferable, Weintraub feels, is a variety of questions, with a different one posed each day. (See the section on weekly reaction sheets in Chapter 7, pp. 134-36.)

He also found that what students were *not* proud of could often be classified as things that they considered their duty.

In a parallel study, however, Weintraub found no growth difference between another fifth-grade class and the five control classes. The two studies were identical, except that in this latter study students were given a sheet headed on one side, "My Last Twenty-four Hours. What I did that made me feel proud, happy," and on the other side, "My Last Twenty-four Hours. What I did that made me feel sorry, ashamed, sad." Also, each sheet had printed on it, spaced along the side, the phrases: "In school," "At home," "At play," and "Other places and times." These phrases were to stimulate thinking, which they did; the former study merely had students write "proud" on one side of a sheet and "not proud" on the other and obtained somewhat fewer responses. No explanation for the differences in the findings was offered.

Shields' College Class

Harry A. Shields carried out a small unpublished study in a philosophy of education course he was teaching in a Catholic college. He undertook to give his group of twenty-eight students a variety of value-clarification experiences over a ten-week period. His class met twice a week during that period, giving him twenty ninety-minute sessions. He used class discussion to ask clarifying questions, he

assigned value sheets such as those in Chapter 6, and he wrote clarifying responses in the margins of student reports that were returned
to students. As a control, he used another class he taught, one that
dealt with methods of teaching. He did not emphasize value clarification in this group.

To measure his results, Shields used two approaches. First, he had
each student in the experimental and control classes complete in
two successive weeks, before the ten-week experiment was begun, a
rating of themselves along eight variables, five presumed associated
with value clarity (i.e., interested and involved in classroom work,
independent, persistent, responsible, and enjoyment of learning) and
three as control or placebo scales (enjoyment of music, participation
in athletics, and being friendly). An average of the two pretests
(whose scores were similar) provided beginning scores. The same
self-rating sheets were used after the experiment and provided
ending scores.

As a second measure, Shields assigned, both before and after the
experiment and to both experimental and control students, papers of
an attitudinal type to write. These papers were unstructured. The
pairs of papers (a pre- and a postpaper for each student) were given
to three independent judges who judged the change in the papers
(improved, same, worse), without knowing whether papers came
from the experiment or the control groups, on the following criteria:
quality, clarity, and depth of thinking; organization and logic; and
quality of the response to the questions the experimenter wrote in
the margins.

The findings of the students' self-ratings were inconclusive. The
growth of the experimental group was perhaps slightly greater than
that of the control group, but the unreliability of the instrument prevented any possibility of the difference reaching statistical significance for a sample of that size.

The judges' ratings of the student papers, however, favored the
experimental group at the .01 level. All three judges saw much more
growth in the papers written by the experimental students. Inasmuch
as the two courses differed in many ways, especially in subject matter, it is impossible, of course, to be certain that the growth in the
experimental papers can be attributed alone (or at all) to the value
experiences.

Dee's Value Sheets in a Technical Course

Frank P. Dee conducted an unpublished study in an adult-education class at Rutgers University that showed that adults studying a technical subject (business organization and management) would enjoy and find "helpful" brief but regular interludes of value discussions.

Dee asked the instructor of the course to distribute value sheets (as in Chapter 6) at the end of each of five successive weekly sessions for students to consider at home, as on optional assignment. These sheets dealt with some aspect of business ethics, financial policy, or sales practices. Students were then given the first ten minutes of each session to discuss, in small groups, their ideas and feelings about the sheet distributed at the end of the preceding week's session. The instructor used this time to prepare his lesson or to counsel individual students. The instructor took no part in the small-group value-sheet discussions.

A comparison class had similar discussions, sparked by similar sheets, but which did *not* contain such value-clarifying questions as "What would *you* choose," "What would make *you* proud," "What have *you* done," etc.

A simple questionnaire completed by both groups indicated that the value sheets were seen as a helpful and enjoyable experience, probably more so than were the similar non-value sheets, and not as an unwelcome intrusion into the technical aspects of the course. Dee suggests that most subject-matter specialists can probably find value sheets that would more than justify the time they take from the regular class content.

Overview of Completed Research

Twelve varied research studies have been reported: four on the college level, two on the high-school level, and six on the elementary-school level. Five of the studies were concerned with the application of the values theory to groups. Seven focused the value-clarification processes on selected students who were hypothesized as being in special need of them.

None of the studies was without weaknesses of design or measurements, and any particular finding is subject to question; but taken as a group, they contributed some support for the assertion that the value-clarification processes *do* make a difference in certain patterns of student behavior. In general, it was found that students became more purposeful and active.

This preliminary research has not, of course, "proved" the theory, nor could it. The theory deals with the relationships between an individual and his surroundings; it is concerned with what a person does with his existence. Based on the assumption that persons—even young ones—*can* have some important measure of rational control over their existences if they have no serious emotional disturbances, the theory hypothesizes (1) that our society does not always present conditions that permit children to effectively develop this control; (2) that persons who do not develop this control over their lives will often relate to their surroundings via certain behavior patterns— apathy, flightiness, indecisiveness, drift, overdissension, overconformity, role-playing, or inconsistency; and (3) that when persons who have not had adequate opportunity to clarify relationships between themselves and their surroundings discover such opportunities, they will often use them to assert more rational control over their existences. Further, the theory hypothesizes seven criteria for experiences that would help clarify those relationships (considering what one prizes, affirming it, choosing from alternatives, choosing freely, considering the consequences carefully, incorporating the choice into actual behavior, repeating the behavior over a period of time) and calls results of such experiences "values."

It should be clear that the theory is more concerned with the process than the outcome. The theory does not say to teachers, "Develop certain values by using this method." It says rather: "Use the valuing strategies. Help students clarify their relationships between self and society. Values will grow naturally and strongly."

In cases like these, research is able to determine to what extent the hypotheses that grow from theory coincide with objective reality. In the case of the value theory, the research has thus far investigated the hypothesis that *if* persons (without significant emotional blocks) had value-clarifying experiences, *then* they would become more purposefully involved with their surroundings (or less apathetic, flighty, etc.). This hypothesis has received some support.

It may be that future thought will produce a more comprehensive or economical description of the relationships involved; but until

then, and in view of the accumulated evidence supporting the use-
fulness of the present theory, it would seem that the value theory
might continue to stimulate and co-ordinate further research efforts
to understand and improve teaching effectiveness in this domain.

THE RESEARCH AHEAD

Without intending to be a detailed examination of what research
problems and prospects face the value theory, a few highlights are
noted that might be of interest to those interested in working in this
area.

The Measurement Problem

J. Raths (1964a) reviews some of the research problems with
values and discusses the difficulty of obtaining valid measures.
Several instruments have been used to measure the values people
hold. There is the well-known Allport, Vernon, and Lindzey "Study
of Values" (1960), which provides a score for the relative strength
of six value areas: theoretical, economic, religious, political, aesthetic,
and social. This instrument, although widely used, has been criticized
as having questionable validity.* A similar instrument has been
developed by Dilley (1957).

Some investigators have used Osgood's semantic differential to get
at the evaluation persons have of various phenomena.† Prince
(1957) developed an instrument called "Differential Values Inventory" which places students' values along a continuum ranging from
the emergent to the traditional. Super (1965) published a "Work
Values Inventory," which measures the relative strength of fifteen
values, such as intellectual stimulation, job achievement, and economic returns. In an earlier study, Hartshorne and May (1928) used
contrived incidents to get at some of the beliefs children have.
Santostefano (1962) also used situational tests. Finally, some
researchers have developed tests which measure what subjects

---

* See, for example, Barton (1959).

† As an example, see Winter (1962).

choose when faced with hypothetical situations. See, for example, Getzel and Jackson (1962), and Grapko (1957).

None of these instruments is very useful for the value theory of this book. As we have said, our concern is not with the values that persons *say* they hold. To us, values are part of a person's behavior pattern, and it seems extremely difficult to obtain a measure of such attributes on a paper-and-pencil test. A pencil-and-paper instrument *validated on behavior* would, of course, be at least as useful as it would be difficult to perfect; the problem of determining the outcome of any approach to value development rests upon the adequacy of measurement.

Thus far behavioral observations, mainly through rating scales of questionable reliability, have been used with this theory. (See Chapter 8 for some samples of these scales.) Improvements in such observational schemes would be extremely helpful.

Perkins (1964) provides a recent study of this problem. See also Gage (1963, chap. ix). The possibilities of using peer ratings, parent ratings, projective techniques, sociograms, and other methods of obtaining reliable and convenient measure of student behavior, especially behavior associated with unclear values, such as apathy, conformity, and so on, need further exploration.

It may be possible, also, to make use of some of the scales contained in standard personality tests for identifying value-related behavioral types and for measuring growth after exposure to the value methodology. For example, the hypomania scale of the "Minnesota Multiphasic Personality Inventory" may be related to the type we call flighty; the achievement scale of the "Edwards Personal Preference Schedule" may be (negatively) related to what we call apathetic behavior. Validity is the problem with such scales and needs careful attention.

The Seven Criteria

The seven criteria for a value grew from a notion of what would characterize a person who was really using his intelligence to guide his life through time and space. The value-clarification process rests on those criteria, of course. For example, one of the criteria for a value is that it be something that penetrates a person's life, that it uses some of a person's limited energy and resources, that it really counts in behavioral decisions. And, therefore, the clarification process uses such questions as, "Do you intend to do something about that idea you expressed?", "Can I help you do something about that?", and "Are there some examples in your life that show how you lived in this way?"

Now the interesting question is: Are all seven criteria necessary? Can one be helped to live an intelligently self-directed life without some of those seven? Hunt and Metcalf (1955) seem to believe that the criterion about incorporating choices into behavior is not vital. Raup (1950), also interested in this area, writes as if the criterion about due thought and reflection was not necessary.

It would not be too difficult to design research that would omit various combinations of the criteria and see if the results indicate that some are unnecessary. It would be a somewhat more creative task to see if *other* criteria, when translated into clarifying operations, augment the seven already identified, thus suggesting that we should reserve the term "value" for something that satisfies more than seven criteria. The decision should be made on the basis of which processes help persons become more purposeful, alive, and intelligent in their relationships with their environments.

For some purposes, it may be useful to describe the valuing methodology in more psychological terms. In that case, the seven criteria may emerge as different factors. One senses, for example, a factor of *thought provocation*. Perhaps a subfactor of that is *stimulation of introspection*. Then there is the tendency to *encourage the use of personal power*, to encourage persons to assert themselves, to put their ideas into practice. Perhaps the *pressure for independence* is significant for those unaccustomed to the decision-making process. There may be other, or different, factors; perhaps something to do with *pride*. It is possible that such a recasting of the valuing process will aid understanding and facilitate study and communication of the ideas.

Values for Whom?

Is there an age before which the clarification process is useless? What are the critical years for valuing, if there are any? Can someone be too old, or too psychologically rigid, to develop clearer values? In his recent work, Bloom (1964) finds that an environmental factor has the greatest effect on a person at the time when the quality in question is in its most rapid period of growth. But when are values most rapidly growing? Our guess would be the years ten to sixteen, but more data are needed.

This raises a question about the relationships between the effect of the clarification process and personality variables. Should everyone get the same process, or are there variations that work best when matched with particular personalities or particular behavioral patterns? (Should the apathetic child be worked with the same way as the dissenting child? Should the apathetic ten-year-old experience the same clarifying processes as the apathetic twenty-year-old, with adjustments only for the level of language?)

The finding reported by J. Raths (1962) that all of the students who did not profit from the value experiences were found to have marked unmet emotional needs raises the question of the relationship between emotional problems and value problems. Can a person whose life is devoid of affection, for example, profit from a value-clarification process? If so, under what conditions? Our original hypothosis is that emotional needs must be satisfied before much progress can be made with the development of clear values. Indeed, we suspect that it may be harmful to confront children who have insufficient ego strength with many decisions, as the value-clarification strategies tend to do.

Do *all* children profit from the value-clarification procedures, no matter how much impetus they get to clarify their personal thinking (as opposed to indoctrination) from home or other sources? Or is it wise to focus upon only those that "need" clarification experiences? Or should all get some and a few get an especially heavy dose? (And how, practically, do this?)

Is there any harm in getting too much, or, like an unnecessary dose of vitamins, does "too much" attention to values leave the organism unaffected?

The theory now identifies eight behavior patterns (apathy, flightiness, etc.) that signal a weak set of personal values. Are there a greater or fewer number that are better signals?

Martin (1960) suggests that some children have more difficulty getting clearer values through a teacher's efforts than do other children. His research suggests that dissenting children and perhaps flighty children are hardest for a teacher to work with because they present special difficulties in the development of an accepting and open teacher-student relationship. Indecisive and posing children are next in difficulty, Martin hypothesizes, with apathetic and over-conforming children the easiest. Is this true? And, if so, does this suggest a technique that emphasizes the development of easy communication *before* the implementation of the value techniques? Or is there some way that by-passes the need for direct communication and still permits the clarification processes to work? The value sheets discussed in Chapter 6 may provide a clue, for example, teaching machines where the teaching is impersonal is a possibility.

The Clarification Process

Some observers wonder if the amount of the attention that the experimental students received accounts for the reported changes rather than the nature of the attention. Lang's study would suggest otherwise, as would many teachers' experiences in dealing with the types of behaviors that have been called value-related. Attention alone has not seemed to work well in the past, but this notion merits more attention.

A more plausible hypothesis is that not *any* attention will bring about value clarification, but that accepting and supportive attention will. This suggests that it is not the kinds of clarifying questions that teachers ask as much as it is the warm way in which they relate to students that makes the difference. Since this accepting climate is a prerequisite to the value approach, it has been a part of experimental designs thus far. The hypothesis in question might be tested by seeing if accepting teachers are successful in helping children who are apathetic, dissenting, etc., even when they do not use value-clarification techniques; or a more contrived study of this hypothesis might be set up. However, it should be noted that teachers who have worked with values have typically reported that the clarification techniques gave them more powerful results than mere warmth or acceptance ever did before.

On the other hand, could it be the *content* and not the atmosphere? It would be useful to know if the accepting atmosphere is unnecessary as long as the right questions are asked. Although it seems likely that a harsh and repressive atmosphere would not suit the development of clear, personal values very well, it might be that a neutral and respectful climate might do. Or perhaps the content has to shift to suit different climates. Certainly the less stringent the requirements for the classroom climate, the larger the number of teachers who will be able to implement the theory easily.

There are also important questions to be faced regarding the sequence of value-clarification experiences. Does it make any difference what comes first or what follows what? Perhaps the power of the process can be magnified by more careful attention to the sequence of experiences.

Similar questions relate to the intensity of clarification efforts. How frequent, strong, and lengthy should they be? The answers to questions like these will likely be situational in nature; it will depend on the particular circumstances. Therefore, a more accurate statement of this question would be: What is the relationship between student, teacher, and situation, and the frequency, strength, and length of value experiences.

Affect, Cognition, and Values

There are many theoretical issues associated with the value theory that remain open. One interesting issue deals with the relationship between the cognitive domain of human activity and the affective domain. The value-clarifying methodology invades both areas and might be seen as one way of synthesizing certain aspects of both. When a person is asked to make a decision, to choose thoughtfully from alternatives, to weight an issue and to decide, he is asked to think. When a person is asked, on the other hand, how he feels about that choice—does he cherish it, is he glad that he made it—he is asked to consider his feelings. A value is a result of activation of *both* the affective and cognitive domains then, and seems to be one of the few connecting links that have been carefully delineated.

With the affective domain of life increasingly due for attention in our schools (we predict), it may be useful to consider the linking that values provide between feelings or emotion and thought or knowledge. When one asks a student who is studying Napoleon what in his own life reflects the kinds of decisions faced by that great man and how he feels about his own decisions, implicit or explicit, one is asking a powerful question, and one is, of course, connecting knowledge with feeling.

What, after all, is the relationship between the two domains? Is some kind of knowledge more useful in enriching feelings? What kind is this? Are there implications here for deciding what subject matter to teach?

And what kinds of affective experiences (see Krathwohl *et al.*, 1964) are educative? Which ones produce growth and which ones either are inert or are deleterious? Can one generalize? These seem to be potentially very important questions for education.

Contagion of Values

We have said that when a child patterns his behavior after those of an adult, when the adult acts as a model of certain behavior, the result may not be a value. Values do not come merely by imitation. It may be, however, that the availability of a model makes it easier for a child to comprehend what a value is actually like in practice, and thus makes it more likely that that value would be chosen, thoughtfully and freely, than would be if the model were not available for observation. Thus, although the familiar phrase "values are caught" has no meaning when we define values as requiring deliberate and free choice, it may well be that the visibility of a value enhances the possibility of its being chosen. Perhaps this would be especially so were the modeled value to be exemplified by someone otherwise respected and were the value perceived as working positively in his life. If this reasoning holds, it would imply that it is still wise for adults to act the way they would prefer students to act, even as they insist on students having free, thoughtful choices about it. Similarly, it may be unwise to model values that will, for one reason or another, be perceived as artificial or dysfunctional, but further study is needed.

Outcomes of Value Clarification

Although it certainly will seem odd to some who are concerned with value study, we have almost no idea of what values the value-clarification methodology tends to promote. We have been largely unconcerned with the outcomes except as those outcomes represent changes in patterns of behavior—less apathy, conformity, and so on, or more seriousness of purpose, more independence, better school grades, and the like. It may be of interest to inquire as to what values do emerge from value clarification. Our guess, based upon the evidence thus far available, would be that they would be those associated with the use of intelligence, the involvement of individuals in group decisions, the openness of communication, and others associated with democracy. Perhaps it will be found that children choose them for the very reason many of us have chosen them. They are the most effective values for providing the kind of life we desire.

Which leads to another issue. What should be the reaction of an adult using the value methodology when a child chooses a value that is unacceptable to the majority? It is not impossible to conceive of someone going through the seven value criteria and deciding that he values intolerance or thievery. What is to be done? Our position is that we respect his right to decide upon that value—indeed every real experience that some children have *insists* that such a value is the only defensible one—but we must often deny him the right to carry the value to action. We believe we have to say, "you may choose what you believe best, but some behavior can't be permitted because it interferes too much with the freedom or rights of others."

Does our restriction prevent such a person from obtaining values? It may be a semantic riddle of little consequence, but since we say that a value must be acted upon and that not all actions are permitted, it may be that we prevent some persons from adopting some values, and thus in fact we guide values more than we say we do. This is particularly relevant for certain subgroups of our society that tend to lead their young naturally and logically to values that the larger society would find intolerant. One thinks of the reasonableness of children in some neighborhoods growing up to be racketeers.

All this leads to another question: Values, we say, cannot result from indoctrination; they require free choice, among other things; but can we call what we "want" an attitude or a belief and feel free to indoctrinate that? Take courtesy, for example. Most parents would probably be happy if their children would be courteous. Some parents might even call that a prime goal of child rearing. Is that not to be trained, rewarded, exhorted, indoctrinated, or otherwise "taught" to the child?

Here, one might say, adults have a choice. They can leave it to the value level—that is, really give the child alternatives, free choice, and freedom to act upon his choices—and trust that the wisdom of courtesy will prevail. If courtesy does prevail, it is likely, of course, to prevail in a deep and satisfying way to the child. But courtesy may not prevail, and then the consequences are as obvious as they are uncomfortable.

The other choice is to remove courtesy from the area in which children are left free to decide things for themselves. Following this road, the adult acknowledges that he is unwilling to take the risk of a child's decision, and so he does not let the child choose. He *teaches* (or indoctrinates) courtesy; he does not *clarify* the issue. The risk here is that he may get courtesy only when someone is looking, or when the rewards are high enough, or at the expense of personal pride and satisfaction, or in other unwanted circumstances.

There is another danger. If too many decisions, like courtesy, honesty, cleanliness, etc., etc., are removed from the child, will there be enough left to give him practice in valuing and the sense of worth that we believe comes with valuing? This is the real danger, as we now see it. It does not seem very serious to us—whatever is done with courtesy or almost any other individual issue. The pattern, however, is of greatest moment. What seems to us of paramount importance is that the child be given a measure of freedom to exercise his intelligence and individuality, and increasingly large amounts as he matures. In general, we would say that the issues that should be left to the child are (1) those that contain alternatives the consequences of which the child is able to grasp to a reasonable extent, and (2) those whose alternatives are neither very distasteful nor dangerous so that any choice can be tolerated.

Values and Non-motivated, Disadvantaged Children

Educators have long been perplexed about how to deal with students who do not seem to be motivated to learn in school or who come from slum neighborhoods and are otherwise unsympathetic to the job of the school. A feverish amount of activity has recently been generated by this problem, especially in view of the difficulties experienced by poorly educated Negroes and school drop-outs of all sorts in the midst of an increasingly technological society.

Of the many remedies suggested, few seem to offer as much as does the value theory of this book. This idea needs to be tested further, but we sense that a good part of the difficulty of these "problem" students stems from feelings of alienation, feelings of not being part of the society that runs the schools and rewards school achievement. And, often, there is no other world of which they do feel a part. If there is something they have *not* done, it is to work out the relationships between self and society.

Thus, perhaps, for more than any other group, value-clarifying experiences—chances to think through what their lives are for in some accepting, aware and realistic fashion—are needed by these children.

We do not believe that the value-clarifying methodology by itself will solve all the problems of such children. We would add a heavy concentration upon their emotional needs and a serious effort to open some doors in the society that have not been open, such as those into the cultural and economic sectors of adult life. But we do believe that the value methodology can be a vital part of any program for the disadvantaged. It may, in fact, be the crucial element in releasing their personal and social productivity.

Also in need of research, and in the same vein, are the possible uses of this methodology with delinquent children, institutionalized children, adult prison inmates, and others who consider themselves outcasts from society. There is some reason to believe that the effects here, too, might be worthwhile.

There are many aspects of the value theory that need further investigation. Although this theory has been used and shown to have positive, significant results, there are still many areas which remain to be explored in greater depth.

At present, we know beneficial results can be brought about by using the value clarification theory. There are difficulties in conducting research, but these problems are not insurmountable. Further research will bring a better understanding of value clarification and its implications for education and this in turn will hopefully lead to better results in the classroom and happier, better integrated, more productive individuals.

Appendix A

Questions for Incomplete Value Sheets

1. "Merry-Go-Round"
    a. When was the last time you were on a merry-go-round?
    b. If you happened to be in line and overheard the incident which takes place in the poem, is there anything *you* might have said to that little boy?
    c. Have you ever experienced anything similar to that boy's feelings?
    d. What prejudice, subtle or otherwise, have you ever personally faced?
    e. If you wanted to *do* something about the problem of "civil rights," what are some things you could do?
       (1.) Right in this school, through some school group.
       (2.) In your town, with some community organization.
       (3.) On the national level.
    f. Perhaps you believe that nothing needs to be done about this problem. If so, state that position clearly and forcefully.

2. Questions for "The Human Being Is Made up of Oxygen, etc."
    a. What is the point of this statement?
    b. Are you serious in believing that you are worth more than $1.00? Explain.
    c. What are some ways we measure the worth of human beings?
    d. Can you list some things you have *done* which show what you think human beings are worth?

3. Some questions for "Louis Armstrong on His Art."
    a. Underline the places where Louis Armstrong tells you what he feels about art.
    b. Circle the statements which he uses to describe "other" artists.
    c. Is there anything you do which you are as dedicated to as Mr. Armstrong is about his trumpet playing?
    d. How does one go about beginning to care that deeply?

4. Questions for "Shuttlesworth's Civil Rights Biography."
   a. Why do you suppose Mr. Shuttlesworth would take all of that?
   b. Maybe it is all right for him to feel that strongly, but what right does he have to involve his children in his problems? Comment.
   c. Could Mr. Shuttlesworth move into your neighborhood? Would you want him to?
   d. If you believe in his cause, are there any things you could do to help it?

5. Some questions for "In Germany they first came for the Communists, etc."
   a. In a few words, what is the central meaning of this statement?
   b. What is the Pastor *for* and what is he *against?*
   c. Which category are *you* in? When would they have come for you?
   d. What are some things going on in our world right now about which you might need to speak up? List them here:
   e. How do you think one goes about speaking up? How do you do it? What are the ways?
   f. Could you pick something you listed in *d* above and work out a strategy by which you could, indeed, speak up for it?
   g. Is there something in your school, some "injustice," about which you could well speak up?
   h. If you are not to speak up, who should do it?
   i. Why stick your neck out? Why not?
   j. We need to *value* what we do and to *do* something about what we value. Do you agree? If so, when was the last time you acted upon one of your values?

Appendix B

Evaluating Value Sheets

Part 1—*Scheme for Evaluating Lesson Plans*

Below are five basic areas which you can use to evaluate your value sheets. You will note that there are three positions on the continuum. *Position one* is considered higher than *position three*. As you reread your plans and come to understand the coding, we hope you will constantly be thinking of ways to lift your ideas increasingly towards the "one" end of the continuum.

T. Topic

1. You have a real live topic and a problem that students are aware of or may easily be made aware of. The topic is likely to touch many students deeply.
2. A mildly live topic, probably of some concern to some students.
3. A topic that may provide some intellectual exercise, but that probably will not penetrate the lives of most students very much.

Th. Thinking

1. Excellent thinking is stimulated here. Plenty of opportunity for reflection is included.
2. Some thinking, but could use more.
3. Routine, rote, or simple responses from students are likely. No real mental exertion demanded.

Alt. Alternatives

1. You have made provisions, broadly, for a consideration of alternatives. Student value-indicators have been elicited consistently.
2. Some consideration of alternatives has been indicated, but student opportunity to examine a wide range of alternatives needs to be increased.
3. This sheet does not adequately involve students in a broad enough consideration of the alternatives available for action or valuing.

A. Action

1. This sheet hits squarely at some present (or near future) action implication. Student behavior will probably change as a result of this lesson. It seems destined to make a real difference in their lives.
2. Some relevance to action here, but the students need to be made more conscious of the behavioral consequences of the lesson, more sensitive to what they can do about it.
3. This sheet may provide intellectual exercise, but it probably will make little difference in the students' lives. Frankly, you are probably wasting your time and theirs.

B. Penetration

1. This topic is handled so that it really penetrates deeply. It touches the emotions, the hidden parts of us, perhaps painfully, but productively.
2. Some penetration, but could be sharper and stronger.
3. Bland, conventional, ambivalent, superficial treatment. Can easily be handled off the top-of-the-head, whereas values cannot be.

Part 2—*Looking at Specific Questions*

As you begin using some of the value sheets in this book, it is hoped you will begin to consider making your own. Drawing up the questions will become easier if you view your questions within the framework of the statements below. Code a few of our sheets, with the letter codes in the left-hand margin. It is good practice for making up your own sheets.

Letter Code		*Working at Specific Questions*
Q	Question narrow:	This is a question for which there is only one answer.
Th	Thinking:	This should stimulate real thinking.
Pr	Problem:	You have identified a real problem here. Good.
M	Moralizing:	Watch it. Moralizing can too easily follow. It puts forth your values and tends to encourage dependency.
CT	Changed topic:	Here you are going off in a new direction before adequately developing the previous emphasis.

Letter Code		*Working at Specific Questions*
Int	Intellectuality:	Provides good intellectual exercise, but probably no real penetration into students' lives. You need to lift this toward reality and toward action.
E	Enough is enough:	You are probably overdoing this point. Pushing too hard may just build up more resistance.
Cr	Criticism:	Either direct or implied, criticism rides the rails of this question or statement. Is there another way of getting at your point?
V-C	Value-clarification:	This will most likely advance the process of clarifying values.
A	Action	This makes a significant bid for some action to grow out of the lesson.
SW	So what?:	I'm afraid that this produces a "so what" in the reader of your plan and may well do the same with a class. It just doesn't seem to matter.

Appendix C

Additional Value Sheets

Pets and You

Dog owners spent $530 million on dog food last year, reports the Wall Street Journal, which adds that this is about 50% more than Americans spend on baby food!

Americans will spend $1.5 billion to acquire pets this year and in addition to the initial investment and the food bill, about $800 million will be spent this year on non-food items for pets. (For dogs: pajamas, cashmere sweaters, mink collars, Halloween costumes and Santa Claus suits; and cosmetics—color shampoo, creme rinses and hair dressing, perfumes, 11 shades of nail polish including lavender and green, a spray dentifrice, tranquilizers, etc.) Not to mention the millions spent on veterinarian fees and boarding kennels. Pets are big business.°

° Charles A. Wells, "Between the Lines, the Wells Newsletter," September 15, 1964.

To think on and to write on:

1. If you have a dog, should you feel badly about the above? Why? Why not?

2. If you don't have a dog, do you spend your money on something which might be written up to sound as ridiculous? Explain.

3. A person who teased a dog owner with the above quotation was found to drive a convertible car with automatic transmission, automatic window lifters, power brakes, power steering, and an automatic headlight dimmer. Comment.

4. Should I come close to starving myself so that others can eat? Discuss.

5. Where do you stand on this issue: "What we spend our money on tells everyone what we value, respect, hold dear, cherish, etc.?"

T.V., Comics and Violence

On the television screen, about 50 actors and actresses (by latest count) keel over gloriously every week. In comic strips, characters are being punched, stabbed, choked and shot to death with approximately the same consistency. In fact, murder and mayhem have become such an integral part of entertainment in this country, that viewers of all ages tend to think of violence as part of wholesome living, like having picnics on Sunday . . .

It is time we stopped recommending brutality as a way of having fun. It takes no particular strength or courage to hit somebody in the mouth, kick him in the stomach, break a piece of furniture over his head. And even a child's forefinger can pull a trigger.*

* From Stephen Baker, "T.V., Comics and Violence," *Today's Child News-magazine*, XII (June, 1964).

To think on and to write on:

1. Really, now, what's all the fuss about?

2. You've watched T.V. and read comic books, and you're not violent. Comment.

3. What policy will you take to your own children about T.V. and comics?

4. Do you do anything to affirm that life is valuable?

5. Does a tabloid like the *New York Daily News* make life seem less valuable? Do you advocate censorship? What can be done?

6. Do your T.V. and reading habits contribute to your immaturity? What IS the impact of your T.V. and reading time? Explain.

The Abrasive Man

I. We have a shortage in teaching of what I shall call the 'abrasive man.' He is obviously a controversial figure. He disturbs the peace of the affluent suburb and the apathetic city. He doesn't fit in. He creates ripples when we prefer calm water. Once the well-rounded man was the well-educated man. Now we are likely to think of him as a smooth, unabrasive fellow, a nice guy. He revolves in a nice little circle, in a nice suburb, where nice people live, 'our kind of people,' you know. It's a good life with one fatal weakness. It often puts these nice people out of touch with the disturbing problems of the city and the rest of the world. To communicate is to share ideas and feelings in a mood of mutuality. We cannot escape the moral and social consequences of noncommunication, of self-isolation from the troubles of the world. In the long run, walling one's self off from our fellow man deadens the personality, makes it insensitive to the aspirations, the pain, the rich pleasure of other people.†

† From Edgar Dale, "Journalism! A New Dimension," *The News Letter* of The Ohio State University, XXX (February, 1965), 4.

Education For Creativity

II. To be creative is to be thoughtfully involved, a concerned and active participant, not a disengaged spectator. Creativity is an experience in depth which transforms pleasure into joy, entertainment into delight, listless apathy into dynamic living. The great tragedy in life is not death but never having lived. The creative person, on reviewing his life, can say with Virgil's Aeneas: "Many of these things I saw, And some of them I was."[*]

[*] From Edgar Dale, "Education for Creativity," *The News Letter* of The Ohio State University, XXX (December, 1964), 4.

To think on and to write on:
1. Which of the above quotations seems to say more to YOU? Why?
2. Are you unabrasive?
3. Does Dale want us to be hostile, aggressive, ornery? Explain.
4. In what events of our time have you participated?
5. List as many ways as possible to avoid ending up life with a large component of mediocrity?
6. Which of the items you listed for #5 are you doing now? When do you start?

Under the Sway of the Great Apes

Edwin P. Young, an uncelebrated philosopher, once observed of football, "After all, it's only a game that kids can play." This is no longer strictly true. If it were, the networks would not have bought it up as a vehicle to sell cigarettes, cars and beer.

The evidence suggests that it satisfies some inner need of the spectator so completely that it can rivet him to his chair through a holiday in disregard of family life or bring him to his feet howling for (Allie) Sherman's head when the outcome fails to gratify.

If sports have ceased to be only games that kids can play and become psychotherapy for the mob, it is too bad, especially for kids who will grow up hating them or busting gussets to achieve therapeutic professional excellence.

What is worse, though, is the distortion of values that radiates throughout the society. For thirty minutes of farce, Liston and Clay can earn more than the entire faculty of a public school can make in a decade[†]

To think on and to write on:
1. Did you watch football on New Years Day?

[†] From Russell E. Baker, "Under the Sway of the Great Apes," *The New York Times*, January 5, 1965. © 1965 by The New York Times Company. Reprinted by permission.

2. Is it a pattern of yours? Is it something about which you are proud?
3. How would you answer Mr. Baker?
4. Do you think the publishers of *Harpers* or *Atlantic* could benefit from taking ads during the televising of a football game? Comment.
5. Does this sheet make you want to do anything different in your life?

Joe College Is Dead

Joe College is dead, and his little anxieties are unrecognizably antique. Indeed, there may still be some refuge which is entirely unaffected, where college remains a place of learning, not a racetrack. But year by year the infection spreads. This generation has been so thoroughly harnessed to the treadmill of the examination that it accepts its servitude as a normal, if strenuous, condition of life. Since education has become a national emergency, it is a patriotic duty to do well in algebra.

The most highly motivated students know that they are engaged in a close race; only the fleetest will enter the desirable colleges. Ahead of them loom the great goals, the College Boards and the National Merit competition. It is a rare teacher who can resist the tendency to turn his classes into extended cram sessions.

Upon entering college, the young people discover that entry into college solves no problems. The place is strange and the conditions of life new, but the race is the same, only the pace is faster.

The goal of college is the same as that of high school—the high score that will open the way to the next stage of competition. Tactics become pre-eminently important. And only the reckless will dare not to know the right answers as the grader expects them, or allow questions to draw their thinking in unexpetced directions. It is vain to point out that success in tests is not necessarily the way to achievement, that the careers of great men do not always begin in the upper tenth percentile, that there are other than competitive values to education.

Young people today secure an admirable training in the techniques of the correct answer. They learn to remember, to be accurate, neat, and cautious. But they are rarely called on to use their ability autonomously or speculatively, to deal with situations in which the answers are not known but must be discovered. With what pain, if ever at all, will they learn how to know what they do not know, how to probe alone beyond the limits of what is handed to them, how to be creative original thinkers! By the time they carry their diplomas away, they will have missed an education—that experience which, by the exposure of one mind to the thinking of others, creates not answers but a lifetime of questions.

We are all sufferers by the losses sustained by this generation of students.°

° Oscar Handlin, "Are the Colleges Killing Education?" *The Atlantic Monthly Magazine,* May, 1962. Copyright © 1962, by The Atlantic Monthly Company, Boston, Mass.

1. Is Handlin talking about you? Why? Why not?

2. Can you do anything about it? Who should do it? How should they go about it? Where do we start? What part can you play?

3. How do you know what's worth fighting for? How do you know what's worth living for? Dying for? What are you doing about it?

4. Is there anything which you care as much about as Handlin does about this?

A Student's Report of a Campus Incident

Someone was caught cheating on an exam in an advanced biology class. The teacher tried to take the paper away, but the boy held on to it. When the teacher finally got hold of the test, several index cards fell out from between the pages. The boy screamed that they were not his. To make a long story short, the teacher informed the student that this would have to be reported to the authorities. The boy threatened to kill the teacher, and they scuffled until other teachers came to get the boy away. The boy had been accepted by a medical school, and this incident meant no med-school for him. His actions were explained by a weak personality cracking under the system. But what amazed me was the reactions of other pre-med students. Their near joy was hard to hide. How awfully sadistic. Or was their joy a sign of relief for not having been caught themselves?

To think on:

1. What is your first, most immediate reaction? (Use free association. Don't write sentences; just put down words.)

2. In what ways do you identify with the boy?

3. In what ways do you identify with the teacher?

4. The author of the incident raises a point about the other students in the class. Comment on that.

5. To cheat or not to cheat? What is the rationalization for each position?

6. What alternatives were open to the student? to the teacher? to the other students?

A Values Sheet for High School Students

Divorce

Divorce was one way out and so they took it—
  escaped from their prison marriage to unbarred air.

Crazy with freedom, two so long cramped and crooked,
  they danced different ways and began to lose that pallor,
  laughing along at last where the wind has no door.

They were like school bent children released into summer
  as if after June there were nothing further to learn—
  chewed candies of whim and swam when the days turned warmer;
  from their lives in the leaves no one could call them home.

Wintered again, they look back at that green illusion,
  pick at their locks and their partners, dreaming a plan
  to tunnel a way through the walls of their own confusion
  and find outside, the woman, the ideal man—
  the god they needn't love, who will worship them.°

To think on and to write on:

° Harold Witt, "Divorce," *Saturday Review*, October 3, 1964.

1. How are you going about finding someone to marry? Describe your approach.

2. What is *your* understanding of the last two lines of the poem?

3. What are some of the pitfalls of this marriage game? List them.

4. What are you going to do about finding a marriage partner?

Graduation Day

Miss Jan Jordan attended Americus, Georgia High School for four years. Her graduation day was in June, 1964. Like other seniors, she invited her friends to the graduation. Unlike other seniors, some of her friends were Negroes.

When they arrived at the gate of the stadium, where the exercises were to be held, they were turned away by police and school authorities. After some efforts to negotiate, Jan, who was then in her cap and gown waiting for the procession to begin, was informed that her friends were not being admitted.

She then stepped out of line, walked to the head of it and said to the faculty member in charge: "I think my friends have as much right to come to my graduation as anyone else's friends do."

With this, she started walking towards the stands, where several thousand people were expectantly waiting for the procession to begin. They watched in amazement as this lone senior, followed by her father and kid brother (her mother stayed at the gate with those who had been barred), walked steadily toward them, slowly climbed to the top of the stands, and sat down. Then the other seniors marched out on the field and seated themselves on the platform facing the stands, and facing Jan and her father and brother.

After speeches by honor students on "Moral Responsibility" and "Reverence," each graduate was called to the rostrum and given a diploma. Jan's name was not called.°

To think on and to write on:

° From J. L. Jordan, the *Koinonia Newsletter*, #29, September 15, 1964, of the Koinonia Farm, Americus, Georgia.

1. What do you think about what Jan Jordan did? Would you do it? Why? Why not?

2. What did she hope to accomplish? Was this a way to do it? What else might she have done?

3. Is there anything you want as badly as she wanted this? Would you be willing to risk your diploma for it? Explain.

4. There is more to the story: "Next day, because she felt that some might not have understood her strange action the night before, Jan placed an ad in the Americus paper. It was headed: "Why I Did Not Graduate with My Class at Americus High," and stated simply that because her friends were not admitted on the same basis as other's, she felt unable to participate."

5. Does this story have *any* implications for your own life? (Use back of this).

Note: As of September, 1964, the Americus Schools were integrated.

An Open-Ended List of Alternatives for a Christmas Vacation

DIRECTIONS: Below are some activities various people were involved in during Christmas vacation. We need some other ideas from *you*. When the list is long enough, we would like to ask each of you to categorize the items in the following ways:

X–This is definitely not for me.

U–Unlikely that I would do it.

N–Neutral or unsure.

P–Possibly I would do this in the future.

A–I affirm this; I will definitely try to build it into my life, if I have not already done so.

_____ 1. Worked up a show and performed it in a hospital ward.

_____ 2. Made up a basket of food and delivered it to some needy family.

_____ 3. Organized a group to go caroling in the neighborhood.

_____ 4. Invited some children from an underprivileged neighborhood to spend a day with me and returned the visit.

_____ 5. Wrote many letters to go out with Seasons Greetings cards to friends in many different parts of the country and world.

_____ 6. Organized a block party for New Year's Eve where everyone brought some specialty of the house to share with neighbors.

_____ 7. Enjoyed it with just my family.

_____ 8. Made the decorations for our tree.

_____ 9. Repaired some broken toys to be distributed to children in an orphanage.

_____10. Solicited friends, relatives and neighbors for old clothes to send to needy children in a migrant worker camp.

_____11. Contributed substantially to a dozen different organizations which appealed for funds.

_____12. Devoted a whole day to helping some other student complete a term paper. *Not* doing it for him.

_____13. At the year's end, evaluated how the year had gone and made plans to make it more significant the next year.

_____14. Made with my own hands almost all the presents I gave.

_____15. Sat down and wrote some letters to public figures affirming some position they had recently taken or acknowledged some beautiful act of some other person.

_____16. Bought a ticket to a play for a child who had never seen one.

_____17. Attempted, without moralizing, to pose alternatives on some basic issues of our time: peace-war, race, economics, etc., to friends and relatives.

_____18. Tried to lift the usual level of family relations to a higher plane in keeping with the season.

_____19. Avoided taking the path of least resistance in present giving, and really tried to find out what the various receivers really would enjoy.

_____20. Went out of my way to help children in the neighborhood capture a less materialistic and more spiritual significance to the holiday season.

_____21.

_____22.

_____23.

_____24.

_____25.

Appendix D

Symbols Useful in Coding Student Papers

E *Extremes* (all, none, every, never, always, etc.). Are you sure? Would you change this on reconsideration?

I *Indefinites* (some, seldom, sometimes, perhaps, a few, might, etc.). Is this unnecessarily vague? Can you be more specific?

VJ *Value judgments* (wasted time, a good lesson, it was unfortunate, a difficult job, a wonderful man, etc.). Are you making a judgment that others might not agree with? Do you want to be more objective here?

AT *Attributing* a situation or a person's feelings on unstated evidence (she overlooked the student; he wanted to cry; she felt badly; he teased her; Sal likes reading; they were afraid to answer; a prouctive lesson, etc.). Are you sure? Have you made it clear to the reader that this is only your inference from the data? Would it be better to omit this, or state the basis for your interpretation?

Alt. *Alternatives* (either we do this or that, if this happens, then that results; John should do thus and so; from the information we can conclude such and such; etc.) Are there other alternatives? Have you considered other possibilities?

G *Generalizations* (since our friends like it, boys everywhere will; after examining three towns . . ., an authority states . . .; after talking to him for five minutes I could tell what kind of person he was; etc.). Have you overgeneralized? Do you have enough data for the conclusions you are making?

OS *Over-simplification* (money leads to happiness; a college education will make a cultured man; Japan started the war; we need more scientists to win the cold war; etc.). Have you oversimplified the situation? Have you inappropriately reduced a complex situation to simple terms?

PR *Projection* (teachers deserve higher salaries; he should quit; they discriminate against people like me; bright students should get more attention than dull students; John cannot be taught anything; etc.). Have you examined your own motives here? Could it be that you are projecting your own feelings into the situation, perhaps not consciously?

D *Dogmatic* (Are you sure? Have you considered alternatives?)

Appendix E

A Programmed Unit On The
Emotional Needs Theory

Lesson A

A-1   It is sometimes said that feelings can get in the way of intelligence, that when emotions are at a high level the mind works less smoothly and effectively.

Think of an incident when you were very, very sad or very, very angry. Can you recapture the feelings of that incident? How effective was the logic of your mind at that time? On a separate sheet of paper, jot down your recollections of this. (No one will see what you write. Don't turn it in, but *do* do it.)

A-2   After you have written your reactions to this, go on to A-3. If you did not write anything yet, take a moment and make the notes as directed above. We ask that you actually *write* your recollections because we believe that writing will help you clarify your thinking more than will casual remembering. Go on to A-3 as soon as you have done the writing.

A-3   Can you think of other incidents in your life that were so emotional that your ability to think straight was impaired? Make private note of some if you can. Just take a few moments on this.

A-4   Would you agree that feelings—especially intense feelings—can preoccupy the mind and make straight thinking difficult?

A-5   Do you think this helps explain why some people freeze up on tests and do less well than they might otherwise do? (Do you?)

A-6   It is often found that a person who becomes anxious when faced with a test remains anxious even though he is *told* to relax, not to worry, etc. Such words do not seem to help a person who is anxious in a testing situation. Is it your experience that words often do not eliminate feelings, especially intense feelings?

A-7   How would you change the following statement to make it more reasonable or more true: Emotions are real to persons having them. A teacher will sometimes find that a child's emotions are interfering with his learning. It would be good if teachers could have a way of helping students free themselves of emotions that interfere with learning.

A-8   Go on to Lesson B *after* you have revised the statement in A-7, if that is necessary. Check with the instructor if you have any questions.

249

Lesson B

B-1 We believe that emotions are very real things, and that they cannot be ignored by a teacher who wants to help children learn and live fruitful lives. But it is difficult to deal with emotions unless you know some relatively workable way to go at it. This unit will try to help you develop some skills in this area.

Go on to B-2 if you are willing to try to learn those skills. If you would rather not spend time at this task at this time, ask the instructor if you might do something else. (Will you give your students this alternative some day?)

B-2 In this unit, the approach to emotions is through the emotional needs theory as developed by Louis E. Raths. There are other ways we could go at it, but this has proven to be a neat and effective theory. Raths has explained how the busy teacher can spot children with emotions so intense that they interfere with learning and living.

Read the first seven pages (up to "What's wrong?") of the booklet Raths wrote with Anna Burrell called *Understanding the Problem Child*. (West Orange, N.J.: The Economics Press) and then, after you have done the reading, go on to B-3. B-3 will help you digest the material in those first seven pages.

B-3 Some children, as you have read, react in strange ways when they have prolonged and repeated emotional disturbances. In a sense, this is fortunate: it tells the sensitive onlooker that something is "wrong" and that help is needed. And so a teacher would do well to know when a student with emotional concerns is signalling for help.

Can you tell which of the following types of behavior listed below, if carried on chronically, might very well be a signal of an emotional problem? Circle those.

a. Chronic stealing of small items, valuable and worthless, and the occasional damaging of property for no apparent reasons.

b. Bragging, belittling others, coupled with a fierce competitive spirit.

c. A nervous child, almost constantly bouncing his feet, shifting in his seat, restless and impatient.

d. Very, very nearsighted child who has to stare at things to see them properly.

e. A child with regular headaches and backaches that physicians seem unable to cure.

f. Keeping to oneself, avoiding contact with others, sitting quietly and doing what one is told to do without complaint.

g. A child who keeps missing the meaning of almost everything that is at all complex, who needs to have things explained carefully and repeatedly.

h. A timid child, quick to permit others to take the lead, slow to protest when others take advantage of him, easily frightened.

i. A loud and boisterous child, negative and bossy in his dealings with the school and teachers as well as with his peers.

j. A child no one seems to notice and who seems to be without friends; the quiet child with no excellent traits apparent.

k. The child with an extremely short attention span; he does this and then that, flitting from interest to interest, not doing anything with much enthusiasm.

l. The child who seems to look for trouble, always in one jam or another, and proud to be the trouble-maker.

B-4   If you have carefully considered the items a-l above, and have circled the appropriate responses, then compare your responses with ours.

It seems to us that all of those behaviors—if they are patterns—would hint strongly at an emotional problem *except* for (d) which, perhaps, is merely an eyesight problem, a health problem. (g) perhaps a problem of intelligence or a lack of experience in thinking, and (k) perhaps a child without purposes and/or with unclear values.

B-5   Many teachers when faced with such behaviors as those listed above would try to reason with the child, explaining why such behavior is unwise. Have you ever seen a teacher do that? How often do you think reasoning is effective in changing behavior such as that listed above?

B-6   Some teachers when faced with such behaviors as those listed above would try to punish such behavior away. "Stay after school until you learn to be more respectful of others!" Does that seem to work?

B-7   What can be done with children who chronically show aggression (through fighting, stealing, belittling, etc.) or who are very submissive, or who are withdrawn, or psychosomatically ill? Will talking or scolding help? We would say, "usually not." But go on to Lesson C for some more specific ideas about this.

But you want to reread B-3-4-5 before you go on, to clarify any questions. You may also want to talk to the instructor about your questions at this point. When you are ready, however, move on to Lesson C.

Lesson C

C-1   Raths, along with other researchers, says that, as we all have physical needs, such as for rest and nourishment, so do we have emotional needs. For example, we all have a need to belong to a group of other persons. And this theory of emotional needs says that if one or more of our emotional needs are unmet, we will feel bad and our growth will be stunted.

If our unmet needs are serious enough, we will likely signal others that we are hurt—and that's what aggression, withdrawal, submission, or psychosomatic illness often is: a signal for help.

The wise teacher doesn't react to such a symptom with punishment or argument, but sees if he can find an emotional need that is not being met and that is prompting that symptom or signal.

To learn more about what our emotional needs are, continue to read in the Raths and Burrell booklet from page 7 to page 20. As you go along, think of when you were younger: pick a time, say when you were in first grade. Do you remember? Or fourth grade? Who was your teacher? When you were younger, were any of these emotional needs unmet *for you?*

C-2   After you have read up to page 20 in the Raths-Burrell booklet, write your name on the board so that groups of three persons can form. If there is a name already up on the board, put your name under it. If there are two names, add your name and circle all three names so that we will know that you are in one group.

As soon as you have a group of three, sit together, exchange some pleasantries, talk over briefly your feelings about the unit thus far—just a few moments on this, please, —and then go on to C-3.

C-3   Below is a list of persons with some behavior patterns described. Read each one and then discuss in your group which of the eight needs, if any, might be unmet. Try to reach consensus for each case below. You may check with our answers (noted in C-4) after each case or after you have discussed them all, whichever your group decides.

NOTE: The needs you hypothesize as being unmet may, in fact, not be unmet at all. This is your best initial estimate. Later we will see how one can tell if one's first estimate is inaccurate. With such incomplete information as that provided below, one can only make guesses. Often, however, a teacher must act on such incomplete information.

1. Anna's mother is an unpleasant woman and is known to be inconsiderate and occasionally mean to her children. Anna gets along well enough with her peers but intensely dislikes her mother, although she doesn't tell people that unless she feels very close to them. Anna has psychosomatic headaches.

2. Bill nags and nags about the phony behavior of adults. He constantly reminds everyone that war is inevitable and almost seems to welcome it. His intense aggression types him as a possible emotional needs case.

3. Carla is out of it—she dresses sloppily, talks strangely, never has money for trips and things, and seems to have no friends, although she doesn't seem to mind. She does fairly well in school and is rather attrac-

tive, if not well washed. But she is so withdrawn that the teacher wonders
if she has unmet emotional needs.

4. Donald is the terror of the school. Nobody has been able to do anything with him. He is surly, nasty, and hostile, yet he is extremely small
for his age, slight and fair, and doesn't seem to have kept up with the
adolescent development of his peers. Nevertheless, punishment seems to
have no effect on Donald.

5. Ernie is also a terror, but he is big and strong, although somewhat
dull. He is sixteen years old and still in the eighth grade. About the only
thing he does well in the eighth grade is frighten children *and* teachers.
He might be an excellent football player, but he is too clumsy to even
clean his glasses without dropping them.

6. Fran is all but invisible. As long as anyone can remember, she has
never spoken to anyone without first having been addressed. She is bright
and gets good grades. She has a very close friend, who is quiet, also. But
she has terrible dreams, frightful and frequent, and is often too frightened
to come to school. No one at school knew this until one teacher stopped to
take an interest in Fran.

7. "Gook" is really named Gerald, but only teachers call him that. He
is the butt of jibes and jokes and reasonably so, usually. He is silly, stupid,
and awkward. Fortunately, he is good-natured; he laughs along with
everyone else at his foibles. But lately a perceptive teacher caught him a
few times crying quietly in the locker room during lunch hour.

C-4 Some possible emotional needs as we see them. (Note: You will, of
course, benefit the most if you have really done the work above.)

1. Anna: perhaps Anna has a need to be free of guilt feeling about her
attitude towards her mother; perhaps she has a need for self-respect
(although we would need more data to check this one); and perhaps
Anna needs to understand that it is possible, and sometimes reasonable,
to dislike one's mother.

2. Bill: Among other needs, he may lack understanding of how difficult it is to be an adult in our crazy world; he may also need to understand the forces that are working to make the world better.

3. Carla: economic security, belonging, and self-respect are likely unmet needs.

4. Donald: this boy may well need belonging, self-respect, and the
understanding that he will eventually mature or, at least, the knowledge
that there is much more to a person than his size.

5. Ernie: There are a lot of children like Ernie, and many of them
need to know something about achievement and self-respect.

6. Fran: Fran is apparently not free of fears; it may take some digging
to find out what fear is operating, however.

7. Gerald: he displays, perhaps, the need for belonging, love and affection, and self-respect.

C-5   After you have discussed these cases, take turns telling the other members in your group what you understand about this needs theory thus far. Check with the instructor if you have any questions. Then go on to Lesson D, which you should work on at home, alone. (Please say goodbye to your group in a way that will not jeopardize the members' need for love, belonging, or, for that matter, talking. There will be time for more of that another day.)

Lesson D

D-1   Working along, now, let's review a bit. Take a piece of paper from your notebook. Make a list of the kinds of behavior patterns that you can think of that might be, in reality, signals of a child who has one or more unmet emotional needs. Really write out the responses. Rely on your memory. Don't refer back to the pamphlet. Write.

D-2   Now, go back to the Raths-Burrell pamphlet and scan the first seven pages. See if you can add *new* behavior clues to your list.

D-3   See how many of the eight emotional needs you can recall. List them.

Now, check with the booklet (a) to complete your list, and (b) to review the meaning of any particular need which is still unclear to you. Go on when you are ready. Nobody is rushing you, or checking you. Find *your* rhythm here.

D-4   Below are eight true-and-false statements. Take this self-grading test and see how many you can answer correctly. (The answers are in D-5, but please don't take the path of least resistance and look at the answers yet.)

  a. A child who is consistently withdrawn and aloof probably suffers from a need for love and affection.

  b. The emotional needs theory provides an explanation of why punishment often does not work with a very hostile or aggressive child.

  c. Many slow learners and many children from slum neighborhoods suffer from a need for achievement.

  d. Stiff tests, difficult assignments, and strict work deadlines strengthen a child and get him ready for college.

  e. Many adults need achievement, belonging, and freedom from guilt about as much as children do.

  f. Many schools are so busy with subject matter that students have little time to get to understand their feelings and growing-up problems.

  g. Often our desire to appear strong and secure makes us disguise our reaction to an emotional hurt, so that, for example, when a student says, "I hate Jimmy," he is more likely saying, "Jimmy made me feel bad."

h. The student who is passive, submissive, and hesitant about trying new things almost certainly needs more friends and companions.

i. Some problems which may look like needs problems may be much more serious and would need to be handled by a trained psychologist.

j. If a teacher incorrectly identifies a need and starts to meet it, serious trouble will occur.

D-5   Some answers as we see them. (At the risk of moralizing, we do hope you have taken the time to write out your T.'s and F.'s.

a. This is not true. Many teachers have a tendency to believe that love will cure all problems, but it is just as reasonable to believe that one of the other seven needs are being unmet. A child could have plenty of love and affection and withdraw from life for other reasons.

b. This is true. In fact, punishment often intensifies pressing emotional needs, and makes them worse.

c. True.

d. False. Many children become frightful, lose confidence in themselves, and suffer from a lack of achievement—just the opposite of the results that would strengthen them and prepare them for college.

e. True. As our physical needs continue all our lives, so do our emotional needs.

f. True. (Was that the case when you were in school?)

g. True. And this may well apply as well to a teacher who says, "I can't stand that kind of student."

h. False. Submissiveness may result from most any combination of unmet needs. See Item a. One must help children obtain the needs that are, for them, unmet: providing opportunities for emotional need satisfaction randomly is not very useful.

i. True. But there are definitely some problems which teachers can handle with perhaps even more success. The needs theory differentiates these carefully.

j. False. What happens is that nothing much happens. If you work on the incorrect need, the behavior persists. If you are sincerely trying to meet needs, it is unlikely that you will do harm.

D-6   How did you do? *Ten* correct: Excellent. A few wrong? Well, perhaps you will want to review the unit or reread the pamphlet. You might do this now or, if you prefer, go ahead and review later. Lesson E, the last lesson, follows. It concerns itself with the Big Question: "What can a busy teacher actually do to help children with their emotional needs?"

Lesson E

E-1   We have talked about *recognizing the symptoms* of emotional deprivation. We have talked about *diagnosing* the situation to identify which emotional needs might be unmet. This lesson considers the problem of *treating* cases that have been diagnosed.

And the first important point to be made is: it does not make much sense to treat a case *before* one studies it, diagnoses it, identifies which emotional needs, if any, are likely to be behind the symptoms.

Have you known teachers who would have definite ideas about how to treat a child just by observing his behavior?

Can you see how it would be better to add to such observations the perceptions of other teachers, of parents, the data in the school records, and the ideas of the student himself—all sifted through the grid of the emotional needs theory?

E-2   Write down in a phrase or two what you sense to be the main point of section E-1.

E-3   And now for action. How does the emotional needs theory get translated into action? It's relatively simple. All one does is . . .

   a. Note symptoms that might be signalling one or more unmet needs.

   b. Study the case and make a preliminary diagnosis, noting what unmet needs may be operating.

   c. Use your control of the classroom situation to provide the child in question the needs meeting he craves, patiently, over an extended period of time.

How can this be done in the midst of a teacher's responsibilities for teaching subject matter, keeping records, keeping order, etc., etc.? To answer this, finish reading the Raths-Burrell booklet. Read it carefully, and then go on to E-4.

E-4   From your reading of the booklet, you have the groundwork of the emotional needs theory. But action lies ahead, and that is the most difficult hurdle. It is easier to understand than to act, as someone must have said once. Teachers' loads are heavy, their psychological training is light, and for all of us, habits are strong. But professional teachers do their best, and we would suggest that you begin by working at one emotional needs case at a time, gradually increasing your efforts as you become more comfortable with the approach. Below are two exercises to help prepare you.

E-5   One of the difficulties in helping children obtain what they need in the way of emotional experiences is *our* lack of self-understanding. Often we are prevented from acting in a professional way because our own needs get in the way. Are you aware of your unmet emotional needs, if any? Think about this, and think about what you might do about it.

As an adult with awareness, you can often go a long way toward getting yourself into positions that will result in better satisfaction of emotional needs. If you need greater feelings of belongingness, for example, you can add activities that will bring you in close touch with congenial people and drop activities that do not. Why not make a plan for yourself in this area of emotional needs?

Make some notes about this. When you feel you have dealt adequately with this issue, go on to E-6. You may want to return to E-5 later.

E-6 Let's try some exercises with children. For each of the cases in C-3 on pages 252-53, *list five things that you could actually do*—and would be comfortable in doing if you had such a child in your class. Be realistic. Include only things you would really do. If you diagnose the situation as including more than one possible unmet need, include five things that might be done for each need so identified. (Use the Raths-Burrell booklet for hints.)

Write the five things you might do (for *each* need or *each* case) on a separate sheet. This may be collected later, so do this neatly and place your name on the sheet.

And to make it more realistic, try to make believe that for each case the following data apply:

For Anna (a): You have a vague feeling of dislike towards Anna. Upon reflection it is because Anna looks much like your younger sister who, when you were growing up, took much of the affection and attention of your family when you needed it. You recognize this and feel that it should not interfere with your reactions to Anna.

For Bill (b): Bill has also nagged at you, and you resent him greatly. He may need one thing, but you feel he deserves a good swift kick in the trousers. What do you do: give Bill what he needs or what he deserves?

For Carla (c): If there are two things you can't stand they are filth and unpleasant odor. Carla has both to a large degree. Do you still help her?

For Donald (d) His beady eyes mystify you. You can't seem to communicate with him. You even hate to look at him.

For Ernie (e) Strange, but Ernie looks a little like your father and reminds you of him. Your father is a big, clumsy man, also, and has a tendency to frighten people who do not know him. In fact, he frightens you oftentimes.

For Fran (f): You like Fran very much. She is your ideal of what a young lady should look and act like in school. You often feel like hugging Fran protectively.

For Gerald (g): Gerald is Negro, with very dark skin and strong features. You are not very comfortable with Negroes. You do not quite know how you feel about Gerald.

E-7 State, in one paragraph of no more than fifty words, the emotional needs theory as you understand it. Add it to the sheet of answers to item E-6, ready to be handed in.

E-8 The real test of the emotional needs theory—whether it is understood and whether you can comfortably work with it—must come during profesisonal role behavior. It is our experience, however, that once a teacher tries it and tastes the satisfactions that come from helping a child become less aggressive, less submissive, less withdrawn, less psychosomatically ill, and less bothered generally by emotional problems—he is likely to work at improving his skills with it. It is satisfying to help children in these ways. Why not try it? Will you?

E-9 This completes the unit. We may ask you to practice the theory on written case studies, children you come in contact with, or one of your friends or relatives. If use of the theory is advisable for these cases, you do not have to fear that you will do harm to the child, although you are relatively inexperienced in the application of the theory. If you provide for a child an experience that is not needed, it will probably have no effect upon him. It does little harm for someone to get *too much* affection, belonging, achievement, self-respect, etc. If you work at one set of needs for a long enough period of time, and the student's signals for help (withdrawal, aggression, etc.) persist, try a new diagnosis. You may not be meeting the *unmet* needs. (Or perhaps you have a case that is too complex or too deep to be reached through the needs theory, and therapy may be demanded.)

When you do provide the right thing to the right person, the gradual but dramatic changes will be clear, and rewarding.

E-10 It might be useful now to review this entire unit and to make note of any questions you have about it. Make notes, also, of things you want to follow up on. Your notes may be useful later for class discussion about this unit.

Notes

The Seven Valuing Criteria

1. Choosing from alternatives
2. Choosing after careful consideration of the consequences of each alternative
3. Choosing freely
4. Prizing, being glad of one's choice
5. Prizing, being willing to publicly affirm one's choice
6. Acting upon one's choice, incorporating choices into behavior
7. Acting upon one's choice repeatedly, over time

Value Indicators

1. Goals or purposes
2. Aspirations
3. Attitudes
4. Interests
5. Feelings
6. Beliefs and convictions
7. Activities
8. Worries, problems, obstacles

Value-related Behavioral Problem Types

1. The apathetic, listless, disinterested person
2. The flighty person
3. The very uncertain
4. The very inconsistent
5. The drifting person
6. The overconforming person
7. The overdissenting person
8. The role-playing person

Ten Value-Rich Areas

1. Money
2. Friendship
3. Love and sex
4. Religion and morals
5. Leisure
6. Politics and social organization
7. Work
8. Family
9. Maturity
10. Character traits

Thirty Clarifying Responses

1. Is this something that you prize?
2. Are you glad about that?
3. How did you feel when that happened?
4. Did you consider any alternatives?
5. Have you felt this way for a long time?
6. Was that something that you yourself selected or chose?
7. Did you *have* to choose that; was it a free choice?
8. Do you *do* anything about that idea?
9. Can you give me some examples of that idea?
10. What do you mean by_____: can you define that word?
11. Where would that idea lead; what would be its consequences?
12. Would you really *do* that or are you just talking?
13. Are you saying that . . . [repeat the statement]?
14. Did you say that . . . [repeat in some distorted way]?
15. Have you thought much about that idea (or behavior)?
16. What are some good things about that notion?
17. What do we have to assume for things to work out that way?
18. Is what you express consistent with . . . [Note something else the person said or did that may point to an inconsistency]?
19. What other possibilities are there?
20. Is that a personal preference or do you think most people should believe that?
21. How can I help you do something about your idea?
22. Is there a purpose back of this activity?
23. Is that very important to you?

24. Do you do this often?
25. Would you like to tell others about your idea?
26. Do you have any reasons for saying (or doing) that?
27. Would you do the same thing over again?
28. How do you know it's right?
29. Do you value that?
30. Do you think people will always believe that?

Twenty-one Clarifying Strategies

1. The clarifying response
2. The value sheet
3. The value-clarifying discussion
4. Role-playing
5. The contrived incident
6. Zig-zag lessons
7. Devil's advocate
8. Value continuum
9. Thought sheets
10. Weekly reaction sheets
11. Open-ended questions
12. Coded student papers
13. Time diaries
14. Autobiographical questionnaires
15. Public interviews
16. Decision-making interviews
17. Voting
18. Five-minute quotes without comment
19. Student reports
20. Action projects
21. An approach to self-conception

Bibliography

Albert, Ethel M. *et al.* *A Selected Bibliography on Values, Ethics, and Esthetics.* Glencoe, Illinois: The Free Press, 1959.

Alberty, Harold *et al.* *Helping Teenagers Explore Values.* Columbus, Ohio: The Ohio State University, Department of Education, 1956. (Mimeographed.)

Allport, Gordon. *Becoming: Basic Considerations for a Psychology of Personality.* New Haven: Yale University Press, 1955.

Allport, G. W., P. E. Vernon, and G. Lindzey. *Study of Values.* Boston: Houghton Mifflin Company, 1960.

Arrow, Kenneth J. *Social Choice and Individual Values.* New York: John Wiley and Sons, Inc., 1951.

Asch, Solomon E. *Social Psychology.* New York: Prentice-Hall, Inc., 1952.

Barrett, Donald N., Editor. *Values in America.* Notre Dame, Indiana: University of Notre Dame Press, 1961.

Barton, Allen H. *Studying the Effects of College Education.* New Haven, Connecticut: The Edward W. Hazen Foundation, 1959.

Best, John W. *Research in Education.* Englewood Cliffs, New Jersey: Prentice-Hall, Inc., 1959.

Bloom, Benjamin S. *Stability and Change in Human Characteristics.* New York: John Wiley & Sons, Inc., 1964.

Brameld, Theodore and Stanley Elam, (eds.). *Values in American Education.* Bloomington, Indiana: Phi Delta Kappa, 1964.

Brinton, Crane. *A History of Western Morals.* New York: Harcourt Brace & World, Inc., 1959.

Brown, Georgia J., *An Investigation of a Methodology for Value Clarification: Its Development, Demonstration, and Application for Teachers of the Elementary School.* Ph.D. dissertation in process, New York University.

Bruner, Jerome S. *The Process of Education.* Cambridge, Massachusetts: Harvard University Press, 1961.

Cambell, Doris Klein. *Difference of Values Among College Students at Different Class Levels.* Unpublished Ph.D. dissertation, University of Florida, 1962.

Carroll, John B. "Neglected Areas in Educational Research," *Phi Delta Kappan,* XLII (May, 1961), pp. 339-43.

Coleman, James S. *The Adolescent Society.* Glencoe, Illinois: The Free Press, 1961.

Conant, James B. *Trial and Error in the Improvement of Education.* Washington, D. C.: Association for Supervision and Curriculum Development, 1961.

Cowley, Malcolm *et al.* *Ethical Problems for the Sixties.* New Britain, Connecticut: Central Connecticut College, 1962.

Dahlke, H. O. *Values in Culture and Classroom.* New York: Harper & Row, Publishers, 1958.

Dale, Edgar. "A Life Management Curriculum," *The News Letter,* XXIX, No. 2 (November, 1963), pp. 1-4.

Dell, William C. "Creativity and the English Curriculum." *The English Journal*, LII, No. 3 (March, 1963), pp. 200-05.

Dewey, John. "My Pedagogic Creed," *The School Journal*, LIV, No. 3 (January 16, 1897), pp. 77-80.

————————. *Moral Principles in Education*. Boston: Houghton Mifflin Company, 1909.

————————. "Some Questions About Value." *Journal of Philosophy*, XL, No. 17 (August 17, 1944), pp. 449-455.

————————. *Theory of Valuation*. Chicago: University of Chicago Press, 1939.

Dilley, N. E. "Personal Values Held by College Students Who Enter a Teacher Education Program," *Journal of Teacher Education*, VIII (September, 1957), pp. 289-91.

Elliott, David L. and Arthur W. Foshay. "Chart or Charter: Recent Developments in Educational Discourse," *Review of Educational Research*, XXXIII, No. 3 (June, 1963), pp. 233-244.

Firth, Raymond W. *Essays on Social Organization in Values*. London: Athlone Press, 1964.

Friedenberg, Edgar Z. *The Vanishing Adolescent*. Boston: Beacon Press, 1959.

Fromm, Erich. *Man for Himself*. New York: Rinehart and Company, 1947.

————————. *The Sane Society*. New York: Holt, Rinehart & Winston, Inc., 1955.

Gage, N. L. (ed.). *Handbook of Research on Teaching*. Chicago: Rand McNally & Company, 1963.

Gagnon, Lawrence. *An Experimental Methodology for Teaching Thinking and Value Clarification*. Doctoral dissertation in process, Wayne State University.

Gardner, John W. *Self-Renewal*. New York: Harper and Row, Publishers, 1964.

Getzel, J. W. and P. W. Jackson. *Creativity and Intelligence*. New York: John Wiley & Sons, Inc., 1962.

Ginzberg, Eli. *Values and Ideals of American Youth*. New York: Columbia University Press, 1961.

Grapko, Michael F. *The Story of Jimmy*, a test of security, Institute of Child Study, University of Toronto, 1957.

Hall, Everett W. *What Is a Value?* New York: Humanities Press, 1952.

Harmin, Merrill and Sidney B. Simon. "The Subject Matter Controversy Revisited," *Peabody Journal of Education*, XLII, No. 4 (January, 1965), pp. 193-205.

Hartshorne, H. and A. M. May. *Studies in Deceit*. New York: Macmillan, 1928.

Havighurst, Robert J. *Human Development and Education*. New York: Longmans, Green and Company, 1953.

Human Values in the Elementary School. Washington, D.C.: Department of Elementary Schools Principals, National Education Association, 1952.

Hunt, Mate G. *Values: Resource Guide*. Oneonta, New York: American Association of Colleges for Teacher Education, 1958.

Hunt, Maurice P. and Lawrence Metcalf. *Teaching High School Social Studies*. New York: Harper & Row, Publishers, 1955.

Jacob, Philip E. *Changing Values in College*. New York: Harper & Row, Publishers, 1957.

Jonas, Arthur H. *A Study of the Relationship of Certain Behaviors of Children to Emotional Needs, Values and Thinking.* Unpublished Ph.D. dissertation, New York University, 1960.

Joncich, Geraldine. "Wither Thou, Educational Scientist?" *Teachers College Record,* LXIV (October, 1962), pp. 1-12.

Katz, Martin. *Decisions and Values.* Princeton, New Jersey: College Entrance Examination Board, 1963.

Klevan, Albert. *An Investigation of a Methodology for Value Clarification: Its Relationship to Consistency in Thinking, Purposefulness and Human Relations.* Unpublished Ph.D. dissertation, New York University, 1957.

Krathwohl, David R., Benjamin S. Bloom, and Bertram B. Masia. *Taxonomy of Educational Objectives: Handbook II: Affective Domain.* New York: David McKay, 1964.

Lang, Melvin. *An Investigation of the Relationship of Value Clarification to Underachievement and Certain Other Behavioral Characteristics of Selected College Students.* Unpublished Ph.D. dissertation, New York University, 1961.

Lepley, Ray. *Value: A Cooperative Inquiry.* New York: Columbia University Press, 1949.

Lerner, Max. *America As a Civilization.* New York: Simon and Schuster, 1957.

Lieberman, Phyllis and Sidney B. Simon. "Vitalizing Student Research Reports," *Social Education,* XXVIII, No. 1 (January, 1964), pp. 24-26.

_____ and _____. "Values and Student Writing." *Educational Leadership,* XXII, No. 6 (March, 1965), pp. 414-21.

_____ and _____. "Topical Issues and Values." *New York State Education.* LII, No. 5 (February, 1965), pp. 11-12.

Lynd, Robert S. *Knowledge for What?* Princeton: Princeton University Press, 1946.

Machnits, Ernest. *A Study of the Relationship of Certain Behaviors of Children to Emotional Needs, Values, and Thinking.* Unpublished Ph.D. dissertation, New York University, 1960.

Macmillan, C.J.B. and George F. Kneller. "Philosophy of Education," *Review of Educational Research,* XXXIV, No. 1 (February, 1964), pp. 22-43.

Martin, Donald. *A Study of the Relationship of Certain Behaviors of Children to Emotional Needs, Values, and Thinking.* Unpublished Ph.D. dissertation, New York University, 1960.

Moral and Spiritual Values in the Public Schools. Washington, D.C.: National Education Association, Educational Policies Commission, 1957.

Murphy, Gardner. *Human Potentialities.* New York: Basic Books, 1958.

Niblett, W. R. (ed.). *Moral Education in a Changing Society.* London: Faber and Faber, Ltd., 1963.

Olmo, Barbara M. *A Study of the Effects of the Value Clarification Method on Uninterested Students.* Unpublished Master's Thesis, Rutgers University, 1964.

Peck, Robert F. and Robert J. Havighurst. *The Psychology of Character Development.* New York: John Wiley & Sons, Inc., 1960.

Perceiving, Behaving, Becoming. Washington, D.C.: Association for Supervision and Curriculum Development Yearbook, 1962.

Perkins, Hugh V. "A Procedure for Assessing the Classroom Behavior of Students and Teachers," *American Educational Research Journal,* I, No. 4 (November, 1964), pp. 249-260.

Perry, Ralph Barton. *General Theory of Value*. New York: Longmans, Green, and Company, 1926.

Prince, R. *A Study of the Relationship Between Values and Administrative Effectiveness in the School Situation*. Unpublished Ph.D. dissertation, University of Chicago, 1957.

Raths, James. *An Application of Clarifying Techniques to Academic Underachievers in High School*. Unpublished Ph.D. dissertation, New York University, 1960.

_____. "Underachievement and A Search for Values," *Journal of Educational Sociology*, XXXIV, No. 9 (May, 1961), pp. 422-24.

_____. "Clarifying Children's Values," *The National Elementary Principal*, XLII, No. 2 (November, 1962a), pp. 35-39.

_____. "Clarifying Children's Values," *Childhood Education*, XLII, No. 2 (November, 1962b), 38.

_____. "Values and Valuing." *Educational Leadership*, XXI, No. 8 (May, 1964a), pp. 543-546.

_____. "A Strategy for Developing Values," *Educational Leadership*, XXI, No. 8 (May, 1964b), pp. 509-514, 554.

Raths, Louis E. "Sociological Knowledge and Needed Curriculum Research," *Research Frontiers in the Study of Children's Learning*. J. B. Macdonald (ed.). Milwaukee: School of Education, The University of Wisconsin-Milwaukee, 1960.

_____. "Clarifying Values," *Curriculum for Today's Boys and Girls*." R. S. Fleming (ed.). Columbus, Ohio: Charles Merrill Books, Inc., 1963.

_____ and Anna Burrell. *Understanding the Problem Child*. West Orange, New Jersey: The Economics Press, 1962.

_____ et al. *Thinking and Teaching*. Columbus, Ohio: Charles E. Merrill Books, Inc., 1966.

Ramp, Bruce R. *The Improvement of Practical Intelligence*. New York: Harper, & Row, Publishers, 1950.

Reisman, David, Nathon Glazer, and Reuel Denney. *The Lonely Crowd*. New Haven: Yale University Press, 1950.

Rogers, Carl R. *On Becoming a Person*. Boston: Houghton Mifflin Co., 1961.

Santostefano, S. "Miniature Situation Tests as a Way of Interviewing Children," *Merrill-Palmer Quarterly*, VIII (1962), pp. 261-270.

Selltiz, Claire *et al. Research Methods in Social Relations*. New York: Holt, Rinehart & Winston, Inc., 1961.

Simon, Marianne P. and Sidney B. Simon. "Dramatic Improvisation: Path to Discovery." *English Journal*, LIV, No. 4 (April, 1965), pp. 323-27.

Simon, Sidney B. *Value Clarification: Methodology and Tests of an Hypothesis in an In-Service Program Relating to Behavioral Changes in Secondary School Students*. Unpublished Ph.D. dissertation, New York University, 1958.

Smith, Eugene and Ralph Tyler. *Appraising and Recording Student Progress*. New York: Harper & Row, Publishers, 1942.

Smith, John E. *Value Convictions and Higher Education*. New Haven, Connecticut: The Edward W. Hazen Foundation, 1958.

Soderquist, Harold O. *The Person and Education*. Columbus, Ohio: Charles E. Merrill Books, Inc., 1964.

Super, Donald E. *Work Values Inventory*. Boston: Houghton Mifflin Co., 1965.

Tisdale, John R. *Psychological Value Theory and Research: 1930-1960.* Unpublished Ph.D. dissertation, Boston University Graduate School, 1961.

Tyler, Ralph W. "The Contribution of the Behavioral Sciences to Educational Research," *First Annual Symposium on Educational Research.* Frank W. Banghart (ed.). Bloomington, Indiana: Phi Delta Kappa, 1960.

Wheelis, Allen. *The Quest for Identity.* New York: W. W. Norton and Company, 1958.

Whyte, William H., Jr. *The Organizational Man.* New York: Simon and Schuster, 1956.

Wiles, Kimball. *The Changing Curriculum of the American High School.* Englewood Cliffs, New Jersey: Prentice-Hall, Inc., 1963.

Winter, W. D. "Student Values and Grades in General Psychology," *Journal of Educational Research*, LV (April, 1962), pp. 331-33.

Witkin, Herman A. *Psychological Differentiation.* New York: John Wiley & Sons, Inc., 1962.

Index

Ackerman, Gary, 100
Acting upon choices, *see* Value criteria
Action projects, 160-62
   example, 160-61
   helpful hints, 161-62
   purpose, 160
Activities, *see* Values indicators
Affirming choices, *see* Value criteria
Allport, Gordon, 9, 205, 220
Anderson, Maxwell, 117, 119
Asch, Solomon E., 123
Aspirations, *see* Value indicators
Association for Supervision and Curriculum Development, 9
Attitudes, *see* Value indicators
Autobiographical questionnaire, 140-42
   form 140-41
   sample questionnaire, 140-41
Automobile, impact on society, 18

Beliefs, *see* Value indicators
Berger, Joseph, 98
Bloom, Benjamin S., 9, 222
Brinton, Crane, 8
Brown's Study, 208
Burrell, Anna, 182

Carroll, John B., 205
Choice, 33-36, 112
   consequences, 34
   free, 34
   importance of alternatives, 34
   personal, 35
Choosing after considering consequences, *see* Value criteria
Choosing freely, *see* Value criteria
Choosing from alternatives, *see* Value criteria
Clarification process, *see* Value processes
Clarifying method, *see* Value clarifying methods
Clarifying question, *see* Clarifying response
Clarifying response, 51-82, 106, 123, 148
   definition, 80
   elements of, 53-54
   examples, 52-53, 53-54
   framework of, 81-82
   intrusion, 76-77
   "one-legged" conferences, 71, 76, 132
   questions, use of, 78-79
   teachers position, 77
   thirty responses, 55-65, 112
   topics to use, 65-72
      examples, 72-79

Clarifying response—*cont.*
  trust, importance of, 81
  what it isn't, 80
Clarity of relationship to society, 4-7
Coded student papers, 138-39, 142
Colton, C. C., 99
Conant, James B., 205
Confucius, 117, 165
Confusion, 18, 67
Contrived incident, 123-25, 141
  examples, 123-24
  purpose, 123, 124-45
Corneille, 99
Cox, Joyce, 91

Daily reaction sheets, *see* Reaction sheets
Dale, Edgar, 186
de Aquado, Bleye Pedro, 101
Decision-making interview, 149-52
  characterized by, 149-51
  decisions suited to approach, 151
Dee's Values Sheets, 218
Devils advocate, 127-29, 141
  example, 128
  purpose, 127, 129
Dewey, John, 7, 9, 206
Dilley, N. E., 220
Disadvantaged children, 228-29
Discussion, use with value sheets, 106, 107
Discussion, value-clarifying contrived incident, 123-25

Discussion—*cont.*
  devils advocate, 127-29, 141
  example, 114-15
  initiating, 116-21
    dramatic scenes, 117-19
    pictures, 117
    questions, 119-20
    quotations, 116-17
    varied sources, 120
  purpose, 113
  role-playing, 121-23
  value continuum, 129-30
  "zig-zag" lesson, 125-27
Dramatic improvisation, *see* Role-playing

Edwards Personal Preference Schedule, 221
Elementary-school Experiments, 209-11
Elliott, David L., 205
Emerson, Ralph Waldo, 99
Emotional disturbance, 3, 7, 76, 182, 191

Family and values, 15-18
Feelings, *see* Value indicators
Foshay, Arthur, 205
Friedenberg, Edgar, 9
Fromm, Erich, 7, 9

Gage, N. L., 221
Gardner, John, 10

Getzel, J. W., 221
Goals, see Value indicators
Grapko, Michael F., 221

Hartshore, H., 220
Havighurst, Robert J., 9, 45, 67
Hemingway, Ernest, 99, 117
Hunt, Mate, 6, 190
Hunt, Maurice P., 222

Inconsistency statements, 5, 20, 82, 88
Interests, see Value indicators

Jackson, P. W., 221
Jacob, Phillip E., 205
Jonas, Arthur H., 209, 210
Jonich, Geraldine, 205

Klevan's College Study, 206-07
    results, 207
    structure, 206-07
Kline, Morris, 102
Kneller, George F., 9
Krathwhol, David R., 9, 10, 226

Lang's Study, 212-13
    results, 213
    structure, 212-13
Lerner, Max, 7
Lindzey, G., 205, 220
Lynd, Robert S., 9

Machnits, Ernest, 209
Macmillan, C. J. B., 9

Mannes, Marya, 84, 85
Martin, Donald, 209, 210, 212, 223, 224
Masia, Bertram B., 9
May, A. M., 220
Metcalf, Lawrence, 6, 9, 190, 222
Minnesota Multiphasic Personality Inventory, 221
Modern life, complexity of, 7, 15
Moralizing, avoidance of, 53, 61, 69, 73, 86, 109, 112, 148, 167, 192

Napoleon Bonaparte, 99
Needs Theory, 197-200, 203-04
    age of appearance, 198
    needs behavior, 200
    pervasiveness and selectivity, 198
    self-help and outside help, 199
    shame and pride, 198
    value behavior, 200

"One-legged" conferences, see Clarifying responses
Open-ended questions, 136-38, 142
    examples, 137-38
    method, 137
    sample questions, 137-38
Osborn, R., 88

Patterns of behavior, see Unclear values

Peck, Robert F., 9, 45, 167
Perkins, Hugh V., 221
Persuasion, 41
Prince, R. A., 220
Prizing, see Value criteria
Problems and worries, see Value indicators
Public interview, 142-49
 examples, 142-44
 frequency of use in classroom, 145
 helpful hints, 146-48
 purpose, 144
 sample questions, 145-46
Purpose, 30-31, 65, 68-69, 80

Quote without comment, 155-56

Raths, James, 10, 211-14, 220, 223
 Campus Elementary School, 213-14
 on underachievers, 211-12
 study, 213-14
Raths, Louis, 182, 183
Raup, Bruce R., 186, 220
Reaction sheets, 134-36
 daily, 135-36
 purpose, 135
 sample questions, 135
 use of, 136
 weekly, 134-35, 142
Reisman, David, 7, 9
Religion, influence of, 19
Repeating behavior, 29, 30, 65

Research about the value theory, 205-29
 Brown's Study, 208
 Campus Elementary School, 213-14
 Dee's Value Sheets, 218
 Elementary-school Experiments, 209-11
 Klevan's College Study, 206-07
 Lang's Study, 212-13
 overview of research, 218-20
 Raths on underachievers, 211-12
 research ahead, 220-29
 Sheild's College Class, 216-17
 Simon's Study, 207-08
 Weintraub's Study, 214-16
Rogers, Carl, 9
Role-playing, 121-23, 141
 discussion following, 122-23
 situations, 121-22
Rothstein, Arnold, 101

Santostefano, S., 220
Schuman, Sima, 99
Security, emphasis on, 23
Seneca, 99
Sheild's Study, 216-17
 results, 217
 structure, 216-17
Simon, Sidney B., 207
Simon's Study, 207-08
 results, 207-08
 structure, 207

Smith, D. E., 101
Smith, John E., 9
Social conditions, changing, 22-24
Sociodrama, *see* Role-playing
Sociometric device, 179
  example of, 179-81
Soderquist, Harold, 9
Streit, Peggy, 99
Student reports, 156-60
  examples, 157-60
  group report, 158
  individual reports, 157-58
  sample questions, 156-57
Super, Donald E., 220
Syrus, 112

Thinking theory, *see* Values and thinking
Thirty clarifying responses, 55-65, 112
Thoreau, Henry David, 116
Thought sheets, 130-34, 141
  examples, 131-32, 133-34
  introducing in classroom, 131
  method, 131
  use of, 132-33
Time diary, 139-40, 142
  sample questions, 139
Tyler, Ralph W., 205

Uncertainty, *see* Unclear values
Unclear values, behavior patterns
  apathy, 5, 81, 166, 175, 179, 202,
  drifting, 5, 82, 176

Unclear values—*cont.*
  flightiness, 5, 81, 175, 179, 202
  inconsistency, 5, 82, 88, 175, 180, 202
  overconformity, 5, 82, 166, 176, 179, 202
  overdissenting, 6, 176, 179
  role-playing, 6, 176, 179-80
  uncertainty, 5, 166, 167, 175, 180, 202

Value-clarifying methods, 51-162
  clarifying response, 51-82
  discussion, 112, 113-30
  value sheets, 83-111
  varied methods, 142-62
  writing, 130-42
Value-clarifying program, initiation of, 165-96
  adapting ideas, 173
  classroom climate, 168-69
  discussing before adopting, 172-73
  encouraging colleagues to join you, 173-74
  experimental design, 174-85
  guidelines, 168-74
  informing others, 172
  measuring value-related behavior, 177-85
  moralizing, eliminating, 169-71
  preparing for conflict, 173
  problems to avoid, 168-74
  starting slowly, 171-72

Value-clarifying—*cont.*
  value-related behavioral
    types, 175-77
  why start program, 166
Value-clarifying, what is worth
    it, 194-96
Value continuum, 129-30, 141
Value criteria, 30-33
  acting upon choices, 29,
    30, 56, 64, 82, 106
  affirming choices, 29, 30,
    56, 82
  choosing after considering
    consequences, 28, 29, 30,
    34, 63, 82
  choosing freely, 28, 30, 34,
    56, 63, 82, 106
  choosing from alternatives,
    28, 30, 34, 63, 82
  prizing, 29, 30, 56, 64, 82,
    106, 112
Value disturbances, 4
Value indicators, 30-33, 65, 66-
    72, 80, 82, 130, 136, 138, 183
  activities, 32, 64, 65, 70-72,
    80, 136, 183
  aspirations, 31, 65, 68, 75,
    80, 123, 138
  attitudes, 31, 65, 66-67, 80,
    123, 136, 183
  beliefs, 32, 66, 80, 136, 138
  defined, 65
  feelings, 31-32
  goals or purposes, 30-31,
    65, 80, 138
  interests, 31, 65, 80, 138
  worries and problems, 32-
    33, 80
Value issues, 187

Value processes
  clarification process, 224-
    25
  components, 30-33, 62-65
  encouraging, 77
  examples of, 72-79
  helping the child, 38-39,
    48
  outcomes, 226-28
  questions teachers ask,
    185-96
Value-related behavior, mea-
    suring, 177-85
  evaluating data, 185
  methods, 177-84
  sample form, 178, 179-81,
    183-84
Value-related disturbances, 8
Values
  are not, 46
  defined, 6, 9-11, 28-30
  development of, 15-26
  factors affecting, 16-17
  family and, 15-18
  indicators, 30-33, 65, 66-72,
    80, 136, 183
  personal nature of, 36-37
  traditional approaches, 39-
    44
Values developing
  clarifying methods, 51-162
  traditional methods, 39-44
Value sheets
  construction of, 94-95
  controversy, use of, 110,
    190
  defined, 83
  directed to, 105

Value sheets—*cont.*
    discussion, using with, 106-07
    do's and don'ts, 109-11
    examples of, 84-85, 86-87, 88, 91-92, 93-94, 95-102
    form of, 103-04, 106
    grading, 110
    incomplete, 103-05
    issues to use, 95, 187
    parents and, 110
    purpose, 83, 110
    sources, 89
    subject matter, 89-104
    teachers' views, 107
    topics, 105-06
    using, 85, 89-91, 106-11, 113-62
        ending units, 90, 108
        incorporated into units, 90, 108
        introducing units, 89, 108
Values and thinking, 200-04
    characteristics of poor thinking, 202
    defined, 201
    thinking theory, 200-02
    thinking processes, 203
Values, unclear, *see* Unclear values
Vernon, P. E., 205, 220
Voting, 152-55
    examples of using, 154
    method, 152, 153-54
    purpose, 153

Voting—*cont.*
    sample questions to use, 152-53

Weekly reaction sheets, *see* Reaction sheets
Weintraub's Study, 214-16
    results, 215-16
    structure, 214-215
Wells, H. G., 99
Wertenbaker, T. J., 101
Whellis, Allen, 9
Whyte, William H., Jr., 7, 9
Wiles, Kimball, 188
Witkin, Herman A., 9
World events, impact on family, 19-20
Worries and problems, *see* Value indicators
Written value-clarification techniques, 130-42
    autobiographical questionnaire, 140-42
    coded student papers, 138-39, 142
    open-ended questions, 135-38, 142
    reaction sheets, 134-36
        daily, 135-36
        weekly, 134-35, 141-42
    thought sheets, 130-34, 141
    time diary, 139-40, 142

"Zig-zag" lesson, 125-27, 141
    examples of, 126, 27
    method, 125